COMPANION TO
THE BOOK OF WORSHIP

COMPANION TO
THE BOOK OF WORSHIP

Edited for the Commission on Worship
of The United Methodist Church

by
William F. Dunkle, Jr.
and
Joseph D. Quillian, Jr.

Published by
ABINGDON PRESS
Nashville and New York

ISBN 0-687-09258-2

Library of Congress Catalog Card Number: 71-120595

Scripture quotations noted RSV are from the Revised Standard Version
of the Bible, copyrighted 1946 and 1952 by the Division of Christian Education, National Council of Churches, and are used by permission.

Scripture quotations noted NEB are from the New English Bible, New
Testament. © the Delegates of the Oxford University Press and the Syndics
of the Cambridge University Press 1961. Reprinted by permission.

SET UP, PRINTED, AND BOUND BY THE
PARTHENON PRESS, AT NASHVILLE,
TENNESSEE, UNITED STATES OF AMERICA

Contents

Contributors

William F. Dunkle, Jr.
Vice-chairman, General Commission on Worship, The United Methodist Church
Wilmette, Illinois

H. Grady Hardin
Professor of Worship and Preaching
Perkins School of Theology
Southern Methodist University
Dallas, Texas

Paul W. Hoon
Henry Sloane Coffin Professor of Pastoral Theology
Union Theological Seminary
New York, New York

Albert C. Outler
Professor of Theology
Perkins School of Theology
Southern Methodist University
Dallas, Texas

Joseph D. Quillian, Jr.
Dean, Perkins School of Theology
Southern Methodist University
Dallas, Texas

David James Randolph, Jr.
Assistant General Secretary, Christian Community Section
General Board of Evangelism
The United Methodist Church
Nashville, Tennessee

Roy A. Reed, Jr.
Associate Professor of Worship and Church Music
Methodist Theological School
Delaware, Ohio

M. Lawrence Snow
Minister, Community United Methodist Church
Poughkeepsie, New York

James F. White
Associate Professor of Worship
Perkins School of Theology
Southern Methodist University
Dallas, Texas

Introduction

"Books," wrote St. Augustine after his conversion, "cannot teach me charity." Neither can books teach us Christian worship that provides a redemptive community in the presence of the Living Lord of history where we truly are "in love and charity with our neighbors" as "new creations in Christ Jesus."

Yet it was the book called the *New Testament* from which Augustine found inspiration and help for his experience of new life in Christ, in whose presence he was taught charity.

So with worship today for secular man, who needs desperately to learn charity, but for whom in too many instances awareness of the transcendence as well as the immanence of God has largely been lost. As a result of this and other difficulties arising from our scientific culture, many today both within and without the church find Christian worship not only difficult but even impossible. With all our scientific achievements, holding promise as well as threat to our existence, we have the imperative to build bridges of understanding between Christian faith, its expression in worship, and our culture.

This book is addressed to that need. It is an ecumenical book on worship, dealing directly with the theological, historical, and practical backgrounds and meanings of *The Book of Worship*, adopted by the General Conference of the former Methodist Church in April, 1964. Nevertheless, it will be equally valuable to members of other churches from whose liturgical heritage *The Book of Worship* has drawn heavily.

A description of the origin and purpose of *The Book of Worship*, as well as this book, which is rightfully called *Companion to The Book of Worship,* may be helpful as an introduction.

The General Commission on Worship of The Methodist Church from 1956-1964, under the able leadership of Bishop Edwin E. Voigt as chairman and Dr. Paul Burt as secretary, with the help of several consultants, surveyed the liturgical heritage of all the major church bodies and drew from them one of the finest collections of worship resources in the Christian world. Acknowledgments in the Foreword of *The Book of Worship* represent forty-eight different sources, including such diverse groups as the Church of South India, the Roman Catholic, the Eastern Orthodox, the various branches of Lutheran, Anglican, and the so-called "free church" traditions.

Some persons think all liturgies considered valuable in the past should be disregarded today in favor of completely new creative or contemporary liturgies. They say, therefore, that *The Book of Worship* came just six years too late. Too bad, they add, that we did not wait at least until after the union of the Methodists and the Evangelical United Brethren, or until we had gone further into the current explosion of contemporary worship before preparing a book with such widespread distribution and use.

I speak for the present Commission on Worship of The United Methodist Church and for many former Methodist and Evangelical United Brethren leaders when I say that we rejoice in the book's early publication. Evangelical United Brethren representatives participated in the preparation of the book; it was with the blessing of their Committee on Worship that the Methodist Commission completed it four years before the 1968 union. The present General Commission on Worship of The United Methodist Church and the predecessor 1964-68 Commission of The Methodist Church have sought to encourage the development and use of new and creative forms of worship. At the same time we have also placed a major emphasis on the widespread understanding and use of *The Book of Worship* and *The Methodist Hymnal* as normative for the worshiping congregations, small groups and individuals, in our larger connection since union.

Why do we make this emphasis? Because we believe in liturgical reform and are thankful for the work done in this direction in *The Book of Worship,* even though the reform did not go as far as some would have desired. Most of us would agree that liturgical reform alone has not been successful in producing a renewal of worship. Reform is helpful and necessary, of course, with good possibilities for clearing away anachronisms that obscure the true meanings of the liturgy. Reform helps man to understand and use the old forms more effectively, but something more is needed than merely rewriting the liturgy.

I join with those who believe that, until we have understood the old forms and the reasons for them, why they were used and what they mean, we have no viable background with which to begin what we may think of as more creative contemporary worship. Indeed, some of the contemporary liturgies prepared by United Methodists and others from the free-church tradition are ineffective because their compilers have not learned to understand and appreciate the worship of Christians in past ages—a rich heritage without which we are impoverished.

This lack of appreciation explains the significant purpose of a *Companion to The Book of Worship*. At our first meeting and after *The Book of Worship* was published, the Commission, having been deluged with requests for explanations and helps concerning the theological reasoning and practical use of the new book, chose capable theological and liturgical leaders to write the chapters on theological meanings, historical settings, and practical suggestions for the most meaningful and effective use of the book in church and home and for personal worship.

There is evidence that the great body of members in the United Methodist Church, as well as in most other churches, is almost biblically, theologically, and liturgically illiterate, with only a smattering of real education—or none —in the meaning of and the reasons for our orders of worship, the forms of the Lord's Supper, Baptism, the use of the Lectionary, and ordination for the ministry. Church members also reflect a lack of appreciation of the rituals for weddings and funerals and other occasional services as genuine worship experiences. Hence the need for this companion book. The chapter on the Ordinal, for instance, is an excellent presentation of the meaning of ordination. We believe it will be of great value, not only to United Methodists and others participating in the Consultation on Church Union, but to all Christians who are concerned with the problem of a common ministry, the principal source of division in the contemporary church.

Companion to The Book of Worship is meant to be an aid and resource book for pastors and other teachers of the laity. It will be helpful, also, to professors of worship in schools of theology who are called to teach their students the rich backgrounds and meanings that can make even traditional liturgies powerfully effective as agents of the Spirit in changing lives and society according to Christ's purpose.

Each of the ten chapters deals with one of the sections of *The Book of Worship*. Each chapter has three parts more or less clearly defined; namely, theological meaning and values, historical origin and relationships, and practical considerations for making the best use of this particular section.

The *Companion to The Book of Worship* is a valuable contribution in two ways:

a) To the use of the traditional forms in such a creative manner that those who seek to worship, believers and unbelievers, may find in them the characteristics of true worship that develop insight and courage in churchmen for their victorious mission in the world. For effectiveness in this mission is always the ultimate test of Christian worship.

b) The development of creative new forms without sacrificing continuity with the past in order to avoid the risks that too often accompany what is called "contemporary" worship.

Some of these risks are:

(1) The loss of intellectual integrity through overemphasis on feelings, which admittedly have been underemphasized in much traditional worship but which may leave us bogged down in feeling without content—an effete aestheticism.

(2) Without an understanding of traditional liturgy the contemporary may stress ephemeral novelty rather than genuine newness of life producing the New Creation in Christ. As Paul put it so well to the Galatians, "the only thing that counts is new creation!" (Galatians 6:15 NEB)

(3) Without an understanding of our continuity with the past, contemporary worship may produce generalized forms of Christian worship that are not specifically Christian. A generalized celebration can never take the place of the celebration of the specific presence and challenge of the Christ.

(4) Without an appreciation for the worship of Christians in the past, "contemporary" worship may produce a multiplicity of forms and lose the unity that belongs in all Christian worship.

One of the great values of this book is that it shows the interlocking relationships of all the parts of the worship of the Christian church. The Lectionary, for example, was constructed from a combination of the lectionaries of all major churches both east and west, the only time this has ever been done to our knowledge. Such unity in diversity is too precious to be lost by forgetting or abandoning our past.

Only as we begin with all the needs of man today, with an understanding of the faith-experienced realities of the past *and* the present, can we compose a liturgy that offers the power of Christian worship to meet effectively today's urgencies. Only then can Christian faith and life be renewed, and the local church as the community of God's people come alive with true joy and effectiveness as a genuine part of the Body of Christ. To this end this book is dedicated.

LANCE WEBB
Chairman, General Commission on Worship
of The United Methodist Church

I

The Order of Worship:
The Ordinary Parts

James F. White

In this chapter we shall discuss the ordinary parts of "The Order of Worship," i.e., those that do not change. In the next chapter our discussion will focus on the proper parts, those that vary from day to day. We shall examine first the history of the basic structure of "The Order of Worship," then the history of the invariable ingredients of the service. After that we shall explore the theology implied by the structure. The chapter will conclude with discussion of the pastoral concerns involved in carrying out the rubrics and in ministering to individual congregations.

I

The 1964 Methodist "Order of Worship" is simply one of the most recent effects of the destruction of the Jerusalem Temple by the Babylonians in 587 B.C. In a sense, this new service is at the same time the most ancient. Changes in the structure and the individual items have occurred over the twenty-six centuries since the Babylonian Exile of the kingdom of Judah. But the basic form of non-sacramental worship represented here was worked out long before the time of Christ, and the essentials have changed little since his time.

The destruction of the Temple of Solomon in 587 B.C. was a major crisis in the history of Jewish worship. Previously worship in the small kingdom of Judah had been nationalized by King Josiah. Sacrificial worship had been eliminated in the villages and high places of the nation and centralized in the Jerusalem Temple. The worship of the Hebrews came to revolve around sacrificial worship conducted in Jerusalem by the priests. The people shared in this cult during pilgrimage feasts or in private prayers at the hours of sacrifice. To the temple cult we owe a number of the psalms. Psalm 24 ("Lift up your heads, O gates! and be lifted up, O ancient doors! that the King of glory may come in!") is possibly a processional psalm from the temple cultus. The daily rhythm of temple sacrifice had become the center of worship in Judah by the beginning of the sixth century B.C.

The Babylonians destroyed all that. The Temple was in ruins, and the priests and many of the people found themselves exiles "by the waters of Babylon." Bitterly they questioned: "How shall we sing the Lord's song in a foreign land?" Our concern is with the answer they and the Christian church have found to that question. Instead of allowing their religion to perish, the Jews developed a new type of cultus. It centered in a new institution, the synagogue, a Greek term for a "gathering-place, place of assembly, congregation, or a meeting." The worship of the synagogue required neither temple, nor priest, nor sacrifice. In modern terms, it was the worship of the scattered church, practiced by the Jews of the diaspora. It was indeed the church in the world, for the synagogue service could be held by Jews scattered anywhere in the world. Essentially the synagogue service was a layman's service no priests or rabbis being necessary. Ten Jewish men over the age of thirteen could hold services wherever they might be. Within Christendom this type of worship has likewise retained its lay character, illustrated equally well by a nun reading her breviary or a lay preacher leading his congregation. It has been the service both of the scattered church and the church gathered.

The synagogue helped perpetuate Judaism during the years after the destruction of Solomon's Temple and continued parallel to the worship in the Second and Third Temples. Essentially the synagogue was both a house of study and a house of prayer, serving two functions: education and worship. These became the means of perpetuating Judaism. Indeed, the modern distinction between education and worship would have been unlikely in the early synagogue. The synagogue probably began as a place of reading and exposition of the traditions of the fathers, i.e. Scripture, in order to preserve a sense of national identity. To this activity were eventually added prayer and praise. These remain to this day the basic ingredients of the type of worship we are discussing: prayer and praise joined to the reading and exposition of Scripture.

Luke 4:16-27 gives a glimpse of this type of worship as practiced by the Nazareth Synagogue. Very likely the service had begun with the recital of the Shema' and some benedictions (prayers) connected with it. A lesson from the Torah was then read and translated. And then Jesus stood up to read the Haftorah and to translate it. Then returning "the book of the prophet Isaiah" to the attendant, Jesus sat down and began his exposition of the lesson. The service ended there, but usually with less tumult than on this particular occasion. The service might also include bits of psalmody. Since the Shema' and the benedictions had a creedal nature and nonbiblical substitutes for psalmody are found in hymns, it will be seen that all the essential ingredients

12

of the "Order of Worship" are found in the synagogue service of Jesus' time. These services evidently were frequented by the earliest Christians (Acts 9:20; 13:15; 14:1; 18:4). Christians were forced out of the synagogue late in the first century when prayers added to the service were so phrased that no follower of Christ could say "Amen" to them. It should be remembered that worship in the synagogue was often a daily practice at dawn and sunset. The early church continued this tradition, at least in some localities. "Thus . . . the influence of the Synagogue upon the worship of the Church is to be seen in the type of worship and the times at which public prayer was held." [1]

The church's use of the synagogue type of service is a double tradition; it appears to this day as the first half of the Eucharist (as the synaxis) and also as a distinct service in itself as in the "Order of Worship." The relationships between the synaxis as a part of the Eucharist, as a distinct service, and private prayers in the first centuries is a hazy area. The Christian Scriptures were added to the Old Testament, and several lessons and a sermon provided the first part of the Eucharist by the second century (Justin Martyr, *First Apology,* 67). From earliest times the Eucharist (Lord's Supper) would be celebrated on the first day of the week (Acts 20:7), and possibly also the agape, a service built around a meal (Pliny's Letter, *ca.* 112). There might be eucharists on Wednesday, Fridays, and Sabbath days depending on the region. Services on other days very likely were modeled on the synagogue service of instruction and prayer. A hint of this is given in the *Apostolic Tradition* of Hippolytus (*ca.* A.D. 217). Hippolytus indicates that in Rome on weekdays there might be "instruction in the word," and each one should go "considering that it is God whom he hears speaking by the mouth of him who instructs. For having prayed with (*lit.* in) the Church he will be able to avoid all the evils of that day." [2] On days when there is no instruction one should read a "holy book" at home. Hippolytus then continues to prescribe a discipline of private prayer. Earlier documents had specified a three-fold obligation for daily prayer (*Didache* 8) but Hippolytus has increased this to seven occasions.

It is not clear as to how widespread morning and evening public services were until the late fourth century. The *Apostolic Constitutions* consider them a firmly established practice. Christians are advised to "assemble yourselves together every day, morning and evening, singing psalms and praying in the Lord's house" (II, 59). They are also expected to assemble on the Lord's day for "the reading of the prophets, the preaching of the Gospel, [and] the oblation of the sacrifice." Similar evidence appears in the *Pilgrimage of Etheria,* the late fourth-century journal of a Spanish lady from her trip to the Holy Land. She notes several daily services in Jerusalem attended by ascetics and ordinary laymen, especially those in the morning and evening. The evidence is scanty

[1] C. W. Dugmore, *The Influence of the Synagogue upon the Divine Office* (London: Oxford University Press, 1944), p. 113.

[2] Gregory Dix (ed.), *The Treatise on the Apostolic Tradition of St. Hippolytus of Rome* (London: S.P.C.K., 1937), p. 61.

but we know that by the sixth century daily public services were being observed in Rome. Possibly the daily hours of private prayer described by Hippolytus had become public services. Best attended by the laity were the services at dawn and nightfall. The other services were more clerical in nature though the laity were not excluded. The recital of psalms, lessons, and canticles, the Lord's Prayer, and other prayers formed the core of these services.

The next great development of this form of worship came to meet the needs of monastic communities, and the history of the offices (as these services are called) is dominated by the ascetics and clergy from the sixth century to the sixteenth. In the west St. Benedict took the lead in prescribing details for the monastics in his *Rule* (*ca.* 543). Most likely he drew upon the daily public offices then current in Rome (matins, lauds, and vespers, plus terce, sext, and none at certain times) and added two services (prime and compline) which St. Basil's *Rule* had already established for eastern monasticism. The basic ingredient of the offices was a weekly recital of the Psalter, usually by monks reciting it antiphonally from the opposite rows of stalls in the choir of the chapel. (The modern divided chancel is a strange survival of a very practical arrangement for the worship of monastic communities.) Lessons, canticles, hymns, homilies, legends of the saints, responds, antiphons, and prayers were also parts of the offices. Saying the eight offices daily was mandatory for groups in religious orders and clergy. Due to the popularity of other devotions and the ignorance of Latin, the laity was usually absent and "the Offices ceased to be in practice, if not in theory, the common prayer of the Christian people." [3] From the sixth to the sixteenth centuries the offices underwent minor modifications in the long thousand years of clerical dominance of this type of worship. During the twelfth century a somewhat abbreviated *modernum officium* came into use by the papacy and curia. The new conditions of life of the traveling Franciscans in the following century brought further changes, mostly abbreviations in lessons and homilies, plus the addition of the Lord's Prayer at the beginning and end of each office. A portable service book, the breviary, was produced through the efforts of the Franciscans. The Franciscan *Breviary* was adopted by the papal curia, and in 1277 Pope Nicholas III, himself a Franciscan, directed its use by most of western Christianity. Thus this breviary formed the basis of the Sarum offices used widely at the time of the Reformation in the southern (Canterbury) province of England.

Dissatisfaction mounted with the breviary, and in 1535 a Spanish cardinal by the name of Quiñones published a drastically revised version at the urging of Pope Clement VII. Quiñones attempted a better distribution of the Psalter, a systematic continuous reading of most of the Bible, and the correction of many faults of the Roman *Breviary* in general use outside monastic communities. Quiñones' first effort, considered too radical, was hastily withdrawn

---

[3] E. C. Ratcliff, "The Choir Offices" in *Liturgy and Worship,* ed. by W. K. Lowther Clarke and Charles Harris (London: S.P.C.K., 1932), p. 266.

and replaced by a more conservative version[4] which ran to over a hundred editions in thirty years before being suppressed in 1558. In 1568 Pius V established a standard *Breviary*. It was revised in 1911 and used till recently throughout the Catholic Church except where the Milanese, Monastic, and Dominican breviaries are used.

A most radical and significant step was taken by Archbishop Thomas Cranmer in attempting to recover the office from its clerical and religious monopoly and in making it truly common prayer. Luther had pioneered the way in reducing the offices to two: matins and vespers. Cranmer's efforts materialized in the first *Book of Common Prayer* (*BCP* hereafter) published in 1549. He had reduced the eight offices to two: matins and evensong. The Psalter was to be read through in the course of a month of daily readings rather than weekly. Most nonscriptural material was excluded so that nothing "be read, but the very pure worde of God, the holy scriptures, or that whiche is evidently grounded upon the same. . . . the rules be fewe & easy." Furthermore "al thinges shalbe read and songe in the churche, in the Englishe tongue, to thende that the congregacion maie be therby edified." The Bible was to be read through in the course of a year and antiphons and responds were abolished as in Quiñones' first breviary. Cranmer even copied portions of Quiñones' preface, evincing a similarity of purpose.

Cranmer's ingenuity is shown in amalgamating the eight offices into two of identical structure. From medieval matins came the Lord's Prayer (now said aloud), versicles, the *Gloria Patri*, "praise ye the Lord," the *Venite*, the psalms, the first lesson, and the *Te Deum*. From lauds were selected the *Benedicite*, the second lesson, and the *Benedictus*. The Kyrie, Creed, and second Lord's Prayer came from prime. Suffrages were borrowed from a bidding prayer used before Mass. Then followed the communion collect for the day, a collect from lauds of the Blessed Virgin Mary, and a collect from prime. Matins ended here abruptly. The same procedure produced evensong, though vespers and compline provided the sources.[5]

Three years later Cranmer produced the second *BCP*. One major change occurred in the addition of a penitential introduction to both services, now renamed as morning prayer and evening prayer. A series of penitential sentences, an exhortation, the general confession, and an absolution were added to the beginning of both services. Cardinal Quiñones had done something similar in moving a confession and absolution from prime and compline and in inserting them at the beginning of his matins.[6] A French Protestant refugee, Valérand Pullain, had a similar arrangement of exhortation, confession, and absolution in his *Liturgia Sacra*, published the previous year in London. The

---

[4] J. Wickham Legg (ed.), *The Second Recension of the Quignon Breviary* (London: Henry Bradshaw Society, vols. 35 and 42, 1908 and 1912).

[5] These may be compared with the Sarum *Breviary* texts in F. E. Brightman, *The English Rite* (London: Rivingtons, 1915), I, 126-67.

[6] *Quignon Breviary* I, 32.

1928 American *BCP* made the penitential introduction optional on most occasions. Minor changes came about in the 1662 English revision: The response, "The Lord's name be praised," was inserted, and the five final prayers were added together with permission for inserting an anthem among them. The effect was that of making the offices perform the function of general intercession formerly left to the litany.

The 1662 offices were the services that John Wesley revised for the Methodists in North America as a part of his book, *The Sunday Service of the Methodists in North America with Other Occasional Services.*[7] Wesley made some major changes in the offices, largely in the direction of brevity and in omitting many psalms and parts of others as "highly improper for the mouths of a Christian congregation." He replaced the absolution making it a prayer for pardon (cf. below). Wesley omitted the *Venite*, the *Benedicite*, and the *Benedictus* (objectionable to the Puritans), the second Lord's Prayer, the suffrages, the anthem, and two of the concluding prayers.

Wesley's service was little used, the Americans being convinced that they could pray better with their books and eyes shut than with them open. In 1792 the 305 pages of the *Sunday Service* were reduced to eight services in 37 pages in the back of the *Discipline*. Morning prayer and evening prayer were not among them. For more than a century Methodist ministers concocted their own order of worship without assistance from official forms. Due to revivalism, evangelistic preaching often dominated the entire service. Quartets and choirs were introduced despite Wesley's distaste for anthems. Hymn singing, promoted by the Wesleys, became a major part of the service. After more than a century, the *Methodist Hymnal* (*MH* hereafter) of 1905 reintroduced an "Order of Worship." Its rubrics directed: "Let all our people be exhorted to kneel in prayer, keeping their faces towards the minister." The sequence is: voluntary, hymn, Apostles' Creed, prayer and Lord's Prayer, anthem, Old Testament lesson (which if a psalm could be read responsively), the *Gloria Patri*, New Testament lesson, notices, collection, hymn, sermon, prayer, hymn, doxology, and benediction. No explanation is given for the strange location of the Creed at the beginning of the service nor of the disappearance of the phrase: "He descended into hell," retained by Wesley. The frequent confusion within Methodism of the psalm with an Old Testament lesson may date from this Order. During the final hymn "an invitation to come to Christ, or to unite with the Church" was prescribed. The Psalter as arranged by Wesley appears in the back of the *Hymnal*. Since 1792 congregational singing had become an integral part of the service but at the expense of the canticles. Drawbacks appear in the clerical monopolizing of prayer, in the lack of relationship between Creed, lessons, and sermon, and in the ambivalence in the service between one designed for a faithful congregation or one for an audience of prospective converts.

[7] (London: 1784).

16

Various twentieth-century disciplines included orders of worship. The *MH* 1935 included four, one being Wesley's morning prayer. The *Book of Worship* (*BW* hereafter) of 1944 capped this with no less than ten! No doubt this proliferation was one reason leading to the second *BW* (1964). In the *Proposed Revisions* (1960) only one "Order of Worship" appears, with the caption: "The following order is adapted from the Sunday Service of John Wesley and is recommended for use every Lord's Day." This service with a few revisions appears as "The Order of Worship" in the *BW* 1964 and the *MH* 1966. In returning to Wesley (and what is almost the same, the 1552 *BCP*), the service is tied directly to its origins in the medieval monastic hours, the offices of the early church, and the synagogue service. At the same time, it includes many developments characteristic of nineteenth-century Methodism: extempore prayer, invitation to Christian discipleship, and hymn singing. Thus it is a curious, though workable, fusion of the ancient Christian tradition of the offices plus nineteenth-century evangelical Protestantism. The twentieth century seems to have contributed little to the structure aside from a general tidying up. But the dual heritage of American Methodism—traditional Christianity plus nineteenth-century evangelical piety—is well represented.

II

The structure of the service is of basic importance. Within it, individual items can be best understood in the light of brief historical explanations. The items are keyed to the "Order of Worship." Letters refer to individual portions of the service and numbers to the rubrics.

A. Prelude: This is a proper of instrumental music. It might be more accurately termed an "opening voluntary," since other types of compositions are used. Such use of music seems to have been a Protestant innovation, cultivated especially in Lutheran circles.

B. Scripture Sentences, or Call to Worship: These have become propers in both the *BW* (cf. Chap. II below) and to some extent in the 1892 and 1928 editions of the American *BCP*. The modern sentences represent refinements over Wesley's five sentences and the 1662 *BCP*'s eleven. In both instances they were definitely of a penitential nature, deriving from Cranmer's 1552 penitential introduction to the office. Cranmer had taken most of them from the "chapters" used in the various medieval hours during Lent. Turning the sentences into a means of introducing the theme of a season or festival certainly is a subversion of Cranmer's use of them, but most modern revisers consider it a definite improvement.

C. Hymn: These too are propers. Two books are necessary to perform "The Order of Worship": The *MH* (which contains the "Order of Worship" as well as hymns) and the *Bible*. The *MH* is mainly a collection of propers, especially hymns, psalms, and canticles. The opening hymn often reflects the current season or festival of the Christian year; otherwise it is likely to be an expression of praise. Office hymns were a part of the medieval hours but were omitted

17

from the *BCP* because of the lack of translations in Cranmer's times. Many were translated in the nineteenth century by John Mason Neale, an Anglican priest whose contributions to the *Hymnal* are second in number only to Isaac Watts and the Wesleys. Many office hymns end in doxologies. Representative examples are *MH* numbers 78, 298, 303, 357, 448, and 814.

D. Invocation: This collect, so prominent in the service, comes from a little-known source. It is the composition of the Rev. William Bright, Regius Professor of Ecclesiastical History at Oxford during the last third of the nineteenth century. It first appeared in the 1861 edition of his *Ancient Collects*. The prayer continues the practice of many ancient collects of reflecting biblical language, in this case King James Version: James 1:17, Zechariah 12:10, and John 4:23. A shortened version appeared among the "Additional Prayers" in the "Family Prayer" section of the 1928 American *BCP*. Methodism seems to have rescued this prayer from obscurity.

E. Call to Confession: This exhortation is a rather subtle form of religious education characteristic of Cranmer. It first appeared as part of the penitential introduction to morning prayer in the 1552 Prayer Book and was scarcely changed in the 1662 *BCP*. Wesley omitted the middle sentence which lists the other acts of worship besides confession: thanksgiving, praise, hearing of God's Word, and supplication. The effect was to render the exhortation entirely penitential and make it serve solely as a spoken rubric. Wesley's passion for brevity was exceeded by his descendants who in the *MH* 1935 carefully pared down the verbiage.

F. Alternate Call to Confession: Following the examples of the 1892 and 1928 *BCP*'s, a short alternate call to confession was given. Between the 1960 *Proposed Revisions* and the *BW* 1964, the word "humbly" was omitted.

G. General Confession: This prayer has survived with very little change from the 1552 *BCP* except for modernizing slightly: "Spare thou them, O God, which confesse theyr faultes. Restore thou them that be penitent." The chief change is the omission in *MH* 1935 of "and there is no health in us" and "miserable offenders." Liberalism evidently could not stomach such a view of man, though Wesley would and did (in his treatise, *The Doctrine of Original Sin According to Scripture, Reason, and Experience*). The prayer itself is a magnificent example of the creative ability Cranmer and his associates had in converting biblical phrases into prayers. From the opening use of Isaiah 53:6 ("All we like sheep have gone astray") onward it combines biblical phrases in an amazingly consistent and beautiful fashion.

H. Prayer for Pardon or Words of Assurance: John Wesley evidently balked at the Declaration of Absolution in the 1662 *BCP* which was a short theological discussion of absolution coming from 1552 almost verbatim. He substituted this prayer, appointed as the communion collect for the twenty-fourth Sunday after Trinity, one of the least used proper collects in the *BCP*. Cranmer translated this very ancient prayer, first appearing in the Gregorian Sacramentary and dating, most likely, from the sixth century. Wesley either resisted the possibility of a layman using a declaratory absolution or, more likely (since he did the same in the communion service), preferred a precatory statement. The words remain the same, except "bands" has become "bonds" and "for Jesus Christ's sake" has become "for the sake of Jesus Christ."

i. The Lord's Prayer: Here begins the service of matins in the 1549 *BCP*. In the Sarum and other breviaries since the thirteenth century, matins had begun with the priest saying silently the Lord's Prayer, but Cranmer's first rubric instructed the priest to "begynne with a loude voyce." The conclusion: "For thine is . . ." was added in 1662 following the Scottish *BCP* of 1637. Wesley changed "which" to "who," "in earth" to "on Earth," and sometime since 1905 the final "and ever" was omitted. The ultimate sources, of course, are Matthew 6:9-13 and Luke 11:2-4. The longer ending appears in a number of ancient manuscripts.

j. Versicles: The first service after midnight in the medieval offices began most appropriately with the words: "Domine labia mea aperies," taken verbatim from Psalm 51:15 as was the following response. The 1552 *BCP* changed "my mouth" to "our mouth." Cranmer retained from medieval matins a second set of versicles from Psalm 70:1: "O God, make speed to save us. O Lord, make haste to help us" and the use of the *Gloria Patri*. Wesley retained these versicles, though neither the American 1789 *BCP* or *MH* 1935 did. The third pair of versicles represent Cranmer's contribution of "Prayse ye the Lorde" in 1549 and the 1637 Scottish and 1662 English *BCP*'s addition "The Lord's name be praised." In the *BW* the versicles lead to the Psalter although in medieval matins and all English and American *BCP*'s they introduce the *Venite,* Psalm 95. Wesley omitted the *Venite* in 1784, possibly in the interest of brevity. Or he may have found the last four verses distasteful, as did the American revisers of the *BCP* who omitted them in 1789 in favor of Psalm 96:9 and 13. Wesley was thus not the only one to censure the Psalter, and there are interesting parallels between his revisions and those in the first American *BCP*.

k. Psalter or Other Act of Praise: The psalms, of course, are propers and will be discussed in the following chapter. They provided the major portions of the daily office of the medieval church, being said through weekly (at least in theory). Cranmer devised a plan for reciting the Psalter through on a monthly basis. Wesley, having expurgated the Psalter as containing much "highly improper for the mouths of a Christian Congregation," retained basically the same pattern. Wesley's version of the Psalter was retained as late as the *MH* 1905, though his scheme for daily reading had long since disappeared.

l. Gloria Patri: One of the oldest non-biblical portions of the service is the *Gloria Patri or* Little Doxology (cf. the *Gloria in excelsis* or greater Doxology). The *Gloria Patri* took its present form after the trinitarian controversies of the fourth century. It reflects such New Testament doxologies as Jude 25 and the baptismal formula of Matthew 28:19. The language has not changed since the 1549 translation. Traditionally western Christianity has sung the *Gloria Patri* at the end of all psalms thus giving them a trinitarian conclusion. The phrase "as it was in the beginning, is now and ever shall be" is a western addition from the sixth century, affirming that the Son is eternal also. The *Gloria Patri* was anti-Arian in origin and has been dropped by modern Unitarians. Liturgically its effect is that of baptizing the psalms, in the terms of Isaac Watts, of making David speak like a Christian.

м. Anthem: This is a proper, though no official collection is provided by the church. The origin of the anthem (a corruption of "antiphon") evidently is a survival of the custom introduced by the Franciscans in the thirteenth century of singing anthems of the Virgin after compline. No mention of anthems appears in early prayer books, but 1662 inserted among the closing prayers the rubric: "In Quires and places where they sing here followeth the Anthem." Thus its use would have been mostly in collegiate and cathedral churches. In accord with his practice of forbidding anthems "because they cannot be properly called joint-worship," Wesley omitted this rubric, as do all three American *BCP*'s.

The anthem raises some acute liturgical problems. There is a measure of truth in Wesley's fear that anthems were not a fully corporate act of worship, as congregational singing was intended to be. There is also the problem that placing the anthem in this position seems to involve duplication of the psalms, already an act of praise anticipating God's Word in the lessons. Either the psalmody or the anthem might have been more appropriately located as a gradual between the two scripture lessons. A third difficulty is caused by the frequent irrelevance of the words and music to the rest of the service or the season. Ideally the anthem should serve as a musical commentary on the appointed lessons. Perhaps a rubric is needed to prevent too subjective or irrelevant musical exegesis. One example is that in the 1928 *BCP* limiting anthems to "the words of Holy Scripture or of the Book of Common Prayer."

N. The Scripture Lessons: These are propers and will be discussed in Chapter Two. In a sense this is the oldest stratum of the service: two lessons (law and prophets) having been read in the synagogue service. Three or nine lessons were provided for in Sarum matins; Quiñones reduced the lessons at matins to three: usually Old Testament, gospel, and Acts or an epistle. Cranmer provided two lessons: one Old Testament, the other New Testament. Wesley paraphrased the rubric of 1662 to require that the Old Testament lesson should be such "as is appointed in the Table of proper Lessons" and specified that there "shall be read in like manner the Second Lesson, taken out of the New Testament." The *BW* 1964 rubric does not intend the exclusion of Revelation or Acts, since lessons from both books are among the epistles provided on pages 62-64. Psalmody, an anthem, or a hymn may be of value between the two lessons though not provided for by the rubrics. It should be kept in mind that the lessons are read as a basic part of the service through which God's word is declared to his people. They are not provided simply as sermon texts. Two lessons are required, Old Testament and New Testament, and would seem particularly needed in a day of widespread biblical illiteracy.

o. Affirmation of Faith: Since no single creed is specified here, this item might be considered a proper, to vary from time to time. However many congregations may consistently use one creed. Hence we shall treat it as an ordinary part of the service. In the *BW* 1964 the affirmations of faith appear on pages 179-81. The creed is essentially a congregational affirmation of God's Word as revealed through Scripture. A strong case could be made for its location immediately after the sermon, emphasizing that God's Word is contemporized in preaching and strengthening the concept of the sermon as the place where God's Word is made incarnate again among his people.

The first affirmation provided on page 179 is the so-called *Apostles' Creed*. Actually it is the old baptismal formula of the Roman Church attested to by Hippolytus in almost its present form at the beginning of the third century. It soon spread beyond Rome and with minor emendations was widely used in the West though not in the East. The most controversial phrase has been: "He descended into hell," the last clause added. It was a stumbling block to the revisers of the first American *BCP* in 1789 (who made it optional) though retained by Wesley. In the *MH* 1905 American Methodists eliminated the phrase. In the ninth century the Apostles' Creed found a place in prime and subsequently in compline. Cranmer simply followed the Sarum *Breviary* in using it for matins and evensong. The ideal place for baptism is immediately after the New Testament lesson (as Cranmer specified). Then the Creed becomes a congregational profession of the faith into which the children have been baptized, or adults, being baptized, may join the congregation in affirming the faith of the church. The spoken rubric introducing the Apostles' and Nicene Creeds on page 179 was produced for the 1964 BW and is not necessary.

The Nicene Creed in its present form dates from the Council of Constantinople in 381. Probably during the ninth century the western church added to the third paragraph the clause "and the Son," though this addition was never accepted in the East. Since the fifth century in the East and the ninth century in the West, the Nicene Creed has been associated with the Eucharist. It was not associated with the daily offices in the *BCP* until a bit of compromise placed it in the 1789 American *BCP* in return for the elimination of the so-called Athanasian Creed. Wesley eliminated any reference to the use of the Athanasian Creed on the fourteen feasts for which the 1662 *BCP* made it mandatory, and this traditional Creed is not used in Methodist worship.

Some serious theological questions may be raised about the other three creeds published in the *BW* 1964. A creed is not a testimony of personal convictions but a profession of the faith of the church. The spoken rubric provided on pages 180 and 181 for these three affirmations is particularly misleading since these declarations of the "holy faith" of the "one true Church, apostolic and universal" are scarcely used outside Methodism. Methodism may have some claim to being one, true, apostolic, and universal, but it certainly has no monopoly on these adjectives. The sentence evidently originated in a *Book of Common Worship* published by Bishop Wilbur P. Thirkield and Oliver

Huckel in 1932.[8] The *BW* 1964 eliminates the words "reverently and sincerely." The "Modern Affirmation" and others represent an attempt to speak to the modern man. It is open to question whether any is more successful than the blunt recital of events in the Apostles' Creed, though none is as abstract as the Nicene Creed.

A Modern Affirmation was written by Professor Edwin Lewis, distinguished Methodist theologian of Drew University, for the *MH* 1935. In a letter dated May 3, 1951, and addressed to Dr. Leon Adkins, Professor Lewis stated that the Creed had been requested by Bishop Thirkield as one that "should preserve the biblical and historical emphases, that the language should have at least a suggestion of the liturgical, and that the statement should be sufficiently general to permit its use in congregations representing somewhat divergent theological views." According to Dr. Lewis, it was accepted "exactly as I had written it."

The Korean Creed was composed by Bishop Herbert Welch for the Methodist church in Korea. It was adopted by the first general conference of the Korean Methodist Church in 1930 for use in worship and as a means of stating the Christian faith in terms comprehensible to non-Christians. It found its way into the *MH* 1935, and the language has not been changed.

A Creed in the Words of St. John was arranged by Henry D. A. Major.[9] It appeared in Thirkield and Huckel's *Book of Common Worship*. The Creed is composed of portions of the Fourth Gospel such as John 4:24, etc. It has never been included in the *MH* but is in both *BW*'s.

P. Salutation: A frequently used exchange in both the Eucharist (at least since the third century) and office occurs in this passage. Ultimately it derives from a Jewish greeting recorded in Ruth 2:4. Prime in the Sarum *Breviary* had it in this position as an introduction to the closing set of prayers, and Cranmer retained it. In 1662 the salutation introduced the *Kyrie*, Lord's Prayer, and suffrages. Wesley eliminated the (second) Lord's Prayer and the suffrages. The *Kyrie* was eliminated in the 1935 *MH* version of Wesley's service as it had been in all American *BCP*'s. The words "Let us pray" are a common spoken rubric in both the Eucharist and office.

Q. Collect for Grace: In all English and American prayer books this has been the third collect of the closing prayers for morning prayer. It is used daily throughout the year. Why it was chosen as the sole collect for the "Order of Worship" is hard to understand since it is appropriate only in a morning service. It is a close translation of a collect from prime and is of ancient origin, coming from the Gregorian Sacramentary. Both 1549 and 1552 ended the

[8] *Book of Common Worship for Use in the Several Communions of the Church of Christ* (New York: E. P. Dutton, 1932), p. 48. Bishop Thirkield (of the Methodist Episcopal Church) was Chairman of the Commission of Worship of the Federal Council of Churches. The Reverend Oliver Huckel was pastor of the Congregational Church, Greenwich, Connecticut.

[9] Principal of Ripon Hall, Oxford, editor of *The Modern Churchman*, and author of *The Church's Creeds and the Modern Man* (London: Skeffington, 1933).

morning office at this point. The 1662 *BCP* added a rubric permitting an anthem and five prayers. Wesley retained the original three collects, eliminated all reference to the anthem, rewrote "A Prayer for the King's Majesty" as "A Prayer for the Supreme Rulers" of the United States, discarded the prayers for the royal family and for the clergy and people, and kept a prayer from the Byzantine Liturgy and the Grace (II Cor. 13:14).

At this point both Anglican morning prayer and Wesley's service ended. No mention is made of a sermon in the rubrics, since morning prayer was a daily service and the sermon was demanded in the holy Communion. From this point on the Methodist "Order of Worship" is independent of the daily office traditions. What follows are basically the adjustments necessary to make the office into the main Sunday service for congregational worship, i.e., that which it was never intended to be. The intercessions, offertory, sermon, and benediction were borrowed from the Eucharist and appended to the office.

R. Pastoral Prayer: Although Wesley did not make provision for extemporaneous prayer in his "Order for Morning Prayer," he did so at the end of his "Order for the Administration of the Lord's Supper": "Then the Elder, if he see it expedient, may put up an Extempore Prayer." This did not mean prayer simply uttered at the time. Wesley asked: "Are not then the words we speak to God to be set in order at least as carefully as those we speak to our fellow worms?" [10] Extemporaneous prayer deserved as much preparation as the sermon and, like it, has the possibility of immediacy and relevancy in expressing the concerns of the congregation growing out of the pastor's encounters with his people throughout the week. The advantages of such prayer are being increasingly recognized today. Within Roman Catholicism the prayer of the faithful in the mass has increasingly approximated the pastoral prayer at its best. It would be most unfortunate for Methodists to abandon extempore prayer, though it obviously needs revitalizing and experimentation in finding means that would enable the congregation to speak concerns from the pews.

A major problem of location is entailed by simply grafting the pastoral prayer, offertory, and sermon on after the office. A permissive rubric acknowledges this tacitly in permitting the offertory and prayers to follow the sermon. This includes all the material after the affirmation of faith, thus allowing the sermon to appear in the context of the lessons and creed as it does in the Eucharist. To intrude the prayers and offertory between these essential halves of the service of the Word is to undercut the basic relationship of God's Word heard in the lessons and sermon. A further advantage is achieved in making the offertory and prayers the final major act in the service, since this position makes it clear that Christian worship leads to Christian service in the world. Indeed, the two cannot be separated without grave danger to both. The offerings of prayer and money are directed for the benefit of the church, for those

[10] *Journal* ed. by Nehemiah Curnock (New York: Eaton and Mains, n.d.) I, 309.

in positions of responsibility, and for those in need. Thus the prayers in this position should be largely intercessory.

s. Offertory: This may include several acts: notices of the concerns of the church and world, scripture sentences, an anthem, the receiving and presentation of the offering, and a prayer of dedication or appropriate service music. Like the sermon, the offertory derives from the Eucharist. In early times people brought forward their own offerings of bread and wine. Cranmer in the 1549 Eucharist indicated that people should bring their money offering "unto the poore mennes boxe every one accordynge to his habilitie and charitable mynde." He also provided for the saying or singing of various scripture sentences as provided for in the *BW* 1964 rubric. Surprisingly no mention of these is made in the present Methodist communion order, though Wesley preserved most of them. Too often the anthem in this position becomes a musical blanket for the action and raises some questions as to how fair this is to the musicians. Offertory sentences and prayers appear on pages 195-99 of the *BW*. Appropriate service music such as *MH* 807-12, may also be used. The most common, no doubt, will be *MH* 809, Bishop Thomas Ken's doxological stanza. The "Topical Index" of *MH* 1966 lists more than a score of doxological stanzas (under "Doxologies"). Many of these can be used effectively at different seasons of the Christian year (e.g., the final stanza of 446 during Eastertide).

t. Hymn: This is the second hymn provided. It could better follow the sermon rather than intruding between it and the lessons. Frequently it will be chosen to reinforce the witness of the sermon or the season of the Christian year at hand.

u. The Sermon: This, we hope, will vary from time to time. Like the pastoral prayer, it contributes an element of spontaneity. It, too, demands experimentation in finding means of getting the sermon out of the pulpit and into the pew. The sermon may be defined as a means by which the power of God is made present in the midst of his people through a contemporary witness to his Word as revealed in Scripture. God's saving power is made present to the hearers through preaching. It is a risk, a radical act of trust that God will use even man's inarticulateness and ineptitude to do his will among his people. Traditionally the sermon belongs with the Eucharist. Preaching is performed through the authority of the church, and Methodist deacons and elders are ordained with the words: "Take thou authority . . . to preach the Word," having been previously licensed "to preach the Gospel in the congregation." The sermon is an act based upon Scripture and performed through the authority of the church. In this sense it is to be distinguished from a statement of personal convictions every bit as much as a creed is. Were the creed to follow the sermon, this might be more apparent. The sources of the sermon are Scripture and life, the authority is from the church, and the power is of God.

v. Invitation to Christian Discipleship: This is a relic of the revivalistc bent of much Methodist worship during the nineteenth century. In some cases it has been replaced with an announcement of the concerns of the church and world during or after the closing intercessory prayers, an invitation to individuals to offer themselves for service to others. In some areas it remains an invitation to walk-in church membership, though increasingly this has been replaced by an invitation to join a disciplined study group preparing for confirmation. In this sense the invitation might be used effectively as the occasion for public enrollment in the catechumenate (those undergoing instruction preparatory to church membership) as in the early church. Baptism and confirmation are more appropriate after the second lesson. In no case should re-Baptism ever be allowed since this completely undercuts the meaning of the sacraments.

w. Hymn: The third hymn is another proper drawn from *MH*.

x. Benediction: Often called the blessing, the benediction, too, comes from the Lord's Supper. Usually it is composed of scriptural passages. Examples appear on pages 205-6 of *BW* 1964.

y. Postlude: Like the prelude, this is a variable piece of instrumental music. It is often called a "Closing Voluntary."

III

We turn now to a brief theological rationale of the structure presented above. A historical understanding is a necessary first part of a theological treatment of worship, and the "Order of Worship" is no exception. We will deal with two theological concerns here: balance and relevancy.

It has been a rather common sport for those who write on worship to analyze it as consisting in three, four, or five basic acts. Wesley spoke of "four grand parts of public prayer; deprecation, petition, intercession, and thanksgiving" (Conference *Minutes* 1766). Other writers have divided the parts differently. The problem with all such divisions is that, necessary though they may be for pedagogical reasons, they are artificial and misleading. Worship, like life itself, is not a particularly tidy affair. All attempts to ratonalize a service of worship come long after the service itself has evolved. And as we have seen, the various orders of worship have been constantly shaped by contingent historical factors. Those items that have survived did so because of a basic adequacy for the conditions of human life and the expression of these conditions. The chief criterion of a service of worship is not that it fits an abstract rational pattern but that it is an adequate representation of man's relationship to God. Consequently what we must judge is the balance of a service in representing the Christian understanding of reality.

This is by no means to insist that sequence is unimportant, since the structure itself will influence the interpretation of the items it contains. But it is to say that one cannot divide a service of worship into neat segments and discern a systematic progression. Where, for instance, does the Lord's Prayer fit into any scheme? It is tempting to isolate certain acts as praise and others as proclamation and so forth. But actually every act of worship is an act of praise, and in every act the gospel is proclaimed. I praise God in listening to his Word, and the gospel is proclaimed when I confess and forgiveness is declared to me. There is the further problem that isolating individual acts of worship tends to make a service more self-conscious. Such a clinical approach may be necessary in lecturing and writing about worship, just as medical students find it necessary to dissect a corpse. But the cadaver should never be mistaken for the living tissue of worship.

Our theological evaluation is directed first of all to the whole of the service rather than to individual parts of it. The question remains: Does the "Order of Worship" reflect the Christian understanding of man's relation to God? Our answer is a qualified "yes." Basically the service presents this relationship as that of man as a sinner who is forgiven and enabled to praise God for the extraordinary and ordinary things done and yet to be done by God on man's behalf. It also depicts God as accessible to his people, both in accepting their praise and in openness to their changing needs and conditions. This God acts in giving himself through his Word and in receiving man's offering of his concerns and service. This analysis will not be dead center on every Christian's understanding of the divine-human relationship. Indeed it would be impossible to find any such consensus wthin the church. But the "Order of Worship" is close to the mark in reflecting the historic understanding of the way God and man relate to each other.

The deficiencies are basically those of balance. Confession is magnified beyond its importance. Acts of confession are basic in understanding man's status as sinner but less important than the praise of God for what he has done. Encounter with Eastern Christians has raised the question in the minds of many Westerners as to whether we have done well to make penitential acts so important in our worship as compared to acts of praise. The praise of God is a more objective act than parading our miserable offenses. The most faithfully preserved part of morning prayer in the "Order of Worship" is the penitential section added by Cranmer in 1552 as something of backlash from Reformed Protestantism on the continent. But Cranmer balanced this with the *Venite* and two canticles of praise that Methodists have omitted. The "Order of Worship" demands that care be taken, especially in the choice of hymns, that an adequate balance of praise and confession be found. What God has done for us is infinitely more important than what we have done against him. The gospel is good news.

Another concern may be raised as to the adequacy of this service, as often conducted, in representing that God is active in the world today. The forms of our worship often seem to suggest that God quit work when the last canonical book of the New Testament was written. The way we worship often leaves the impression that God has been dead since the second century. The sermon and pastoral prayer are the two elements in the service in which the reality of God as acting in our midst and in the midst of the world can be affirmed. The lack of serious intercessory prayer in much of Methodist worship is one of the worst indications of failure to acknowledge the activity of the God whom we worship. Unfortunately there is no rubric demanding intercessions for "all sorts and conditions of men," and this lack leaves the service often suggesting that God's actions are all past tense rather than present and future.

Related to this is an underplaying of man's responsibilities in God's world, i.e., the relation of worship to mission. While this might be comprehended under the "Invitation to Christian Discipleship," that act is usually conceived in a more narrow sense. Yet the fulfillment of love of God comes in relation to one's neighbor. The kiss of peace (act of reconciliation) once expressed this in the Eucharist, but direct reference to mission is not adequately represented in this service. We need strenuous rethinking of the forms of pastoral prayer, notices, offertory, and invitation to Christian discipleship.

Our other concern is that of relevancy. Just how relevant is the "Order of Worship" to the conditions of modern life? We have seen that basically the "Order of Worship" is a Bible service, and a new Catholic version is simply called the "Bible Service." Within Judaism it developed as a means of instruction in the traditions of the people. Throughout most of its history in Christianity it has been the private preserve of the clergy and religious communities, men whose piety was nourished and shaped by the constant reiteration of Scripture on a daily basis. Cranmer took the radical step of making it accessible to the laity and succeeded, perhaps better than he intended, in making it a popular service in which the congregation could participate to a remarkable extent. It was primarily a biblical service, woven around the monthly recital of the Psalter and yearly coverage of almost all the Bible. The English clergy were bound to daily recitation of the two offices. Cranmer had intended that the Eucharist would remain the chief service of the congregation, but through a number of historical accidents this did not endure. Wesley prescribed the reading of morning prayer "every Lord's Day," the "litany only on Wednesdays and Fridays," and extempore prayer on "all other days." But he also advised "the elders to administer the supper of the Lord on every Lord's Day." The office was to be balanced by the sacrament.

A major problem today is the biblical illiteracy of the average Christian. Are we justified in using the office that takes such a literacy for granted? Or is it an effective means of imparting biblical literacy? Neither question is easily answered. But at any rate the adequacy of the divine office as a basic pattern for congregational worship has been widely questioned. What alternative do we have? The Eucharist has since New Testament times been the primary act of congregational worship, and this was the intention of Cranmer. Wesley's sermon on "The Duty of Constant Communion" makes clear the importance he placed on frequent communion. It has been claimed by some recent writers that the Eucharist is a more missionary type of worship than the office, in that it conveys the very heart of the gospel in dramatic form Sunday after Sunday as opposed to the fragmentary exposition of it week after week in the office. The message of the Eucharist is instantaneous; the office is intended to be cumulative.

Ideally one could wish for both. The Methodist Communion order lacks the use of the Old Testament lesson, a vital part of the Christian faith. And it has no psalmody from the basic book of Christian praise. Yet the Eucharist supplies movement and action, elements of communication lacking in the tradition of the offices. The problem is largely that of communication. We need elements of the office to proclaim and rejoice in the whole history of God's acts. But modern man who participates so much in the communications revolution also needs to be shown what God has done, to be drawn into acting out the drama of salvation himself. The name of a children's game may best sum up the ways of making Methodist worship more relevant: "Show and Tell." After almost two hundred years we may yet catch up with Wesley's realization that we can get through to men by combining the traditions of the office and the Eucharist.

IV

We turn now to discuss pastoral concerns in conducting the service according to the rubrics provided and to speak of the context of the local congregation.

Three general rubrics precede the service.

1. Most laymen are untrained in using silence in worship in a creative fashion. What frequently occurs here is speaking in many tongues in a most nonbiblical sense, the babble of people exchanging pleasantries. Yet they can hardly be blamed when nothing is provided for them but a stern: "Be silent." Some churches call people's attention to the "Prayers for Use on Entering the Church," items 715-18 in *MH*.

2. This refers to the propers discussed in the following chapter.

3. The congregational "Amen" is a relic of Hebrew, meaning something firm or certain. It has been used within Christian worship since the first century (I Cor. 14:16). The Amen provides a congregational form of affirmation, a "me too."

We shall treat briefly the specific rubrics that follow.

4. The scripture sentences would normally be said by the minister or sung by the choir. Only one is necessary.

5. Standing to sing or for any other act of worship is basically a gesture of respect for the presence of one greater than ourselves. One could argue that except for prayer of confession it is a suitable posture for prayer as well as hymnody and psalmody.

6. Architecture will determine whether a procession is necessary. Many new churches locate the choir so that a procession is not needed. There is nothing particularly edifying about a choir procession, though we have often contrived to make a virtue out of the mechanical necessity of getting the choir in and out of a too conspicuous location. If the minister is in the procession the sentences can usually be heard when spoken at the back of the church.

7. It is both appropriate and convenient for the people to stand for the invocation. There does not seem to be any great reason for limiting the recital of this prayer to the minister.

8. & 9. The call to confession is a spoken rubric usually said by the minister while standing and facing the congregation.

10. If a posture indicating humility is desirable anywhere during the service, it is at this point. During the nineteenth century, Methodists generally knelt for prayer, though they have become more comfortable since by relaxing in upholstered pews. It is most appropriate that all join in saying this prayer.

11. The minister prays for forgiveness of sin, but the very fact he does so is a declaration of God's willingness to forgive. Some would insist that this act (and the benediction) belong especially to the ordained ministry as appropriate to those authorized by the church to exercise a representative ministry. Others would insist these acts belong equally well to all baptized Christians.

12. The Lord's Prayer as the exemplar of all Christian prayer ought always to be congregational. Musical settings should be avoided unless all can participate. The posture is not indicated, though it would be the same in 10, 11, and 12.

13. There are three standard ways of saying the psalms: as a dialogue between minister and people, as a dialogue between halves of the congregation, or in unison. The second of these is the most effective and joyous though not the easiest to organize. Standing is the obvious physical expression for an act of praise. Ideally the psalms deserve to be sung, and various experiments such as the Gelineau psalms or the chants 663, 664, 667, 669, 671, and 672 *MH* could be used. The *Gloria Patri* may be sung to several settings such as 792, 793, and 794 *MH*.

14. Two lessons are prescribed, one from each Testament. The reader is not specified, and there is no reason why a layman coming from the congregation cannot act as a lector for one or both lessons, provided he has been carefully selected and trained. The lessons may be read in the midst of the congregation, from the lectern, or from the pulpit.

15. The Creed has a doxological character, and standing is appropriate. When the Creed is followed by the sermon and the sermon by a hymn there is a good physiological opportunity for standing before settling down and after waking up. The doxology may seem redundant, though it ought to highlight the doxological nature of the Creed.

16. This may be ministerial or in unison. Standing would be especially appropriate for this and the pastoral prayer as an expression of respect for God's presence.

17. The notices can easily degenerate into commercials for the church program. Some of this may be necessary but too much promotionalism is self-defeating. If we took seriously the world as our parish the notices might have a radically different (and more significant) function in worship.

18. Offertory sentences and prayers appear on pages 195-99 of the *BW*. Various publications are available on the training of ushers. There is nothing wrong with placing the offering plates on the altar-table after the offering has been received. Indeed they are more appropriate than flowers and candles,

since the plates are used for and do represent the sacrificial aspect of worship. Appropriate musical elements at the presentation of the offering are 807-12 *MH*.

19. This has been discussed (and strongly urged) above.

20. & 21. Standing, the doxological posture, is appropriate for the hymns.

22. There does not seem to be any great advantage to remaining seated during and after the benediction unless the people have been trained in silent prayer. Items 768-72 *MH* or pages 206-7 *BW* may help here. There is nothing especially edifying about watching the candles be extinguished. Further architectural and liturgical experimentation needs to be done with regard to making the process of scattering into the world a meaningful culmination of Christian worship. Some have argued that the congregation ought to be on their feet during the benediction with the sense of being sent forth to continue their service in the world.

Obviously adaptation will have to be made from congregation to congregation corresponding to the sociological factors of each community. Too much standing may be impossible for churches of elderly parishioners. Changes in wording may be helpful for young people. Worship and sociology are intimately connected. There is nothing holy about uniformity. The invention of printing made it possible; the invention of television may have made it superfluous. We are concerned with the involvement of a specific community of people, not with people in general.

Our concern here is with pastoral liturgy, and if liturgy is to be truly pastoral it must relate as effectively as possible to the unique individual congregation by which it is used. The rubrics present us with an example of excellence. One ought not depart from them except for clear theological, historical, and pastoral reasons. But the glory of the free church tradition is that we can adapt rubrics to local circumstances. The tragedy is that most Methodists have not even been aware that there are rubrics. The burden of proof is upon whoever wishes to depart from the rubrics. But when substantiated by solid theological, historical, and pastoral concerns, changes are hard to forbid.

In addition to the problem of adapting the service for local congregations there is the problem of preparing the congregation to understand the "Order of Worship." This will vary considerably from congregation to congregation. Ideally changes should not be made until the congregation is persuaded and instructed to the point that it wants them. In some congregations that might be never! Worship demands a tremendous teaching ministry, especially among adults. This is a long slow frustrating process but important.

Various ways can be used. A Commission on Worship can function largely as a study group, spreading ideas to other members of the church. Various groups in the church can discuss worship. Interpretations may appear in the bulletin and newsletter. Sunday School classes may discuss worship. One may occasionally do the service as a demonstration service with the minister or someone else explaining the meaning of each part. Such efforts are often very much appreciated and help people to worship with understanding.

II

The Order of Worship: The Proper Parts

James F. White

Two thirds of the *Book of Worship* is devoted to propers that can be used in the "Order of Worship." The propers are the items that vary from Sunday to Sunday or from day to day. Most of the items in the *BW* under Part II, "Aids for the Ordering of Worship," and Part III, "Acts of Praise," are provided to follow the seasons and festivals of the Christian year. The exceptions are provided to follow the seasons and festivals of the Christian year. The exceptions are in the "General Aids to Worship" under Part II. These are propers, too, but not organized on the basis of the Christian year. Thus the use of the majority of the propers provided depends upon the sequence of the Christian year. We will begin, accordingly, with a discussion of the history and theology of the Christian year.

I

The Christian year is based on Jewish customs adapted for the use of the church. The basic unit of cultic time is not the year but the week. The origin of the Jewish seven-day week is obscure; possibly it came from Canaanite sources. Its original purpose among the Hebrews seems to have been humanitarian rather than cultic; the fourth commandment forbids the work of self, children, slaves, beasts of burden, and travelers on the seventh day (Exod. 20:8-11). The justification of this is that God himself rested on the seventh day of creation. In the course of time the Sabbath came to be a cultic occasion, and in the first century A.D. Tuesday and Thursday were also observed by some Jews as days of fasting.

The early church simply adopted the seven-day cycle of Judaism with one basic change. Christ had risen from the dead on the first day of the new week or the eighth day of the old. Hence the second week of creation began with the resurrection. The commemoration of the beginning of the new creation replaced the commemoration of the completion of the old. Sunday looks forward to the events of new creation, just as the Sabbath looks backward. At the same time, each Sunday is a commemoration of the resurrection. It cannot definitely be concluded that Sunday had become the normal occasion for Christian worship in New Testament times, though this is suggested by Acts 20:7-11 and Revelation 1:10. It is indicated in a letter of Pliny ca. A.D. 112 and by Justin Martyr ca. A.D. 155 that Sunday had become the normal occasion for the gathering of the Christian community. Wednesday and Friday might be observed as days of fasting, but Sunday remained the great day of rejoicing and public worship. Each Sunday was a little Easter. And as the day of resurrection, Sunday remained a day of joy, always a feast day even during seasons of penitence. The Eucharist, as the church's great thanksgiving, has remained the normal Sunday service for most Christians throughout the church's history.

From Judaism the church also derived its two earliest and greatest annual festivals: Passover-Easter and Pentecost. The origin of both festivals is hazy. Possibly Passover was originally a nomadic spring migration date and at a later stage a spring harvest (unleavened bread), while Pentecost came from a wheat harvest festival. At an early date Passover was historicized as a commemoration of the deliverance from bondage in Egypt. Pentecost, or the Feast of Weeks (the fiftieth day after seven times seven weeks), at a much later date was historicized to commemorate the giving of the law at Mount Sinai. Whether or not the Last Supper was the Passover meal, the climactic events of Jesus' ministry occurred in the context of the Passover. Until the fourth century, Easter commemorated all the events of Holy Week. As suggested in Acts 2, the reception of the Holy Spirit was associated with the festival of Pentecost, and this Jewish festival came to be considered the birthday of the Christian church, just as the reception of the covenant at Mount Sinai represented the beginning of Judaism. Between Easter and Pentecost the early church kept the great fifty days, Paschaltide or Eastertide. Tertullian speaks of this as a time during which Christians neither fasted nor knelt. It was the earliest and most important season of the Christian year.

The third festival to emerge was that of Epiphany, possibly developed during the second century in Egypt as a Christian challenge to a pagan winter festival. Fixed on January 6, it has since represented the baptism of Jesus and his first miracle at Cana among eastern Christians, while Christians in the West preferred to commemorate the visit of the Magi. The three oldest Christian festivals—Easter, Pentecost, and Epiphany—were joined by the cult of martyrs in various local churches. There is evidence of this as early as A.D. 156

in the "Martyrdom of Polycarp." Local churches celebrated the anniversaries of the death of local heroes of the faith, their heavenly birthdays being far more important than earthly birthdays.

Not till the fourth century were important additions made to the calendar. Then the three major feasts split into a variety of feasts commemorating a series of events. Christmas apparently originated in Rome during the fourth century. It was fixed at the time of the winter solstice (another pagan festival) while Epiphany was narrowed to a commemoration of the Magi (in the West). Eight days later (January 1) would have been the Circumcision (Luke 2:21). After forty days (February 2) came the Presentation in the Temple (Luke 2:22) or Purification of Mary or Candlemas. In the seventh century a process of biological reasoning set the date of the Annunciation or Lady Day nine months prior to Christmas on March 25.

The same type of splintering occurred with Easter and Pentecost. Evidence indicates that these great changes originated in Jerusalem, very likely under the guidance of Bishop Cyril of Jerusalem during the latter half of the fourth century. The Peace of the Church led many pilgrims to visit the Holy Land. The prominent holy sites were identified and, in a pattern not totally dissimilar from that used today by aggressive chambers of commerce, special days and services were developed focusing on the sacred places. Though Easter had previously included the commemoration of the crucifixion, now the previous Friday was associated with the veneration of the true cross, relics of which soon found their way throughout the world. The result was our Good Friday. The Church of the Holy Sepulchre was the focus of worship on Easter Eve and Day, and small Easter sepulchres were built in churches across Europe where the consecrated bread might be kept during the hours Christ was entombed. Etheria, the Spanish pilgrim, also describes services forty days after Easter. Special services were subsequently held on the Mount of Olives, the site of the Ascension according to Acts 1:12. The feast of Pentecost originally included the departure of Christ and arrival of the Spirit. Maundy Thursday also became a separate commemoration as did Palm Sunday, each with appropriate services on special spots. Thus by the end of the fourth century the great festivals of the Christian year had developed according to two annual cycles: the sanctoral, those on fixed dates (such as December 25) and the temporal, Sundays and days dependent upon the date of Easter (such as Ascension Day).

The history of the calendar since has seen constant addition and subtraction of Saints Days and christological and Marian feasts. Most of the modern calendar had been worked out by the end of the fourth century, and modern reforms have tended to reject many subsequent accumulations. The medieval offices appointed propers for both the temporal and sanctoral cycles. The 1549 *BCP* eliminated propers for the saints except for the chief Marian feasts, Apostles, Evangelists, St. Stephen, Holy Innocents, St. John the Baptist, St. Mary Magdalene, St. Michael and All Angels, and All Saints. John Wesley eliminated even these "as at present answering no valuable end." America has contributed

Thanksgiving Day, deriving from the Plymouth Harvest Thanksgiving of 1621. In addition to special days, the church has long observed special seasons. Eastertide, the great fifty days, is the oldest and most important of these. It is a season of joy in the resurrection. Lent had its origins in the second century through the catechetical and penitential preparation of candidates for baptism at the Easter vigil. By the late fourth century the Roman Church had developed a six-week Lenten season, and in the sixth century its beginning was established on what came to be known as Ash Wednesday. The season had become one of penitence, associated with recollection of Jesus' sufferings. Sundays during Lent (as little Easters) are not numbered among the forty days that constitute Lent.

Among Eastern Christians the Christian year begins with Easter. After the fourth-century introduction of Christmas at Rome it became common to reckon Christmas the beginning of the church's year. It seems likely that areas in the West that had not yet adopted Christmas were already observing a season comparable to Lent in preparation for Epiphany. A shortened version of this was eventually adopted in Rome as the season of Advent, beginning with the fourth Sunday before Christmas. By the eighth century the first Sunday of Advent was considered the beginning of the Christian year. Advent combines both penitential and joyful preparation for Christmas. Not only does Advent prepare one for the feast of the Nativity, but it also contains a theme of anticipation of the second coming of Christ in judgment. Advent looks back to the past and ahead to the culmination of God's work.

The twelve days between Christmas and Epiphany fall mostly within the octave (eight days) of Christmas. (Since 1955 the Roman Catholic Church has observed octaves only for Christmas, Easter, and Pentecost.) Protestants refer to the twelve days of Christmas as Christmastide. Traditionally this brief season had been filled with commemorations of saints (Stephen, John, Holy Innocents, Thomas of Canterbury, Sylvester, and their octaves) as well as the Circumcision. Most years there are two Sundays within Christmastide, otherwise only one. Christmastide is a season of joy in the nativity.

The Sundays following Epiphany were slow in developing the character of a season. Since its length is determined by the date of Easter each year, Epiphanytide can be anywhere from four to nine Sundays. Methodists do not observe the so-called pre-Lenten Season (the Sundays of Septuagesima, Sexagesima, and Quinquagesima), and very likely it will soon be shelved by much of Christendom. The theme of the Epiphany season is the manifestation of Christ to the world both in the past and present. Wesley eliminated both the Epiphany season and Lent, numbering Sundays (besides Advent) after Christmas, Easter, Ascension, and Trinity Sunday.

Pentecost concludes the great fifty days of Easter. Sundays were numbered after Pentecost throughout much of the history of the church. During the tenth century the first Sunday of Pentecost was set aside as the Feast of the Trinity. Resisted at first by the papacy as being a theological feast rather than a historical one, the Feast of the Trinity received papal sanction in the four-teenth century. During the Middle Ages it became customary in northern Europe to date Sundays after Trinity, and the term Trinity Season derives from this. Rome followed the older custom and in 1570 made it mandatory to number Sundays after Pentecost. Meanwhile Anglicans and Lutherans had retained the medieval practice of numbering Sundays after Trinity Sunday. The Methodist calendar follows the older Roman practice. The keynote of Pentecost is the presence of the Holy Spirit in the church till the end of time.

The most recent season appearing in the Methodist calendar is that of Kingdomtide. It was adopted in the 1930's by the Federal Council of Churches and reflects the influence of the Social Gospel. Apparently The United Method-ist Church alone retains this season, though American Presbyterians are experi-menting with a season of God the Father (from the first Sunday of October till Advent) in an attempt to give a Trinitarian pattern to the Church year. Kingdomtide begins on the last Sunday in August and can have thirteen or fourteen Sundays. Due to its short history, it is difficult to interpret or to find appropriate symbols for Kingdomtide. It does break the long dry spell of Pentecost and misses by only one Sunday the effective beginning of the academic year and hence of renewed church activity. Perhaps it should be called the "on-season"!

Theologically there is much to be said for the observance of the Christian year. First of all, it provides a means of recalling the important events in Christ's ministry. The Christian year is primarily christological, a factor em-phasized in recent Roman Catholic reforms. Through the annual cycle of the Christian year we relive the significant events in salvation history, and they become our contemporaries. Sacred history becomes a part of us as we participate in the community that shares in this history. The objective re-presentation of these events in worship helps us appropriate them as parts of our own history.

Secondly, the observance of the church's year gives the pastor a balance that is greater than any individual's apprehension of the gospel. The church year is not a tidy or systematic affair, but it does capture what the church has considered vital in the life and work of Christ. All of us have partial and fragmentary understandings of the Christian faith. The Christian year gives a catholicity of understanding that is deeper than any of us. It helps us preach the whole gospel rather than those portions that thrill us particularly. Every pastor knows how easy it is to get into a rut in his preach-ing. The church year, especially through the use of the lectionary, is one of the most effective means of getting away from this hazard.

The mechanics of the use of the Christian year is very simple. The Christian year is simply a means of providing the suitable propers for any service of Christian worship. The chief peril of the Christian year is that it can become wooden and mechanical. The Puritans abolished it altogether since they pre-ferred to read the books of the Bible through in course and felt the year could be idolatrous. We may not wish to exaggerate the faults of the year so much, but must observe that without proper instruction the use of the Christian year means very little to most people. Yet there are genuine values in using the Christian year as a means of proclaiming the whole gospel. Education is a large part of this ministry and the various ways of reaching people—bulletins, newsletters, Sunday school classes, Woman's Society, Worship Commission, choir, etc.—can be used to explain the meaning of the festivals and seasons of the year.

It has been found that the traditional visual symbols of the feasts and seasons are excellent means of education for children and often lead to their raising questions with their parents. The United Methodist Church has adopted basically the Roman Catholic sequence of colors as evolved since the twelfth century. This includes purple for the penitential seasons (Advent and Lent), white for the seasons of joy (Christmastide and Eastertide), green for the seasons of less distinct character (Epiphany and Kingdomtide), and red for Pentecost. The use of red throughout Pentecost was present in the Ambrosian rite of Milan and has been adopted by United Methodists and Presbyterians. These colors may be used in the textiles for altar-table, lectern, or pulpit hangings, in banners, and in dossals. Some firms supply well-designed bulletins reflecting the seasons and feasts of the Christian year. Certain ancient customs have the effect of heightening people's awareness of the season. The Advent wreath with four candles has become popular in churches in recent years, though originally more domestic than ecclesiastical. During Lent the custom of placing a veil of black or purple cloth over the cross or statues in a church focuses attention on the sorrowful mysteries. And the large paschal candle during Eastertide witnesses to the triumph of the Light of the World over death. When well used these visual devices can be made effective helps in proclaiming the gospel and of living the year with Christ. Otherwise they can become mere toys, a fashionable form of idolatry.

The sequence of the Christian year is outlined on page 61 of *BW* or *MH* 674. A calendar and lectionary appear on the following pages. If one plans to introduce the year it might be well to begin interpreting it to the congregation in September and then actually begin a systematic use at the beginning of Advent in early December or late November. Commercial practices have changed the traditional Christian custom of celebrating Christmas during the twelve days *after* December 25. Today few churches want to wait till Christmas to begin the celebration of the Nativity. But Advent can be an effective way of preparing for a more christological commemoration of Christmas than the department stores provide. After the joy of Christmas, Epiphany has been ecclesiastically something of an off-season, and this fact we do share in common with the stores. Methodists have taken Lent increasingly seriously, and it frequently becomes a season of more intense study of the faith. But why not make even more of the much more significant season of Easter? Christianity is good news after all! The chief events of the Christian year are crowded into the six months of December through May.

Page 64 *BW* lists special days rather indiscriminately. Some of these are of much more importance to ecumenical Christianity than others. It is amazing how often the sentimental Mother's Day (now camouflaged as the Festival of the Christian Home) is observed with care and the second greatest Christian feast, Pentecost (which sometimes coincides with it), ignored. The traditional feasts (Ascension Day, Trinity Sunday, and All Saints' Day) deserve first-class consideration. Universal Bible Sunday is the second Sunday in Advent due to the propers Cranmer chose. Not till the eighteenth century did this country deem January 1 the beginning of a new year. Race Relations Sunday, we hope, will someday be obsolete but in the meantime is an appropriate occasion for penitence. Aldersgate Sunday is, in effect, the only Methodist "saint's day," though Wesley abolished all such days. Independence Day, Labor Day, and Thanksgiving Day are national holidays and reminders of the intersections of civil and ecclesial life. Reformation Day may soon seem too narrow, and World Order Sunday and Commitment Day are often meaningless bits of denominational clutter. These call for the use of considerable discretion. On page 65 is a table dating Ash Wednesday, Easter, Pentecost, and the first Sunday in Advent, and indicating the length of Epiphany, Pentecost, and Kingdomtide until long after The United Methodist Church, we trust, shall have been fused into a wider Christianity.

II

We turn our attention now to examine the use of specific items in Parts II and III of the *BW*. Obviously there is much too much material to treat each item separately. The source of some materials is identified in the index in *BW*. We shall discuss the major categories, and a few individual items of special interest will be briefly noticed.

The use of Scripture provides the basis for a great number of the propers. This is obvious in the Scripture sentences, psalms, and lessons, but that is only the beginning. The language of many ancient collects is based upon fragments of Scripture and the same is true of versicles, salutations, benedictions, words of assurance, offertory sentences, litanies, and many types of prayers. Frequently the scriptural source is indicated in italics, but there are many biblical passages not so identified.

One of the most important sections in *BW* is "A Lectionary for Public Worship" on pages 62-64 and reproduced as *MH* 674. Combined with the lectionary is a table of the psalms and other acts of praise appropriate to each Sunday and certain other festivals.

The lessons are read in public worship as the declaration of God's Word. They are read for their own sake and not merely to supply the text for the sermon. It is amazing that we lament the biblical illiteracy of modern Christians, yet many churches do not bother to read more than one lesson. It is quite appropriate to preach on the lessons or to read a different text immediately before the sermon and to preach on it. The lessons should be chosen, usually with the lectionary, to give an orderly coverage of the most important parts of Scripture rather than subjecting the congregation to a repertoire of the pastor's personal favorites.

The church has used lectionaries since at least the fourth century. The most important festivals were the first to receive designated lections (readings), and eventually separate lectionaries were developed for the Eucharist and the office. At one time the eucharistic lections included one from the Old Testament, and it seems likely that this practice will be recovered in the Roman Catholic Church plus the epistles and gospels presently read at Mass. The Methodist lectionary provides three lessons. All three may be used in either the "Order of Worship" or the Lord's Supper. Presumedly Methodist worship should take Scripture as seriously as the Roman Church. In any case, the "Order of Worship" prescribes no less than two lessons: "one from the Old Testament, and one from the Epistles or Gospels." The Lord's Supper states: "If two lessons are read, let one be the Epistle and the other the Gospel." This lectionary serves for both the "Order of Worship" and the Eucharist. The Old Testament lesson is read as a basic part of the history of God's actions since the gospel can hardly be understood without it. There is no reason to perpetuate the Marcionite heresy of the second century by excluding the Old Testament from our worship. The term "epistle" is used in the lectionary in a liturgical sense; it includes portions of Acts and Revelation as well as letters. The gospel lesson, drawn from one of the four Gospels, has always been treated with the greatest respect as often containing the words of Jesus. In some denominations it is customary for the congregation to stand for the gospel lesson.

The Methodist lectionary is the product of careful study, drawing upon a wide sampling of traditional and contemporary lectionaries. It is possibly the most ecumenical lectionary ever compiled. Unfortunately the length of the lections was rather arbitrarily limited. And like all one-year lectionaries, it suffers from the necessity of excluding many passages that could not be included in the 76 dates for which lections are provided. The 89 chapters of Gospels in the New Testament can hardly be reduced to 76 lessons of ten verses each. It is also a pity that a daily lectionary has not been provided for seminaries, conferences, and private reading. But as a one-year Sunday lectionary this one is unsurpassed and ought to have wide use within and beyond Methodism.

It is only for the sake of convenience that the table of psalms, canticles, and other acts of praise appears at the same place as the lectionary. These items make up Part III of *BW*. The psalms belong in the "Order of Worship" as acts of praise and certainly not as substitutes for either of the lessons. In the early church psalmody was interspersed with the lections as a response of joy and praise for God's works as narrated in Scripture. Ever since, the Psalter has been the basic hymnbook of the Christian church. The monastic office read it through weekly and the *BCP* provides for a monthly recitation. John Wesley felt it necessary to expurgate the imprecatory psalms. Yet 115 psalms or portions thereof survived his blue pencil and were printed in *MH* as late as 1905. The 1935 *MH* substituted a patchwork of Scripture passages, but the 1966 *MH* and *BW* have restored 53 psalms (many abbreviated) in a form easily used by the congregations. We may wish that more had been provided, but the return of the Psalter may well be the most important single improvement in both books. Except for Psalm 23 (King James Version) the Revised Standard Version has been used.

A canticle is a song from the Bible other than the psalms. The *Te Deum* (page 283) is not from Scripture but is also referred to as a canticle. It was written, most likely, by Bishop Niceta of Remesiana who died *ca* A.D. 414. Some of the acts of praise following page 283 are also psalms: items 54, 58, 60, 62. These are based on Coverdale's translation of the Vulgate on which portions of the Great Bible of 1539 were based. Other passages are drawn from the Lucan canticles and various other portions of the Old Testament, Apocrypha, and New Testament. Some are simply blue-ribbon portions of Scripture printed to be read responsively (e.g., 87, 90) or as a monologue (e.g., 99, 107). Several postbiblical litanies, both ancient (113) and modern (115), are also provided, the sources being indicated in the "Index of First Lines."

In practice either a psalm or other act of praise would be used, preferably the one listed for the occasion in the table accompanying the lectionary. Since most of this material appears in *MH* conveniently numbered (554-661) it can easily be used by the congregation. It should also be noticed that *MH* provides a musical setting for ten of the canticles (663-73) and instructions for chanting *MH* 662. These may be easily learned by many congregations and used effectively. Above all the psalms should be used as the supreme expression of the praise of God.

III

The largest section of Part II is entitled "The Christian Year." We shall look briefly at the services it provides for the seasons and special festivals of the year.

The *BW* furnishes four basic types of propers for most of the seasons: Scripture sentences or calls to worship, invocations, collects, and prayers of petition and intercession. There is a number of items peculiar to individual seasons as well. The Scripture sentences or calls to worship are simply inserted at the beginning of the "Order of Worship." Not only do they open the service but in many cases reflect the central concern of the season at hand. Only one is necessary for each service, and it is well to vary them from Sunday to Sunday during any given season. Occasionally they are in the form of versicles and would need to be printed in the bulletin. A few of the sentences appear in *MH* (676 and following).

The *BW* does not make the use of the invocations clear. We may presume that the invocation in the "Order of Worship" is a common invocation to be used at any time but then find that proper invocations are scattered throughout the section on the Christian year. Evidently one may take his choice, either a common invocation or proper ones, though the rubrics do not make this choice apparent.

The position the collects would occupy in the "Order of Worship" is also not clear. There is no rubric there or in the Lord's Supper calling for proper collects. The Anglican tradition would place the Collect for the Day after the Creed and before the fixed collects for peace and grace. The equivalent position in the "Order for Worship" would be either before the Collect for Grace or in its place. Since the Collect for Grace is a morning prayer, it would seem justifiable to substitute other collects in its place at services occurring at other times of day. The traditional spot for the collect of the day in the Eucharist in the West has been after the *Gloria in excelsis* and before the epistle. This spot would not make much sense in the Methodist Communion order since a long penitential section and the intercessions have been dropped in between the *Gloria in excelsis* and the epistle. No rubrical provision is made for proper collects at the Eucharist, but if used they would logically precede the epistle lesson. The great advantage of the proper collect in the Eucharist is that it highlights the season at hand and focuses on this theme in the lessons. Wesley followed the *BCP* in providing specific collects, epistles, and gospels for the Eucharist on all the Sundays of the year.

The *BW* may not make clear rubrically as to how the proper collects are to be used, but at least it supplies a magnificent collection of them. Some of them date from the sacramentaries of the sixth century. A collect is a definite literary form, usually consisting of five items: an address to God ("O Lord, our heavenly Father . . ."), a relative clause ("who hast safely brought us to . . ."), the prayer itself, usually a petition ("defend us in . . ."), a result clause ("that all our doings . . ."), and a christological termination ("through Jesus Christ our Lord"). Originally the people were "bid" to pray by the deacon, prayed in silence, and then in a collect the bishop summed up (collected) their petitions in a spoken prayer. The term has survived but not the original definition. The new Presbyterian and United Church of Christ liturgies have returned to the ancient practice of bidding, silence, and collected prayers.

Prayers of petition or intercession are provided for several of the seasons. Again it is not made clear as to what use is to be made of these prayers. We can presume that they might be used in the "Order of Worship" as part of the pastoral prayer. Again they might be used in place of the prayer for the "Whole State of Christ's Church" in the Communion service. Prayers are provided for special occasions such as Race Relations Day (page 88). Certainly these prayers of petition or intercession should not replace extempore prayer though they may provide a good school of prayer for the pastor in preparing his pastoral prayer. Rather they ought to be used to complement pastoral prayer in dealing with relatively fixed and static elements of human life. The prayers should also have wide use in personal devotions. Prayers of petition are primarily for ourselves and those identified with us. It is prayer for "our daily bread." Intercessory prayer is prayer for others. It is, in a sense, the most worldly kind of prayer since it comprehends all mankind. Public prayer ought to include both types as well as such kinds as invocation, thanksgiving, offering, and others.

Unique to the Advent season are a set of Advent antiphons on page 70. Antiphons are responses as when two groups say a psalm responsively. Or antiphons may be a verse sung before and after a psalm or before and after each verse of the psalm. Usually they are chosen from a verse of the psalm itself, and since different verses can be used as antiphons at different times they tremendously increase the interpretations that can be highlighted in the psalms. The Advent antiphons are used in the first sense and may be read as a dialogue of the minister and congregation or between two halves of the congregation.

The short season of Christmastide has several unique features. There is "An Order for Worship for Christmas Day," pages 71-73, featuring the Benedictus, commonly used in Anglican morning prayer. Sentences, collects, and invocations are provided for the end of the civil year or the beginning of the new year. (In this context the Covenant service pages 382-88 should also be consulted.)

Since the theme of the Epiphany Season is the transmission of the gospel throughout all the world, a modern "Litany for Missions" from The Kingdom, the Power and the Glory (the so-called "Grey Book," an Anglican collection of the 1920's) appears in this context as well as other prayers for missions.

Lent, the chief penitential season, has a number of special services for important occasions. These begin with the Ash Wednesday service, parallel to the 1892 "A Penitential Office for Ash Wednesday" in the American BCP or the English BCP's fierce "Commination, or Denouncing of God's Anger and Judgments Against Sinners." Both of these feature Psalm 51, but BW chooses Psalm 130 instead. The BCP services replaced the medieval distribution of the ashes and discipline of penitents. Appropriate propers are provided for Passion Sunday, Palm Sunday, and all the days of Holy Week. The Three-Hours' Service is furnished for Good Friday. This practice comes from late seventeenth-century Peru. It is organized on the basis of the seven last "words" of Jesus. Fragments of much earlier services appear in the "Order of Worship for Good Friday Evening." The "reproaches" (pages 109-10) probably date from tenth-century France and are an excellent example of the fusion of drama and liturgy. Much earlier would be the "adoration at the cross" (page 110), deriving from the veneration of the cross in fourth-century Jerusalem. During the Middle Ages a cross would have been put in the Easter Sepulchre on Good Friday as a symbol of Christ's burial. It is here observed with the singing of appropriate hymns (*MH* 416, 420, 418, 435, and 124). This service is a good example of the highly dramatic forms of communication found in some early practices.

As we might expect, Easter Day has its own propers. The theme of the whole season is Alleluia. An "Emmaus Litany" is provided for Eastertide, based on Luke 24:13-36. The three Rogation Days immediately prior to Ascension Day date from the fifth century and focus on the blessing of crops. Ascension Day itself dates from fourth-century Jerusalem. The Festival of the Christian Home and Church Loyalty Sunday, by contrast, are modern inventions.

In Pentecost *BW* provides a hymn, "Veni, Creator Spiritus," an office hymn of the ninth century used since the eleventh century in ordination rites (cf. *BW*, pages 51 and 56). By coincidence, most Methodist ordinations occur at this time of the year, and its use in congregational worship may mean more when this is made apparent. Trinity Sunday has its own propers, as do Memorial Day, Student Day, and Independence Day.

Kingdomtide includes propers for Labor Sunday, Opening of School, Church School Rally Day, Reformation Sunday, All Saints' Day, Veterans' Day, and Thanksgiving Day, about as odd a lot as one could find anywhere. All Saints' Day, which may date from the seventh century, ought to be taken more seriously. It is the church's parallel (with All Souls' Day) of the secular Memorial Day. The "Order of Worship for All Saints' Day" features the *Te Deum* and two excellent hymns (*MH* 302 and 536). Thanksgiving Day also has a special service featuring a modern "Litany of Thanksgiving and Intercession." These conclude the section on "The Christian Year."

The remainder of Part II is filled with "General Aids to Worship." These are not directed toward any particular season or occasion in the church year but most of them are appropriate at any time. The "Prayers for Use on Entering the Church" might well be printed on the back of the bulletin or on cards in the pews. Many ministers have used similar "Prayers with the Choir" before beginning the opening procession. The "Scripture sentences and invocations" supplement those provided under the seasons of the Christian year. The "Prayers of Confession" may very well be used in rotation with the General Confession in the "Order of Worship." "Words of Assurance" and "Prayers for Pardon and Forgiveness" are evidently intended to be used likewise, though this ought to be done with caution. Many of the "Words of Assurance" are not explicit enough to replace the prayer for pardon. We have already discussed the "Affirmations of Faith" in Chapter One. "Prayers of Thanksgiving" and "Prayers of Petition and Intercession" can be used in the pastoral prayer. The "Order of Worship" calls for the use of "Offertory Sentences and Prayers," and a good assortment is provided. For good measure, collections of "Versicles" and "Salutations" are thrown in too. The "Communion Table Dismissals" belong elsewhere, and the use of the "Ascriptions of Glory" is unclear. Most of the "Benedictions" are biblical. They are basically declarations rather than prayers. "Prayers for Use Before Leaving the Church" might well be printed in the bulletin on pew cards.

This section concludes with a collection of "General Prayers." They include "Litanies," other prayers, and somehow "Table Graces" have wandered into this section. One is reminded of the author who, growing tired of punctuating, printed several pages of periods and commas at the back of his book and advised readers to "salt and pepper as they pleased." These prayers may be used at appropriate occasions and in personal devotions. The concluding element, "A Form for Family Prayer or Worship in a Small Group," is a condensed outline of the "Order for Worship."

III

Baptism: Historical, Theological, and Practical Considerations

David James Randolph

Baptism is the event in which one comes to life in the family of God. Baptism is the sacrament by means of which the grace of God makes us partakers of his righteousness and inheritors of everlasting life. It is through the event—the word, the water, the pastoral acts, the personal encounters, the faith of the congregation, and the continuing commitment of the participants—rather than in some substance that God's grace is active in baptism. Our Lord expressly pointed out the place of infants in the family of God when he said, "Let the children come to me, and do not hinder them; for to such belongs the kingdom of heaven" (Matthew 19:14). Baptism is not for infants only, however. Adults who receive this sacrament are also taken into the life of Christ's holy church.

Historical Considerations

The church accepts baptism as a sacrament instituted by Jesus Christ himself. The baptism of Jesus at the hands of John was spoken of as a "baptism of repentance for the forgiveness of sins" (Mark 1:4b. For accounts of Jesus' baptism compare Matthew 3:13-17; Mark 1:9-11; Luke 3:21-22). The baptism which Jesus instituted has connections with the Old Testament tradition of "washings" for purification. However, as John the Baptist himself indicated,

44

the "one who comes after" baptized not only with water but with the Holy Spirit. Some scholars regard as the clearest New Testament evidence of Jesus' authorization of baptism his word to Nicodemus, "Unless one is born of water and the Spirit, he cannot enter the kingdom of God" (John 3:5). The baptism which Jesus initiated is a means by which the Holy Spirit is communicated. As such, it is a sign of entrance into the new age inaugurated by Jesus Christ and becomes an essential part of the mission of the church. This is the significance of the church's record of the gospel commission, "Go therefore and make disciples of all nations, baptizing them in the name of the Father and of the Son and of the Holy Spirit, teaching them to observe all that I have commanded you; and lo, I am with you always, to the close of the age" (Matthew 28:19-20). Evidences of how this command was carried out are found in the Day of Pentecost (Acts 2:38), in Philip's experience with the Samaritans (Acts 8:12), and elsewhere.

Infant baptism has been practiced by the church since the earliest times. The silence of the New Testament on this point has been interpreted by some to mean that infant baptism was simply taken for granted, while others have assumed otherwise. There is no doubt, however, that baptism of infants belongs to the oldest traditions of the church. Cyprian (ca. 200-258) gives positive approval of the practice. Tertullian (ca. 155-222) was in favor of delaying baptism, but his language makes clear that the custom of the time was to baptize infants.

In the years prior to A.D. 500 baptism was held in even higher esteem than was the Communion, according to the historian J. W. C. Wand. The ceremony normally was held only at Easter, thus marking a clear association between baptism and the "dying and rising" with Christ. The creedal and doctrinal significance of baptism was of major importance in the early ages of Christian history. As the "Apostolic Tradition" of Hippolytus makes clear, an examination of a candidate's faith was conducted in connection with baptism, and out of this arose some of the earliest creedal confessions of the church.

Toward the close of the sixth century the ceremony became more complex. For example, the bishop would divide the waters of the font in the form of the cross and breathe three times upon the water. The medieval service became longer still. The devil was adjured to come out of the child; the child was anointed on the breast and between the shoulders and was invested with a white cloth or robe called a chrisom.

The first prayer book of Edward VI, issued in 1549, retained the form of exorcism, anointing, chrisom, and trine immersion. These were all omitted in the prayer book of 1552. The Protestant Reformation had the effect not only of diminishing the number of sacraments to the two instituted by our Lord but of reducing to essentials their administration. The brief writings of John Wesley on baptism are largely a summary of the essentials practiced by the Church of England. Methodists in America always have permitted infant baptism although the order of service recommended by Mr. Wesley has been abbreviated.

Although baptism often has been a controversial subject, Methodists usually have occupied a middle ground, practicing infant baptism but recognizing the validity of adult baptism also. There are records which have survived from frontier days of lengthy debates between Methodists and others, but of late, Methodists have seemed more aware of their mediating position and have tended to become less argumentative.

Recently the ecumenical discussions of baptism have become increasingly important. There were those who felt that baptism might be the controversial rock against which the ecumenical ship would shatter. On the contrary, baptism emerged from the discussions of the World Council of Churches as one of the central rallying points of Christian unity. Moreover, the Second Vatican Council reaffirmed baptism as a "sacramental bond of unity linking all who have been reborn by means of it." Thus the phrase "one Lord, one faith, one baptism" is both one of the oldest and one of the most recent affirmations of the central importance of baptism to the life of the church.

Theological Considerations

Baptism should be seen in the context of the whole of Christian doctrine and not in isolation.

Infant baptism has been normative for Methodists. Infant baptism tells us more about God than it does about infants. This act tells us that the God of the Christian revelation is a God of grace who reaches toward us and draws us to him while we are yet helpless. A little baby kicking in his crib is loved by God. Baptism shows us that God's love is poured out upon us not because we are worthy but because we are needy.

Grace is free because God offers it voluntarily, without compulsion, and because no offerings of man could purchase it. But grace is not "cheap." The cost of discipleship was, and is, the cross. In baptism we acknowledge that the God who loves us and receives us into his family is the God who makes us "heirs . . . and joint-heirs with Christ."

Infant baptism also tells us about man. The First Epistle of Peter tells how God called us out of darkness into his marvelous light: "Once you were no people but now you are God's people" (I Peter 2:10). This claim can be made for the one who feels the waters of baptism. He who was "no one" now bears a Christian name. He who was a nobody is now a somebody in Christ Jesus. He has been given a title and a name in the kingdom of God. The nothingness, the anonymity, the alienation—which are some of the contemporary understandings of original sin—are washed away in baptism. The baptized child is born to new life in Christ.

Some are puzzled because ever since John Wesley's day Methodists who practice infant baptism also believe in an evangelism which emphasizes adult conversion. They ask, if a person is "born again" into the family of God at baptism, why is it necessary for him to have an adult experience of regeneration?

At least two truths contribute to the answer. First, life is dynamic, not static. Life moves, shifts, changes, and people develop. In adult conversion new areas of life discovered by adult experience are claimed by Christ.

Second, God is God and man is man. A conversation takes place between God and man, not a merger. God never fails to keep up his end of the conversation, but man is often tempted to lapse into silence. This is the reason John Wesley emphasized that baptism saves us *when* we "live answerable thereto—if we repent, believe, and obey the gospel." The fact of baptism is indelible. Once baptized, we are always baptized, and this act need not be repeated. But if the meaning of baptism is to be understood, we must continue answering to God for it. That man fails to answer God or answers wrongly and behaves defiantly marks his sinfulness. For this man needs the forgiveness of God and the chance for new life. For this also he needs the continuing grace of the Lord's Supper, which is itself both a renewal of baptism and a converting agency. "Repent and believe" are words relevant after as well as before baptism.

Far from denying the efficacy of infant baptism, therefore, adult responsibility is its necessary consequence. *Because* we have been baptized, new areas of life are to be offered up to Christ, and we are to repent of our sins.

Infant baptism tells us about the home and the church. Where infant baptism is stressed as it is in Methodism, it is necessary likewise to stress the importance of the parents and the congregation. Baptism is more than a "dedication" of the child by the parents inasmuch as a real transaction between God and the child is acknowledged. The vows of the parents to lead godly lives and their pledge to bring up the child in the way of the Christian faith are heightened by the sublime significance of this transaction. The vows parents take are not mere "ceremony" associated with getting a baptism "done." They are part of a serious covenant, and the church has a right to expect them to be fulfilled. The family should be regarded as a primary unit by which the mission of the church reaches into the world.

The congregation as a whole also takes on responsibility for the baptized, even though the person is baptized into Christ's whole church and not merely a local congregation. The congregation pledges to care for the child and to surround him with love. In fact, Christian parents represent the congregation when presenting a child for baptism, and not themselves only. Where parents are not practicing Christians, perhaps the congregation should be represented by other sponsors. In some cases where a child has been orphaned, members of a local congregation have sometimes become "like a mother and father" to him. But often in less dramatic circumstances the love and guidance of church members have lifted the level of life and broadened the horizons of the young. It is a high moment when the congregation pledges itself to the nurture of the baptized child.

Baptism tells us not only about God and about man but about the church where God and man meet. When the child is baptized, he becomes a member of the church of Jesus Christ. Methodism uses the term "preparatory member."

Confirmation is the service in which persons who have been baptized confirm the vows which were made in baptism and commit themselves to accept their responsibilities in the household of faith. Confirmation classes are held to help prepare persons for these new responsibilities. Almost invariably the pastor learns a great deal from the young people as well. One girl summed up her training in such a class with the poignant words, "I have found what I have always been looking for, and his name is God." Confirmation is a sign of our finding the God who has found us in baptism.

While infant baptism is normative for Methodists, it is not exclusive. Baptism of youth and adults is fully acceptable when it is desired. Methodist worship provides an order of baptism for youth and adults which is distinguished from the other principally in that the persons themselves profess their vows. In some cases it is a family's choice to follow the practice of adult baptism. In other cases, for various reasons, a person may simply not have been baptized. In no case should an adult be embarrassed in any way by seeking baptism, for adult baptism clearly has been part of the church's tradition from the earliest times.

Practical Considerations

Two things are essential to Christian baptism: the application of water and the administration in the name of the Trinity. In addition, the tradition and practice of the church emphasize the importance of the following practical considerations.

1. Pastors should teach their congregations the meaning and purpose of baptism and urge that children be presented for baptism at an early age. Pastors should meet with parents in advance of baptism to interpret the meaning of the sacrament and to clarify parental responsibilities. Whenever possible, pastors also ought to meet with the sponsors, when such are to participate.

2. The pastor in charge of the congregation to which the baptized person is to be related should perform the sacrament of baptism unless he invites another qualified minister to do so. In The United Methodist Church, an elder has full authority to baptize, but deacons and unordained supply pastors may baptize only under certain circumstances (see *Discipline of The Methodist Church*, 1964, paragraphs 318, 392, 402). An ancient understanding of the church is that in an extreme emergency any Christian may baptize.

3. Baptism should be administered in the presence of the congregation at a stated hour and place of worship since it marks the entrance into the

Christian fellowship. However, the sacrament may be administered at other times and places in urgent cases or under extraordinary circumstances. Since the Orders for baptism set forth in Methodist worship are placed within the context of regular worship, scripture reading could well be added to the appropriate order if the baptism is administered outside the regular service of worship.

4. Every church should provide a baptismal font. In addition to its obvious function, a font serves as a constant reminder of the prime significance of baptism. The placing of the font is a matter of considerable discussion. Some hold that it should be placed near the entrance to the nave, associating baptism with entrance into the church. Others hold that it should be placed in a chapel or alcove at the side of the nave, emphasizing the uniqueness of the act of baptism. Others believe the font should be placed prominently in the front of the nave. Still others would insist that a simple bowl is adequate; when placed on the Communion table, it emphasizes baptism's integral relation to the sacrament of the Lord's Supper. A fundamental guideline should be that since baptism is an event in which the whole congregation is involved, the font should be so placed that the acts of baptism are visible and the words audible to the whole congregation so that maximum participation by all worshipers is assured.

5. Baptism may be administered by sprinkling, pouring, or immersion. Although Methodists recognize baptism by immersion, they generally have not provided facilities for it. In future church planning and building perhaps consideration should be given to correcting this oversight.

For sprinkling, a small basin (traditionally in the form of a shell, a symbol of baptism) should be located within the font. A pitcher or ewer of fresh water ought always be kept near the font. Infants are usually cradled along the minister's left arm and shoulder while the water is administered with the right hand to the infant's head or forehead. Adults usually kneel for baptism by sprinkling.

In the case of pouring, a pitcher or ewer is necessary along with the font or some other receptacle to receive the excess water. The water is poured over the head of the person baptized as the words of administration are spoken. Infants may be held by the minister so the water may be poured from the forehead back, while adults may kneel and bow so that the water may be poured from the back of the head forward.

In immersion, either a baptistry inside a church or a natural body of water is used. Normally the minister stands behind the person to be baptized with a towel to be placed over the person's nose and mouth as the candidate is immersed backward, then lifted forward.

A thoughtful chancel guild will see that a towel is conveniently at hand to dry the minister's hands following a baptism and will in general assist the minister in making all necessary arrangements for this sacrament.

6. Water used in baptism is "simple" water in the sense that it need not

be "consecrated" or "holy water." However, water is never "simple" altogether, inasmuch as God the Creator has already made it as part of his good creation. The symbolism of water is infinitely rich, and while no magic inheres in its properties, there are significances which go deeper than those of ordinary usage. Poetic meanings of the use of water need not be reserved for pagan mythologies only.

7. "Christening" refers to that part of the service of baptism in which the name is given. "Christening" is not appropriate as an act or service apart from the sacrament of baptism. In the giving of the name only the Christian name is used, not the surname. This name is then used throughout the Christian career of the individual: in confirmation, marriage, ordination, and burial, for example.

8. Sponsors may join with parents in presenting a child for baptism, standing before a congregation as its representatives and uniting with the parents (but not substituting for the parents) in taking the vows audibly. An ancient tradition is to have three sponsors, two of the same sex of the child and one of the opposite sex, none kin to the child or each other. In earlier times when disease more often orphaned children, this was an insurance that a child might have at least three foster homes available. It was thought that a boy should have two "godfathers," and a girl two "godmothers."

9. It is necessary to administer baptism only once. Appeals to be rebaptized (for example, "in water from the River Jordan where our Lord was baptized") are to be rejected as gratuitous.

10. If stoles are worn by the minister, the appropriate color for baptism is white.

11. If a child does not have two parents who can be present (as, for example, in war time), a steward or senior member of the church may be willing to stand with the other parent if called upon.

12. In the act of confirmation, the laying on of hands is traditional although the shaking of hands is also acceptable.

13. Photographs, if desired, should be taken afterward and not during a service.

14. A pastor should see that the names of all baptized children are properly listed as preparatory members on the permanent church records, and the parents or sponsors of each child should receive a certificate of baptism. Baptized infants should be reported annually as preparatory members until they are confirmed. When families transfer from one congregation to another, names of baptized children should be included with the certificate of transfer.

15. Methodist ceremony ought not to become rigidly uniform. However, such purely individualistic pastoral practices as using a flower to sprinkle baptismal water or publicly kissing a baby after baptism increasingly are considered sentimentalities which weaken baptismal worship.

IV

The Lord's Supper or Holy Communion

Joseph D. Quillian, Jr.

If a convocation of world religions were held at which the representatives of each faith would conduct its most characteristic service, the Christians would celebrate Holy Communion. The prayers, Scripture lessons, creed, sermon, hymns, and actions of this service embody the content and spirit of the Christian faith. Holy Communion is the fully normative service of worship of the Christian community of faith. For almost twenty centuries this sacrament has maintained the identity of the Christian community, and has renewed and sustained countless Christians in the grace that it provides.

History of the Service of Holy Communion

The Beginning

On the night that he was betrayed, Jesus ate supper with his disciples in an upper room in a private home in Jerusalem. It was a meal with a special purpose. It was to celebrate the Passover.

The Passover received its name from God's "passing over" the houses of the Hebrews in Egypt, all of which were marked with the blood of a lamb killed for that purpose, the night that death struck all the firstborn of the Egyptians (Exod. 12). The Passover actually had come to mean for the Jews the joyful and thankful remembrance of the whole action of God in delivering them out of Egyptian slavery and leading them through the wilderness to the Promised Land.

Jesus gave a new meaning to the Passover supper in that upper room by taking, blessing, breaking, and giving bread to his disciples, saying that this bread was his body; and by taking a cup of wine, giving thanks, and passing it to his disciples, calling it his blood of the new covenant (Matt. 26; Mark 14; Luke 22). After the supper, Jesus went to the garden of Gethsemane, and there he prayed the "passion prayer," was betrayed by Judas, and arrested. In less than twenty-four hours, he was reviled, tried, sentenced to death, and hanged upon a cross between two crucified thieves until he died; and his body was taken down from the cross, anointed, enshrouded, and laid in the tomb of Joseph of Arimathea.

On the third day from his death and entombment, Jesus Christ was raised from the dead. On the resurrection day, two of his disciples were going to the village of Emmaus, when Jesus joined them and walked along with them. They did not recognize him, even when "beginning with Moses and all the prophets, he interpreted to them in all the scriptures the things concerning himself" (Luke 24:27). When they came to Emmaus, the disciples invited their unknown companion to stay with them that night.

When he was at table with them, he took the bread and blessed, and broke it, and gave it to them. And their eyes were opened and they recognized him; and he vanished out of their sight. They said to each other, "Did not our hearts burn within us while he talked to us on the road, while he opened to us the scriptures?" And they rose that same hour and returned to Jerusalem; and they found the eleven gathered together and those who were with them, who said, "The Lord has risen indeed, and has appeared to Simon!" Then they told what had happened on the road, and how he was known to them in the breaking of the bread. As they were saying this, Jesus himself stood among them. (Luke 24:30-36.)

There were, then, two suppers. There was a passion supper and there was a resurrection supper. Between the two suppers, the heart of the great redemptive act in Christ had taken place: the Passion–Crucifixion–Resurrection. When the disciples came together for further fellowship meals within and following the week after the Resurrection, they must have remembered both suppers with their Lord: the one as he came from his ministry of preaching, teaching, and healing and moved toward his passion and death; the other as he came from his resurrection and moved toward his ascension and eternal lordship.

The passion supper meant that the Passover Lamb of the Old Covenant was now replaced by the Lamb of God of the New Covenant. The resurrection supper meant that the Lamb of God was the Risen Lord, forever to be among his followers when they came together "to remember him." The "two suppers become one supper" meant that the atoning sacrifice of God in Christ was at once and inseparably the sanctifying victory of God in Christ!

There is evidence that the early Christians were more mindful of the Resurrection emphasis in the fellowship meal than they were of the Passion–

Crucifixion emphasis (Acts 2:42-47; 10:41; John 6; 21; Rev. 3:20). Some of them seem to have been so overly exuberant in celebrating the resurrection meal that Paul had to remind them that the One who was raised from the dead also was the One who sacrificially died for them and many (I Cor. 11:17-24). The *one supper*, the *one* sacramental, memorial meal, was to be a celebration of profound joy and thanksgiving, for Jesus Christ's death clearly was indispensable to the meaning of Jesus Christ's resurrection. God's "mighty act of redemption in Christ" was "death–resurrection," one and inseparable.

Paul's corrective warning to the Corinthians has obscured to many later Christians the joyful and thankful awareness of Jesus Christ's resurrection and coming again, an essential aspect of the celebration of Holy Communion. Consequently, the service focused only on the passion and death often has taken on a somber and rather doleful tone. The Corinthians needed Paul's word. We also need a word, and Paul might well say to us, "I would not have you grieve as those who have no hope. Remember that your Lord who suffered and died also rose from the dead!" (See I Thess. 4:13-18.) "Do you not know that all of us who have been baptized into Christ Jesus were baptized into his death? We were buried therefore with him by baptism into death, so that as Christ was raised from the dead by the glory of the Father, we too might walk in newness of life" (Rom. 6:3-4). The one great act of redemption that is the meaning of the sacrament of Baptism is also the meaning of the sacrament of Holy Communion. Both sacraments whenever observed are to be celebrated, giving thanks to God for his gracious gift of life to us through Jesus Christ.

The early Christians probably came together for a sacramental meal within days after the Emmaus supper, certainly not later than the next Sunday. It is not irresponsible fancy to suppose that since the Resurrection Day itself not a single Sunday has passed when Christians have not come together to celebrate the Supper of their Lord, the Holy Communion, the memorial feast, the great thanksgiving. In fact, since before the end of the first century A.D., probably not a day has passed without Christians somewhere gathering to do what our Lord commanded to be done in remembrance of him.

Development of the Service

Quite early in the life of the church, the service of Holy Communion assumed a simple fourfold form:

1. The offering of bread and wine (the offertory).
2. A prayer of blessing and thanksgiving (the prayer of consecration).
3. The breaking of the bread (the fraction).
4. The distribution of the bread and wine (the distribution or administration of the elements).

The Communion service normally was held with only full members of the church, "the faithful," in attendance. A different service, consisting of lessons from the holy Scriptures, sermon, prayers, and hymns, was attended by the faithful as well as by those who were in training to become church members (the catechumens, or those being catechized or instructed). After this was done, all those who were not full members of the church were dismissed just before the offertory, so that only "the faithful" remained for the Communion proper.

The service of the early church was developed into fuller services as the years went by, with variations being apparent in the Eastern or Greek church, and the Western or Latin church. Speaking very generally, the Eastern services were lengthier and more elaborate, with the emphasis on the Resurrection as well as on the Passion and Crucifixion. The Western services tended to be simpler, with the emphasis quite largely on the sacrificial death of the Lord.

The Methodist Service

The Methodist service is rooted in the Western tradition. The service of Salisbury Cathedral (the *Sarum Missal*) was the basis used by Archbishop Cranmer in shaping the first Protestant (Anglican) service in England. With the *Sarum Missal* as the core, Cranmer drew from Lutheran and Greek Orthodox services to design this first Anglican service in 1549. The service was revised in 1552, 1559, 1604, and 1662. The 1662 revision also drew on the Scottish service of 1637. In 1784, John Wesley abridged the 1662 Book of Common Prayer of the Church of England, made a few changes and additions, and entitled it *The Sunday Service of the Methodists* in North America, and sent it from England for use in this country. From the Communion service in *The Sunday Service*, all the American Methodist services have come. The Methodist Episcopal Church made revisions in 1792 and 1844. After the two separations, the Methodist Episcopal Church, the Methodist Episcopal Church, South, and the Methodist Protestant Church revised their services from time to time, drawing on one another's respective services. After reunion in 1939, two services were provided for alternative use in The Methodist Church. The 1964 service of Holy Communion of The Methodist Church is intended to be evangelical in content and spirit, a thankful celebration of the whole gospel of Jesus, which embodies at once the meanings of the passion supper and the resurrection supper.

The Meanings of the Service

Christians call their sacramental meal by several names—the Lord's Supper, the Mass, the Holy Communion, the Holy Liturgy, the Holy Eucharist. While each name carries its own characteristic emphasis, the same basic content is found under each name.

We may spell out this basic content as:
1. Remembrance
2. Proclamation
3. Offertory

4. Participation
5. Thanksgiving

We cannot say that one basic aspect is essential and the others are of secondary importance. Rather, each aspect may be thought of as an arc of a circle; if one arc is omitted or shortened, then the circle no longer exists. In its stead, there is only a broken curved line which at best may be only suggestive of a circle. Therefore a full and sound service of Holy Communion is the entire service which adequately expresses all five aspects of the basic content.

Remembrance

"In remembrance of me"—these may well be the most familiar of all the words related to the Lord's Supper. These words appear on thousands of altars and communion tables across Methodism, reminding us that what we do in this sacrament is done in obedience to the Lord's own command, "Do this in remembrance of me." In the oldest account of the Jerusalem supper (I Cor. 11:23-26), Jesus is said to have given this command twice—once in connection with the bread and once in connection with the wine.

But *who* is it whom we remember? We remember more than a young prophet on the night before his death. We remember that he was more than a prophet, for we are aware of his birth when angels sang their song of glory; of his baptism when God expressed his pleasure in his well-beloved Son; and of his words of teaching and deeds of healing when men marveled at what he said and did. We remember more—so much more than can be contained within the usual meaning of "remembrance." It is more nearly "revealed awareness" than simply "remembrance." For we are aware, by God's revelation, that the Lord whose command we obey is the preexistent Word who was with God in the beginning, who was God, and through whom God made all things (John 1:1-5); the Incarnate God, wholly God and wholly man; the obedient Son of God in his baptism, preaching, teaching, and healing, as well as in his passion and death; the Son of man, representing us all in his temptation, suffering, death, and resurrection; the atoning Messiah, the Lamb of God, in his passion, crucifixion, and death; the mighty Savior in his resurrection; the Lord of lords, King of kings, and heavenly Advocate in his ascension and eternal rulership; and the Judge of all men in his coming again.

The second coming, in its essence, means that God will at last complete through Jesus Christ the redemptive victory which he has begun through Jesus Christ. Creation and second coming are "God's great acts" of the beginning and the end, the Alpha and the Omega, and the meaning of it all is caught up in the birth, obedient life, passion, crucifixion, resurrection, and ascension of the One whom we remember as we celebrate together the sacred meal.

The Lord's Supper, then, is no simple "memorial" centering on the Lord's death. It is a wondrous remembrance, a revealed awareness, of God's purpose

55

in Christ in creation and coming again, whereby our lives in the present have meaning and hope.

Proclamation

Paul said, "For as often as you eat this bread and drink the cup, you proclaim the Lord's death until he comes" (I Cor. 11:26). To "proclaim" is to "set forth strongly and clearly"; it is to "bear witness with confident assurance." That which it proclaims, "the Lord's death until he comes," stands for the whole person and work of Jesus Christ. To say "he died for us" is to mean "he gave his life for us." So the whole meaning of Jesus' death includes all that we mean by the remembrance of him. Therefore, when Christians celebrate the Holy Communion, they proclaim the whole gospel of Jesus Christ, both to themselves and to all men.

As a specific act, the Holy Communion is our principal witness to the gospel. It is sound and right that every celebration of this sacrament should include a lesson or lessons from the holy Scriptures and a sermon, as well as an offertory; prayers of praise, confession-intercession-consecration, commitment and thanksgiving; and the distributing and partaking of the bread and the wine. In the whole service of Holy Communion the whole gospel is proclaimed, the entire meaning of "the Lord's death until he comes."

Offertory

At the heart of the Christian faith, there is a mystery. The mystery is a Person. The Person is at once divine and human—truly God and truly man. He is Jesus Christ. This is the witness of the church in the holy Scriptures and in the historic creeds. The Christian mystery is an offense to the human mind trying to act of itself, simply because mystery cannot be contained within rational sense. The Christian mystery is the greatest of all blessings to human faith because this mystery is revelation, meaning, and hope, and indeed makes living sense (I Cor. 1:18-25). The Christian testifies that he knows God only through Jesus Christ, and that he knows himself only through Jesus Christ. So in his work of revelation Jesus Christ reveals God as he is and man as he ought to be and may become. But more than this: Jesus Christ is God's offering of himself to men through Christ, men's offering of themselves to God man's offertory of perfect obedience to God.

The Holy Communion is the celebration of the great double offertory: God's offering of himself to men through Christ, men's offering of themselves to God through Christ.

Offertory is the real meaning of Christian sacrifice. Sacrifice is willing, purposeful self-giving. Jesus Christ is, "by the one offering of himself, a full, perfect, and sufficient sacrifice for the sins of the whole world." This is God's sacrifice, his willing, purposeful giving of himself for the sake of his children. At the same time, it is Jesus Christ through whom we offer to God "ourselves, our souls and bodies, to be a reasonable, holy, and lively sacrifice" unto him.

Methodists are accustomed to emphasizing the rededication of their lives to God in the sacrament of Holy Communion. A genuinely Christian rededication involves us in the "great offertory." We can offer to God our hearts and the fruits of the labor of our hands only as we accept his offering of redemptive love through Jesus Christ, and in turn make our offering to God through the same Jesus Christ, our Savior and our Lord.

It is the Holy Spirit who enables us to accept God's offertory of saving love. It is the Holy Spirit who enables us to offer ourselves to God in response to his love and to know the blessedness of being accepted by him, thus being renewed in our relationship to him as his children who desire above all else to do his will. The great offertory, then, is completed as the Holy Spirit, the divine guiding and sustaining Power, goes with us into our daily work, our homes and our civic and social activities, thereby making possible our continuing response to God in joyful obedience to him in all our living.

Participation

"The cup of blessing which we bless, is it not a participation in the blood of Christ? The bread which we break, is it not a participation in the body of Christ? Because there is one loaf, we who are many are one body, for we all partake of the same loaf" (I Cor. 10:16-17).

Because we participate in Jesus Christ, because we are related to the human nature of Jesus Christ in a mystical and real way, we can claim his righteousness and his perfect obedience to God as representing us. He has done for us that which we could not do for ourselves by his life, death, resurrection, and ascension. He has effected our forgiveness which we now are to accept and live.

The heart of participation in the Holy Communion is the acceptance of Jesus Christ's gift of salvation. As we accept his gift, we are reconciled to God and to one another (Rom. 5:6-11). We are made to know that we are members of the great company of believers of all time, those who have gone before and those who will come after, as well as those of our own day. So it is that in the celebration of the Lord's Supper we praise God "with angels and archangels and with all the company of heaven." This is the *Holy Communion,* the being in community of living faith with God and with all fellow Christians. This is the celebration of restoration to the relationship with God and men that was God's very purpose for us in creation. Consequently, redemption *from* sin (sin, which is self-centeredness and estrangement at its heart) is redemption *to* God's "creation-purpose" which will at last be realized in the coming again. Through Jesus Christ we are made participants in God's victory.

Thanksgiving

Sometimes the prayers in the service of Holy Communion, beginning with "Lift up your hearts" (the *Sursum Corda*), and continuing through the prayer of consecration, are called "the great thanksgiving." It is thanksgiving for the great offertory, for the One remembered, for the proclaimed gospel, for participation in the death and resurrection and ascension of Jesus Christ. The thanksgiving looks with confident hope to the messianic banquet, the Holy Communion of all his children with God when he will complete the victorious redemption.

Every observance of this sacrament, then, is a thankful celebration of God's redemptive work through Jesus Christ. The term "eucharist" means "thanksgiving." Charles Wesley almost always referred to the Holy Communion as the Holy Eucharist, and John Wesley frequently did so. "Eucharist" is especially compatible with the Methodist spirit of joyful, experienced salvation.

Through Holy Communion we most completely celebrate even now the final victory of God for which "the trumpet shall sound" (I Cor. 15:52-57), and this with a joyful thanksgiving that meets with the song of the morning stars at creation, the glory hymn of the angels on the birthnight of the Lord, and the *Sanctus* of the heavenly creatures around the eternal throne of God.

Holy Communion is the great continuing revival in which we remember our Savior, proclaim his whole gospel, participate in the great offertory, and give thanks to God for the wonder of his redeeming love in Jesus Christ, that we, even we, "should be called the children of God!" (I John 3:1.)

Conducting the Service

The service of Holy Communion belongs to all the people gathered together for the celebration. The service should be conducted in such a manner that the meaning of the sacrament be most fully secured to the people through their participation in word, action, and spirit.

Rubrics and Their Meanings

The directions for conducting and participating in the service are called rubrics. In many of the orders of worship, the directions are printed in red and so acquire the name "rubrics" from the Latin word for "red earth for coloring." In other orders, the rubrics are printed in italics.

Rubrics are of two main sorts, general and specifically directive. The general rubrics pertain to the entire service and appear at the beginning of the Order for the Administration of the Sacrament of the Lord's Supper or Holy Communion. The specifically directive rubrics are interspersed throughout the parts of the service. Some rubrics are mandatory and are worded "shall." For instance, the sermon rubric is mandatory: "Then *shall* follow the sermon." Other rubrics are permissive and read "may." This means that the elder may either include or omit the portions of the service to which a permissive rubric applies. For instance, the rubric pertaining to a hymn after the sermon is permissive: "A hymn *may* be sung."

The reason for having mandatory rubrics is to insure the inclusion of those portions of the service, by word and action, which the church deems desirable in all normal celebration of this sacrament.

In the outline of the service which follows, an "M" is placed to the left of each portion that is governed by a mandatory rubric, and a "P" is to the left of each portion to which a permissive rubric applies.

The Service in Outline

P   Prelude or opening voluntary

P   A hymn

M   The Sentences

M   A Versicle ("The Lord be with you . . .")

M   The Collect for Purity ("Almighty God, unto whom our hearts are open . . .")

M   The Lord's Prayer

M   The Gloria in Excelsis ("Glory be to God on high . . .")

M   The Invitation ("Ye that do truly and earnestly repent . . .")

M   The Prayer of Confession ("Almighty God, Father of our Lord Jesus Christ . . .")

M   The Prayer for Forgiveness ("Almighty God, our heavenly Father, who of thy great mercy . . .")

M   The Comfortable Words

P   The Pastoral Prayer or the Prayer for the Whole State of Christ's Church

M   The Scripture lesson or lessons

P   An anthem or a hymn between the lessons if two lessons are read

P   The Creed or Affirmation of Faith

M   The Sermon

P   Parish notices or announcements

P   A hymn

The Consecration Movement

M   The Sursum Corda ("Lift up your hearts . . .")

M   The Sanctus

M   The Vere Dignum ("It is very meet, right . . .")

P   The Proper Preface (variable with the seasons of the church year)

M   Introduction to the Sanctus proper ("Therefore with angels and archangels . . .")

M   The Sanctus proper ("Holy, holy, holy . . .")

M   The Prayer of Consecration ("Almighty God, our heavenly Father, who of thy tender mercy . . .")

M   The Prayer of Humble Access ("We do not presume . . .")

P   The Agnus Dei ("O Lamb of God . . .")

M The Distribution of the Elements (the bread and wine)

M The Peace Versicle ("The peace of the Lord . . .")

M The Prayer of Thanksgiving ("O Lord, our heavenly Father . . .")

P A hymn

M The Peace Benediction ("The peace of God . . .")

P Postlude or closing voluntary

The Elder

The service is under the direction of an ordained elder of the church as a fully authorized representative of the church of Jesus Christ. The elder has responsibility for maintaining the wholeness and distinctiveness of the service, that it be rightly celebrated in content and spirit.

Each elder should know the service in its entirety by heart. Though he normally will use a book in leading the service, the book should be necessary only as an unobtrusive prompter. The prayers are not to be simply read; they are to be prayed. The elder properly is so familiar with the service that there is no uncertainty as to what comes next. The naturalness and the unself-conscious participation of the elder will do much to put the people at ease and enable them to take part in the service.

The Deacon

The deacon is the first assistant of the elder, leading in those portions of the service that the elder assigns to him. The only part of the service that the elder always must take is the Prayer of Consecration. Normally the elder also will preach the sermon, but another may do so.

It is best for the service not to be shunted back and forth between the elder and the deacon, or if others also are leading portions of the service, among several leaders. One workable plan is for the deacon to take the service from the beginning through the creed, and for the elder to take the service from the sermon through the benediction. Variations are appropriate, of course, and some may prefer for the elder to pray the Prayer of Forgiveness and give the Words of Assurance.

The Sub-deacons

The sub-deacons are assistants in the service who normally function in helping to distribute the elements. Sub-deacons may be ordained deacons or may be laymen.

The Rubrics in Detail

The rubrics provide guidance for *what* shall be done in the service. They do not provide guidance in most instances as to *how* things shall be done. In fact, the wording often is deliberately general so as to allow for appropriate variations under different circumstances of physical arrangement and occasion.

As we go through the rubrics one by one, we shall not attempt to indicate a large number of variations but only some of the more obvious and useful ones.

The General Rubrics

The general rubrics are the first six at the beginning of the service.

1. *It shall be the duty of the pastor to administer the Sacrament of the Lord's Supper at regularly appointed times to the people committed to his care, remembering the charge laid upon him at the time of his ordination: "Be thou a faithful dispenser of the Word of God, and of his holy Sacraments."*

A major responsibility of a pastor is to see that the service of Holy Communion is provided for his people at appropriate intervals. Vital understanding and participation in this sacrament is essentially definitive of the office of the ordained minister.

Practices vary broadly as to how often Holy Communion is celebrated. The two most usual patterns in The United Methodist Church are each first Sunday of the month and once a quarter. A number of larger churches have Holy Communion once a week in an early service or in a vesper service on Sunday. Some few Methodists feel that this sacrament should be celebrated at each major regular service of the church. A reasonable practice is to follow the custom of the region and of the particular local church as to the frequency of Holy Communion and the regular service (usually either monthly or quarterly) and to provide additional observances of this sacrament at times seriously desired by members of the congregation. More frequent services normally would be on Sunday, but in light of the changing weekly schedules of many church members, mid-week services may meet with appreciative response.

2. *The order for the administration of this Sacrament to the sick, to those confined to their homes, or to others in circumstances where the full service is impracticable, should include the Invitation, the General Confession, the Prayer for Pardon, the Comfortable Words, the Prayer of Consecration, the Prayer of Humble Access, the Words of Distribution, the Prayer of Thanksgiving, and the Benediction.*

This rubric simply indicates the portions of the service that normally should be included when the service is conducted under unusual circumstances. In very extreme cases, such as at the bedside of a person who is seriously ill and quite weak, a simple Prayer of Consecration, the Words of Distribution, and the Benediction may suffice. Most church members who find great meaning in the service, however, are likely to prefer the inclusion of all the portions indicated in the rubric, even under unusual and informal circumstances.

3. *At the time of Holy Communion, the Lord's Table shall have upon it a fair white linen cloth. The elements of bread and wine shall be placed thereon. The pure, unfermented juice of the grape shall be used.*

The "fair white linen cloth" is merely a table covering that is appropriate for this central sacrament of the church. The cloth may be placed on the table before the service, the elements of bread and wine placed on it, and the elements covered with another white cloth. Many now prefer for the cover to be on the table before the service begins but for the elements to be brought forward by members of the congregation at the time of the offertory and handed to the minister who then places them on the table.

The United Methodist Church follows the practice of using the unfermented juice of the grape rather than fermented wine. In liturgical usage, however, the grape juice is referred to as wine.

4. *It is our custom to deliver the elements into the hands of the people while they kneel before the Lord's Table. But at the discretion of the minister, the elements may be served to any or to all of the people while standing, or while seated in the pews.*

The people may receive the elements kneeling at the chancel rail or standing at the chancel rail, or the elements may be distributed to the people while they are seated in their pews, depending upon the physical arrangements, the number of people, and circumstances.

If the elements are distributed to the people in the pews, it is obvious that laymen will assist in passing the bread and wine from pew to pew. There is no reason why laymen may not also assist in distributing the elements when they are members of the general ministry of the church. As many persons as needed, whether ordained or lay, should serve so as to allow the service to proceed as smoothly and naturally as possible without extended delays that tend to weigh it down. (More detail concerning distribution will be given in connection with that rubric in the service.)

5. *Upon entering the church, the people shall bow in prayer and shall remain until the entire service is concluded.*

This rubric directs that everyone shall participate appropriately in the service from beginning to end. It intends to discourage the leaving of the service by a person immediately after he himself has received the elements. Meditation after receiving the elements, the Peace Versicle, Prayer of Thanksgiving, and Benediction are essential parts of the service. Leaving after receiving the elements also tends to rupture the sense of corporate worship and to make communion to appear erroneously as individual devotions.

6. *All people who intend to lead a Christian life are invited to receive this holy Sacrament.*

The intention of this rubric is to make clear that all Christians of any denomination are welcome at a United Methodist service of Holy Communion. This rubric also indicates the absence of a confirmation requirement for admission to Communion. Some feel that children should not receive communion until after confirmation. I interpret this rubric to mean that it is not improper for children and others to receive communion prior to confirmation.

The Specifically Directive Rubrics
1. *The service may begin with a prelude.*

Most services of worship begin with a prelude or opening voluntary. This rubric simply indicates permissively that the Service of Holy Communion may begin in this fashion.

2. *A hymn may be sung, the people standing.*

The hymn also is the permitted option and may either follow the prelude or precede the service.

3. *Or the minister may begin the service with one or more of the following or other suitable sentences from the Scriptures.*

The service may begin with one or more of the following Sentences; or prelude, hymn, and Sentences may all be used; or only prelude and Sentences; or only hymn and Sentences. At any rate, it appears to be the intention that a Sentence or Sentences always shall be used.

It is not usually desirable to read all the Sentences. The one or ones most appropriate to the theme of the sermon may well be selected. Also, special festival occasions of Holy Communion may indicate the appropriateness of one or another of the Sentences.

4. *Here the minister, facing the people, shall say,*

This rubric is a mandatory one and controls the versicle which begins the section of praise preceding the invitation and confession. Versicles are something like traffic signals of the service indicating a turn from one part of the service to another.

5. *Then, kneeling or bowed, the minister and people together shall say,*

The inclusion of the Collect for Purity and Lord's Prayer is required. The attitude of prayer is indicated by the rubric and will vary according to whether kneelers are provided in the church or whether people simply bow in their pews.

6. *Then, standing, all shall sing or say,*

The Gloria in Excelsis is the oldest of all communion hymns and is one of the highest hymns of praise of the Christian faith. It can be sung or said appropriately only by standing. It is always desirable that the congregation learn to sing the Gloria in Excelsis, rather than the choir alone. Since it is the high hymn of Christian communion, it is more appropriate for the Gloria in Excelsis to be said by all than sung by a few.

7. *The minister, facing the people while they remain standing, shall say,*

Depending on his position in the chancel, the minister will either step forward to offer the invitation while the people remain standing after the Gloria in Excelsis, or he will remain standing at the same place. Since it is the custom in most churches to turn toward the table or altar during the singing of the Gloria, this rubric is specific in directing the minister to turn and face the people as he offers the invitation. It also makes clear that the people are to continue to stand as they receive the invitation to the entire service which now follows, though the invitation ends with the specific call to confession.

8. *Then the minister, kneeling and facing the Lord's Table, and all the people, kneeling or bowed, shall make together this general confession.*

The minister normally will kneel in front of the table facing toward it with the people as he unites with them in this prayer. If the physical appointments are such as to make it more natural to kneel at the end of the table and at right angles with the people, it is entirely appropriate to do so.

9. *Then the minister shall pray, saying,*

The Prayer for Forgiveness was originally in the form of absolution with the minister saying, "Have mercy upon *you.*" It now is a part of the movement whereby we accept the forgiveness which God has promised to us. The Prayer of Forgiveness should be prayed with reverent and firm declarative tone.

10. *The minister, standing and facing the people, shall say,*

The minister then stands while the people remain seated and says to them the words introducing the scriptural passages of assurance. "Comfortable words" actually means "strengthening words." They signify the giving of God's grace to us.

11. *Then the minister shall say one or more of the following sentences,·*

It is not necessary that all the sentences be read. Each in its own way carries the force of the certainty of God's forgiveness. Having made our confession and asked for God's forgiveness, we now in this moment gladly and thankfully accept his forgiveness and look toward the new life which to share we have been invited.

12. *Here, the minister may offer a pastoral prayer, or he may say,*

Let us pray for the whole state of Christ's church.

13. *Then may follow this prayer, the minister beginning, the people responding:*

Neither the pastoral prayer nor the Prayer for the Whole State of Christ's Church is mandatory. Normally, one or the other will occur, however. The alternative is intended to allow for an extempore pastoral prayer when the circumstance and occasion would seem to make it more appropriate.

14. *Then shall be read the lesson (s) from the Holy Scriptures. If two lessons are read, let one be the Epistle and the other the Gospel. An anthem or a hymn may be sung after the first lesson.*

It is a centuries-old tradition that an Epistle and a Gospel lesson be read in the Communion service, and that the people stand for the Gospel. In liturgical usage any biblical passage other than the Gospel is referred to as the Epistle. If an Old Testament passage is selected for the Epistle, the reader may say, "In the stead of the Epistle, the first lesson is from such and such a chapter and book."

The rubric in this service does not direct that the people stand for the Gospel. The prevailing custom in the particular church might best be followed. Some persons raise a question about standing for the Gospel as being inconsistent with our doctrine of the wholeness of the Holy Scriptures. They feel that we should either stand for all Scripture lessons or sit for all of them. The matter is unresolved, and one is entirely free to follow the traditional custom of standing for the Gospel or not.

The rubric provides permissively for an anthem or hymn after the first lesson. This is a good position for an anthem or hymn and tends to keep the scripture reading from seeming unduly long when two lessons are read.

15. *Here the minister and people may say the Apostles' Creed or another of the Christian affirmations of faith, the people standing.*

The Apostles' Creed is the traditional baptismal creed while the Nicene Creed is the traditional communion creed. The intention is to allow for the alternative of the less familiar Nicene Creed as well as for other affirmations of faith besides the Apostles' Creed.

While the use of any creed or affirmation of faith in this service is permissive rather than mandatory, it is provided that all shall stand if a creed or affirmation is used.

16. *Then shall follow the sermon.*

The sermon is mandatory. Sermon and sacrament are in nowise to be set over against each other. The sermon is an essential part of the entire service of Holy Communion.

A sermon may be three minutes long, or thirty minutes or more. The sermon in the Communion service should be brief and direct. It should be devotional and declarative. There is much to be said for a strong one-point Communion sermon of not more than ten or twelve minutes. The two things that bog down a Communion service more than anything else are unduly long sermons and awkward procedures in distributing the elements. With a ten-minute sermon and an effective method of distribution, there is no necessity for the entire service involving 1,500 people to take more than an hour.

17. *Here parish notices may be given.*

Essential announcements are provided for at this point and should be considered a proper and natural part of the service rather than an intrusion.

18. *A hymn may be sung. The minister shall uncover the elements, and shall proceed to receive the offering from the people. When the offering is presented, the people shall stand, and a prayer of dedication shall be said or sung.*

This rubric has to do with the offertory of the elements of bread and wine and the offertory of money.

In the early church, the people brought offerings of bread and wine and produce of various kinds. Some of the bread and wine was then consecrated for use in the service.

The hymn is permissive but usually occurs while the offering of money is being received or an organ voluntary is played or an anthem or solo is sung.

Obviously there are various procedures that may be followed at this point. The elements may already be on the table at the start of the service, and only the offering of money is brought forward. If there is room on the table in addition to the elements, the offering plates may be placed there. If not, the plates, after being received and acknowledged by prayer or a sung response, may be placed on a side table or on side tables.

Another procedure that is an ancient one and that now is coming into considerable use again is for the elements to be placed at the back of the church on a small table before the service begins, and at this point to be brought forward by previously designated members of the congregation and handed to the minister who places them on the table. When both the offering of elements and the offering of money are presented from the midst of the congregation, the elements should be brought forward first with the offering plates being brought immediately behind. The minister first places the elements on the table and then receives the offering plates and places them at the most appropriate and convenient place.

As the rubric indicates, the people always stand when the offering is brought forward and remain standing through the Sanctus.

19. *Where custom prevails, an offering may be left by the people at the chancel when they come forward to receive the elements.*

In some churches, instead of the plates being passed to the people in the pews to receive the offering of money, the people simply leave the offering at the chancel when they come forward to receive the elements.

20. *The people shall remain standing, and the minister, facing the people, shall say,*

Having stood when the offering was presented, the people continue to stand. The minister, who may have been facing the table if it is in an altar position against the wall, would now turn to face the people for the Sursum Corda. If the minister has been standing behind a free-standing table and facing the people across it, he simply continues to stand in the same position for the Sursum Corda. If he is beside the table at the lower level of the chancel, he stands in that position facing the people.

21. *Then the minister, facing the Lord's Table, shall say,*

This rubric deliberately provides for many variations. If the minister is behind a free-standing table, he faces the table and the people at the same time. If he is at an altar against the wall, he may face the table directly in the center with his back to the people during the time of the presentation of the offering and so is facing the altar table with them. If the physical situation makes it more natural for him to face the table from the side, as is often the case when the table is at the lower level in front of the pulpit and behind the chancel rail, it is appropriate to do so. In any event, the minister stands at this point while facing the table.

22. *Here may follow the proper preface (see The Methodist Hymnal No. 831 or The Book of Worship, page 23), or else the minister immediately shall say,*

The proper preface may be inserted here for appropriate special occasions or seasons. It is immediately followed by the preface to the Sanctus, of course, so is not confusing to the people when inserted. The proper preface always is optional but does serve usefully to focus and heighten the emphasis of a festival occasion.

23. *Then shall all sing or say:*

While standing, all join in the Sanctus. It is best sung by all, but if the people are not prepared to join fully in the singing of the Sanctus, it is better said by all than sung by the choir only.

24. *The people shall kneel or bow; the minister, facing the Lord's Table, shall offer the Prayer of Consecration.*

If kneelers or cushions are provided, the people kneel. Otherwise they remain seated and bowed for the Prayer of Consecration.

The minister normally stands for the Prayer of Consecration, but this rubric deliberately leaves that point vague. The minister may stand behind a free-standing table facing the people; in the center or to one side at a table against a wall, with his back to the people; or he may stand at the side of the table at right angle to the people. If the minister kneels, he may do so in front of the table or to the side of the table. He does not ordinarily kneel behind a free-standing table. Again, the traditionally proper position for the minister during the Prayer of Consecration is standing.

25. *[Here the minister may take the bread in his hands]; [Here the minister may take the cup in his hands].*

This is a permissive rubric, and many feel that it is an unfortunate one. The people are bowed in prayer and are not participating by sight in the breaking of the bread if done at this point, or in the blessing of the cup.

The preference of many is to break the bread (called the Fraction) and bless the cup either immediately following the Prayer of Consecration or just after the Prayer of Humble Access. The people then look at what is going on. When the minister breaks the bread, he may say, "The bread which we break, is it not a participation in the body of Christ? Because there is one loaf, we who are many are one body, for we all partake of the same loaf." When he blesses the cup he may say, "The cup of blessing which we bless, is it not a participation in the blood of Christ?" Variations of these words are appropriate.

26. *The minister shall kneel before the Lord's Table. After a brief silence, the minister and people together shall pray, saying,*

If the minister has been standing behind the table facing the people during the Prayer of Consecration, he now comes from behind the table and kneels in front of it facing with the people toward the table for the Prayer of Humble Access. If the minister has been standing facing a table against the wall with his back to the people, he now kneels in front of the table facing it. If his necessary position is at the side of the table, he simply kneels there. The major point is that he unites with the people in this prayer rather than performing a representative act as is the case with the Prayer of Consecration.

The brief silence allows everyone to appropriate in meditation the meaning of the Prayer of Consecration and further to prepare himself to receive the elements.

27. *Here may be said or sung,*

The Agnus Dei is one of the church's oldest hymns associated with Holy Communion. It is appropriate for the elder to serve himself while the Agnus Dei is being sung or said, and also to serve those who are assisting him. Some may prefer to wait until after the Agnus Dei is concluded before proceeding to serve.

28. *The minister shall first receive the Holy Communion in both kinds, and then shall deliver the same to any who are assisting him. Then the minister or those assisting him shall deliver the elements in both kinds to the people.*

The elder serves himself first, both bread and wine. He thereby acknowledges himself as "chief of sinners"—that is, that he lives by God's grace and needs the forgiving, reconciling, and strengthening love of God given in this sacrament. He next serves the deacon in both kinds. The elder then distributes the bread to the sub-deacons and the deacon gives them the wine. It is now time for the people to receive the elements. A simple, natural, and efficient method of chancel distribution of the elements is the continuous table (envision a church with a center aisle and two side aisles). Under other physical arrangements, simply make commonsense adjustments.

Let the minister indicate to the people that they are to come to the chancel by the center aisle, filling the chancel to both sides, and after receiving both the bread and the wine they are to return to their pews by the side aisles to continue there in prayer or in the singing of hymns. As soon as there are three or four people kneeling at either end of the chancel rail, the serving should begin. Two servers work from each end of the chancel, one serving the bread and the other serving the wine. The servers work toward the center until they meet and then return without delay to their respective ends of the chancel rail to continue serving immediately. There are no table dismissals under this form of distribution. As soon as one person arises from the chancel rail, another quietly takes his place.

Ushers should be especially unobtrusive during communion. In fact, they seldom are needed when using a continuous table. The people simply stand in the center aisle until there is a place for them at the chancel rail. For a smooth and natural use of the continuous table, the people possible should not be ushered up to the chancel by groups. Simplicity and naturalness should prevail.

This method is faster than any except pew distribution, but at the same time it provides personal ministration in distributing the elements, retains a sense of corporateness in the communion, and has an easy kind of spirit and tone.

Many appropriate variations may be used, of course. Whatever method is used, a feeling of impersonal or mass production should be avoided. Also, dull repetition of table dismissals should be abandoned. If only a half-dozen tables or so are to be served, worshipful dismissals are available in *The Book of Worship*. If there are more than six or eight tables (a table is a full chancel rail of people in this present reference), table dismissals tend to become leaden and mechanical.

The bread for communion is in several forms. Whole loaves, small squares of unleavened bread, small squares cut from loaf bread, and wafers are used. Increasingly, the whole loaf is being preferred by many. The symbolism in the breaking of the whole loaf is stronger, of course. When the bread is served, the minister breaks off a small piece of the loaf and places it in the communicant's hand.

The wine in Methodist services most frequently is in small glasses. A number of churches now use the chalice (a large cup, usually silver). One convenient way to serve the bread and wine when the loaf and chalice are used is the method called "intinction." The server places the bread in the communicant's hand. The communicant holds the piece of bread until the cup comes to him, then dips the bread in the wine and places it in his mouth.

The server of the cup may well carry a paper napkin in his hand to allow each person to touch it lightly with the bread after it has been dipped in the wine and so avoid the danger of a drop of wine falling on the floor or on clothing or chin.

Whatever method is preferred in distributing of the elements, whether trays of small glasses or the chalice, or whether small bits of bread or wafer or the whole loaf, the simplest and most efficient procedure should be used. Actual haste or the appearance of haste should not occur.

29. *During the distribution of the elements appropriate hymns may be sung or played.*

A listing of hymn numbers to be sung during the distribution may be provided on the hymn boards, in the bulletin, or on a separate sheet. A broad range of hymns should be selected, not just the hymns that refer specifically to Holy Communion. Music often is more silent than silence. That is, it catches us up in the meaning of what we are doing and obscures distracting sounds. Many congregations have adopted the practice of singing hymns during the distribution and feel that it is a major improvement in the service.

This rubric is clearly permissive, of course, and silence, or a series of scripture sentences read during the distribution, is appropriate as well as hymns or organ voluntaries.

30. *When the bread is given, one or both of the following sentences shall be said; When the cup is given, one or both of the following sentences shall be said.*

The words of distribution often are said in the process of serving four or five people, the server saying words slowly as he moves along. Sometimes the words are said by the elder to the entire congregation just before the people are served, and then the serving proceeds without the Words of Distribution being said any further. Either method is allowable under this rubric.

The words can be said quite easily and naturally while hymns are being sung during the distribution, so the choice of whether to say the words during the distribution need not depend on whether or not hymns are used.

31. *When all have communed, the minister shall place upon the Lord's Table all that remains of the elements, covering the same.*

The servers and the elders should all stand quietly until the last communicant has left the chancel rail. The unused elements should then be brought to the elder and handed to him so that he may place them on the table. There should be no haste. After the elements are in place, they usually are covered with any metal or other covering provided, and then the whole table holding the elements and vessels is covered with a white cloth. In those instances in which the containers have adequate and sightly metal or other covers, it is not mandatory to use the white cloth covering.

As to the ultimate disposition of the unused elements, they may be used for home or hospital communion later in the day, not as "reserve sacrament," but simply as convenience. Even so, there still is likely to be some bread and some wine left over in any event. It is appropriate for the elder and others, after the service, to consume all that is left over, or if this is not preferred, the wine might be poured upon the ground and the bread buried or burned. It does not seem appropriate for the consecrated elements to be poured down the drain or deposited in a garbage pail.

32. *Then the minister, standing and facing the people, shall say,*

This rubric brings us to the Peace Versicle that leads into the closing movement of the service. In some churches, the peace is "passed" at this point. That is, the elder takes the right hand of the deacon between his hands, and the deacon places his left hand against the elder's right hand. In other words, a double handshake, and the elder says, "The peace of the Lord be with you," and the deacon replies, "And with thy spirit." Then the deacon and elder do the same with the sub-deacons who go up the center aisle passing the peace to the end-most person in each pew who then turns to pass the peace to the person next to him in his pew, and so on.

When the peace is passed, the elder does not then start at the beginning of the versicle before the prayer, but begins, "Let us give thanks unto the Lord."

33. *Then the minister, kneeling before the Lord's Table, and the people, kneeling or bowed, shall pray saying,*

The minister returns to the same position as for the Prayer of Humble Access and units as one with the people in offering thanksgiving for the sacrament and offering themselves to God as living gifts.

34. *Then a hymn may be sung.*

A brief hymn usually is best at this point in the service. Sometimes a doxology is used most appropriately.

35. *Then the minister shall let the people depart with this blessing.*

The Peace Benediction is especially associated with the Holy Communion. It is at once a blessing and dismissal and sends us out to live the life represented by this sacrament.

The minister appropriately steps toward the people to take the position where he will stand to give the benediction. The minister's raised hands are symbolic of being placed on the head of each person in blessing and benediction.

36. *A postlude may follow.*

More and more congregations remain seated through the postlude or closing voluntary. When this is done, the people may be seated to receive the benediction, or they may become accustomed to sitting down immediately after the benediction if they have continued to stand after the hymn. The preceding rubric is deliberately vague concerning details so as to allow for variations.

In the experience of many, the postlude or closing voluntary may contribute much in securing the meaning and spirit of the service to the people.

V

The Order for the Service of Marriage

Paul W. Hoon

I. Introduction
    The marriage service is unique in the church's worship in that it is both
    a religious and a secular act. The minister represents both ecclesiastical
    and civil authority. The marriage order itself likewise includes elements
    from both Christian and secular traditions. These elements can best be
    identified and the service itself best interpreted by noting at the outset
    its threefold structure.

    1. The *betrothal* consists of the address to the congregation, the
        charge to the couple, the questions to the couple and their responses
        which are often referred to as the espousal, the giving away of the
        hand of the bride. The betrothal derives in part from the rites of
        sponsalia in the Roman Empire and is paralleled by Jewish rites.
        It preceded the actual marriage or nuptial rites by an interval of
        months or even a year or more. This separation is still reflected in
        the future tense of the verbs: "Wilt thou have . . . . Wilt thou
        love . . . , etc.?"

    2. The *nuptial* or marriage acts are of similar origin, including the
        joining of right hands, the consent and pledging of the couples'
        faith to one another, the giving and receiving of the ring or rings.
        This is the decisive and validating action of the ceremony.

    3. The *ministry of the church* includes the pronouncement by the
        minister, prayers, and blessing.

II. Historical
    A. Evidences of secular, even of pagan, origins abound in present
        marriage customs and in certain parts of the service. For instance,

groomsmen and bridesmaids are modern equivalents of ancient surety witnesses. The bride's veil was once thought to shield her from evil spirits; the bridesmaids' attire, resembling and yet differing from the bride's, was thought to deceive and deflect the evil spirits from the bride, and bells were rung to drive the evil spirits away. Rice is a symbol of fertility, and the throwing of rice indicated good wishes of friends for many children. The bridal wreath (called *subarrhatio*), the crown of flowers, comes from the Romans. Likewise the giving of a ring derives from similar Roman usage in making legal contracts (mentioned by Pliny); joining of right hands (*dextrarum iunctio* found in Xenophon and Cicero) signifies fidelity; the wedding feast (*coena nuptialis*) including sharing in the wedding cake derives from the Roman custom of offering a sacrifice to Jupiter Farraeus.

B. *Christianization of the marriage ceremony.* There was no liturgy of matrimony in the primitive church corresponding to Baptism and Holy Communion, although from the beginning there was a Christian conception of marriage (Paul's phrase in I Cor. 7:39, "married . . . in the Lord" probably meant "before the Christian community"). Through about the first three centuries, marriage civilly contracted by baptized Christians was considered to be a Christian marriage. The first reference to the church entering into the secular domain and prescribing the nature of the service is in a letter of Ignatius asserting that marriage should be "under recognition of [i.e. witnessed by] the bishop." Tertullian admonished Christians to celebrate the Eucharist at marriage as a substitute for the Roman custom of sacrifice to Jupiter. From the fifth century on, certain church ceremonies including ecclesiastical benediction were prescribed, but in general marriage was still civilly validated. For the first thousand years, Christians followed secular customs but infused them with Christian meaning. In the latter part of the twelfth century, marriage became one of the important sacraments of the church, although it was not regarded so important as Baptism or Holy Communion. It was officially designated a sacrament by the Roman Church in 1439, and its sacramental character was dogmatically defined at the Council of Trent in 1563.

C. *The beginning of the rite as generally practiced in the Church of England* appears to be recorded first in laws of King Edmund (A.D. 946). The presence of a priest was required. Cranmer's revisions which became normative for Anglicanism in 1549 and from which our Methodist order comes, drew chiefly on the rite used in the diocese of Salisbury which we call the Sarum rite, but they also included elements from the York rite, elements from the writings

73

of Archbishop Hermann von Wied of Cologne, Germany, entitled "Pious Consultations," and certain phrases from Luther.

D. *Methodist history.* John Wesley greatly admired the Book of Common Prayer. The marriage order in the 1784 service book which he prepared for American Methodists followed Cranmer's Anglican order as it had been revised in 1661, but deleted the giving in marriage of the woman and the ceremony of the ring. The former was restored by the Methodist Episcopal Church in 1916. The latter ceremony was reinserted by the Methodist Episcopal Church in 1864, and by the Methodist Episcopal Church, South, in 1886. Other alterations from time to time included the omission in 1854 of the betrothal and its restoration by the southern church in 1910 and by the northern church in 1916, the dropping in 1854 of the publication of the banns and of concluding prayers (after the pronouncement) which Wesley had retained from the Anglican Order. Before the Uniting Conference in 1939, the orders were quite similar. Influenced by the 1928 Book of Common Prayer of the American Episcopal Church, the slightly longer service of the northern church was adopted. The 1940 order changed the phrase "fear of God" to read "love of God" (which had been made the reading of the northern church in 1932), and the 1944 order revised the language of the charge to the couple and inserted the prayer of blessing upon the giving of the rings taken from the 1928 Book of Common Prayer of the Protestant Episcopal Church.

E. *Notes on elements of particular historical interest or importance.*

1. The positions of bride and groom, with the man at the minister's left and on the woman's right, were specified in the ancient Sarum rite. This provision probably has two sources: the interpretation of tradition deriving from Genesis 2:21-23 that Eve was fashioned from Adam's left rib, and the English tradition of designating the right hand as the place of honor.

2. The opening address to the congregation is a statement by the church of its understanding of the meaning of marriage. It also is a vestige of the legal requirement of the publishing of the banns, publicly announcing a marriage on three successive Sundays before it is performed. This practice dates from the time when the priest had the duty to inquire legally into the qualifications of those to be married. American Methodism inherited the custom of publishing the banns from Wesley and followed it until about the middle of the nineteenth century, when the state superseded the church as examiner in such matters. This address, and the last sentence especially, imply the important question of whether impediments to marriage are known to exist, and the church rightly has always taken

this question most seriously. Canonical impediments have traditionally included blood relationship in varying degrees (called "consanguinity"), mistaken identity, mental deficiency sufficient to prevent intelligent choice, insanity, impuberty, known impotence or sterility, a previous marriage still existent, fraud. Inquiry into certain of these has been taken over by civil authorities, but the minister still has the duty to inquire into the couple's qualifications on behalf of the church, and the congregation's silence after the question, "If any man can show any just cause . . . ," indicates their function of approval in both an ecclesiastical and civil sense.

3. The bride's promise to "obey" and "serve" has not appeared in any Methodist order since the early part of this century. It originated with Luther, was appropriated by Cranmer, retained by Wesley, but eliminated by the northern church in 1864 and the southern church in 1910 as inconsistent with the status of equality of women.

4. Note the import of the verbs embodied in the betrothal and espousal vows: "live together," "love," "comfort" (i.e. strengthen as well as console), "honor," "keep," "to have and to hold" (a legal term deriving from marriage contracts), "'cherish," "pledge" (originally "plight"). Nine in all, they are from the 1661 revision of Cranmer's 1549 order.

5. The ceremony of the ring is a survival of ancient usage among both Jews and Romans. The ring was originally a symbol or seal by which power or authority or both were transmitted, as by a king to an officer, becoming changed into a symbol of love and respect. Its round shape is considered to symbolize endlessness, perpetuity, and therefore the enduring nature of marriage. Ancient practice called for it to be placed upon the fourth finger (in our modern parlance the third finger), because it was thought that a vein from this finger led directly from the heart. The Puritans eliminated the ring from the marriage ceremony because it was felt to be idolatry of an object, and doubtless for this reason Wesley deleted the giving of the ring from his 1784 order. It was restored in mid-nineteenth-century American Methodism, and the prayer of blessing on the giving of the ring has been taken from the 1928 order of the American Protestant Episcopal Church. To speak accurately, we should conceive this prayer as a "prayer of blessing upon *the giving* of the ring," rather than upon the ring itself.

6. The parent's giving of the hand of the bride was originally a custom of the Teutons, appropriated from them via the York

75

rite by Cranmer, incorporated into the Anglican order, omitted by Wesley, and restored by the Methodist Episcopal Church in 1916. The father is the parent who always gives away the hand of the bride, acting for himself and the mother and probably for the whole clan. When the father for any reason cannot serve in this capacity, it is appropriate for a male member of the family or for someone else to serve in his stead. When the father says "I do," he is speaking representatively as well as personally, so it is both unduly sentimental and inappropriate for the simple "I do" to be replaced by "her mother and I do."

7. The pronouncement by the minister, "Forasmuch as N. and N. have consented together . . . ," was adopted by Cranmer via the Sarum rite from a Gallican rite used by Archbishop Hermann von Wied. By this forthright, dignified pronouncement, the minister voices the acknowledgment by the church that the marriage union has been officially undertaken, and in the words, "those whom God hath joined together, let not man put asunder," restates the pronouncement of our Lord himself in his own language.

8. The prayer, "O eternal God . . . ," was originally located after the giving of the ring and before the pronouncement in both Cranmer's and Wesley's orders and continued to be so located through at least 1924 in American Methodism. The present order wisely places it immediately after the pronouncement of marriage, following it with the Lord's Prayer, thus making prayer the first act the couple perform after their marriage. In the spirit of prayer they go forth into their life together. This prayer is a skillful blending of two prayers, one taken from the English Book of Common Prayer and the other from the 1928 American Book of Common Prayer. The Lord's Prayer, interestingly, was not originally included in Cranmer's marriage order but reserved for the subsequent Communion service, but Wesley inserted it in a position after the pronouncement in conjunction with other prayers before the benediction. Note that all—congregation, couple, and minister—participate in the Lord's Prayer. As part of his pastoral instruction, the minister can helpfully go through the Lord's Prayer, phrase by phrase, explaining to the couple how its meanings apply to their married life. Observe also that while free prayer is not specified, it also is not disallowed. If employed, it should be conceived and cast in a form whose dignity is congruous with the prescribed prayers.

9. Sermon and sacrament: Toward the end of the second and

76

about the beginning of the third centuries, the distinctively Christian element introduced into the ceremony was the celebration of Holy Communion, with a solemn benediction of the couple, first mentioned by Tertullian. Cranmer included both sacrament and sermon as mandatory in the 1549 Prayer Book; the 1661 order softened the imperative, making Communion optional if "convenient"; and Wesley's 1784 order for American Methodists omitted all reference to Communion whatsoever. (The 1928 American Protestant Episcopal order also dropped the nuptial Eucharist as mandatory, although it provided collect, epistle [Eph. 5:21 ff.] and gospel [Matt. 19:4-6] lessons if Communion should be desired.) The present rubric makes Communion optional and specifies celebration at a time other than the wedding service proper. Participation in the sacrament is to be encouraged, but never on grounds of mere sentiment or aesthetics; rather, the sacrament should be celebrated only if the minister is assured of the couple's integrity in desiring it. With regard to the sermon, note that it is not specified nor disallowed. This illustrates well the intention underlying the composition of the *Book of Worship* as stated in the Preface: ". . . to provide significant structure for the worship of the Church," but not "in any way to fetter the spontaneity or reject the reliance upon the Holy Spirit which have characterized Methodist worship throughout its history." Grounded in the gospel and based upon a passage from the Bible, a brief sermon, properly located, is appropriate. It can best come as the conclusion to an opening sequence of processional or the processional hymn, brief invocation, Psalter or scripture reading, sermon, before the marriage order itself with the opening address to the congregation is begun. Alternatively, a sermon may be inserted immediately before the charge to the couple, or, perhaps preceded by a hymn, near the end of the service after the prayers and before the benediction, although this may anticlimactically stall the service. In any case, it is essential not to interrupt the theological integrity and the liturgical movement of the nuptial section of the order, that is, from the pledging of the couple's faith to one another through the pronouncement and prayers.

III.   Pastoral

Interpreting the historical nature of the marriage service is only part of the minister's responsibility to instruct the couple in their duty to understand the Christian significance of marriage. Instruction also means counseling the couple in order to interpret to them "the standards of the church" and to inquire whether these standards, as well as those of the state, have been complied with. It is to be understood that if a couple request a Christian minister to conduct their marriage ceremony, they do so on the church's terms, and it is the minister's duty likewise to counsel them in the name of the church and to convey the concern of the Christian community that their marriage be understood and entered upon as a Christian marriage. It is assumed that the minister will set a sufficient number of appointments, before and if necessary after the ceremony, and that the couple will comply with this requirement, to ensure that this purpose is achieved. The welfare of the couple as well as the discipline of the church is involved here. A plan widely followed includes four appointments in all, although circumstances may suggest a larger or smaller number: before the wedding, one with the couple together and one separately with each some weeks after the wedding, one conference with the couple together. Pastoral counseling will deal with such areas as:

A. Assurance that the "laws of the state" have been complied with, including requirements having to do with the legality of the marriage, length of residence, blood tests, possession of license, etc.

B. Spiritual, personal, and psychological matters that properly concern the church, such as the couple's readiness for marriage, their maturity and health, their awareness of the adjustments marriage and homemaking inevitably demand, identification of problems and of the resources for dealing with them, their understanding of and attitudes toward sexuality, their conception of parenthood and their plans for family life, their church relation, the practice of prayer and stewardship in their home, their understanding of their Christian vocation in the world. If necessary, the minister and the couple will not hesitate to solicit the help of a physician, professional counselor, or therapist in order better to prepare the couple for marriage. The minister may also wish to examine with the couple the statement of The United Methodist Church on Christian marriage and family life as set forth in the *Discipline*.

IV. Theological
Instruction in "the Christian significance of the holy estate" of matrimony requires above all a religious, or what we may call a theological, understanding of marriage and family life. The marriage order states this understanding by means of a number of affirmations both explicitly and implicitly, and at a number of points in the service, which taken together provide a coherent framework of Christian interpretation.

A. *The divine nature of marriage* is intentionally and unmistakably marked by important usages of language: "holy matrimony," "instituted of God, and signifying unto us the mystical union which exists between Christ and his Church; which holy estate Christ

78

adorned and beautified with his presence in Cana of Galilee. It is therefore . . . to be entered into . . . in the fear of God. . . . If these solemn vows are kept inviolate, as God's Word demands, and if steadfastly you endeavor to do the will of your heavenly Father, God will bless your marriage, will grant you fulfillment in it, and will establish your home in peace . . . according to God's holy ordinance. . . . Those whom God hath joined togther, let not man put asunder. . . . God the Father, the Son, and the Holy Spirit bless, preserve, and keep you . . . ." Through all these usages, indeed from the beginning to the end of the marriage order, the church defines marriage as unqualifiedly grounded in the nature of God, as expressive of the purpose of God, as sustained by the grace of God, and as bringing man to know his true destiny in God. This profoundly religious view of marriage is at an opposite pole from those views which understand marriage as merely a secular contract between parties, or as having its ground in the biological fact of sexuality as part of the natural order.

1. In this respect the church's understanding only reflects the biblical understanding of marriage. The biblical understanding of marriage, however, cannot be reconstructed on selected proof texts. (The most important texts are Gen. 1:26-31; 2:18-25; 3:5-7, 15-20, and our Lord's teaching in Matt. 19:5-15; Mark 10:2-16; Luke 16:18; and I Cor. 6:15-20; 7:1-40; II Cor. 11:2-4; Eph. 5:21–6:4; Rev. 19:6-16.) The whole tenor of the Bible must be borne in mind, including the way in which the Old and New Testaments employ marriage symbolism to convey the mystic relation between God and his people (see esp. Song of Sol.; Isa. 54:5 ff.; Jer. 31:31 ff.; Hos. 2; John 2:1-11; 3:29, as well as the references cited above in Cor., Eph., and Rev.). Throughout the wedding order as throughout the Bible, God is understood as the Founder of marriage. Marriage and sexuality are his way of ordering the manifoldness of life (the phrase, "after God's ordinance," is Luther's), and in marriage a man and a woman participate in the divine plan for human existence. The affirmation that sexuality and marriage are part of the creation clearly marks them as good (see Gen. 1:27-28, 31), and as primary in a way in which celibacy is not primary. Marriage is thus to be understood as a vocation; to be called to be a husband or wife or parent is as sacred a calling as there is.

The divine nature of marriage is given a distinctively Christian emphasis in the reference to Christ's presence at the marriage in Cana of Galilee (John 2:1-11), to Christ's words, "Those whom God hath joined together, let not man put asunder" (Matt. 19:6), and to Paul's daring use in Ephesians 5 of the symbol of marriage as a simile of the mystical union which exists between Christ and his church.

2. The Cana narrative suggests that Christ affirms and hallows marriage, that his glory is present in it, and that his presence can richly alter the very nature of marriage as radically as water was once symbolically changed into the more vital and sparkling wine. In the salvation history culminating in him, the secular nature of marriage has been taken up and transfigured, so that it is not too much to say that the heights of meaning in marriage can only be known and experienced in relation to him.

3. In the very important passage in Matt. 19:4-6, Jesus reaffirms sexuality as part of the goodness of creation; he abrogates the Mosaic toleration of divorce in order to restore marriage to its original place in God's plan; he specifies the union of man and woman in their total being as "one flesh" as the core of marriage, and he enjoins marriage as normally indissoluble and exclusive.

4. The phrase, "the mystical union which exists between Christ and his Church," is taken from Paul's teaching in Ephesians 5:21-33, and gathers the divine ordination of marriage into a still higher sanctity. For the Christian, the union of husband and wife becomes a mysterious experience of the union of Christ with his people. From their relation with each other, husband and wife can richly learn of their relation with God as he gives us life through his Son in the community of the church, and reciprocally, from their relation with God in the body of Christ, the church, they can learn how to live out their relationship to each other in marriage. Each, marriage and church, holds intimations of meaning for the other.

B. *The holy nature of marriage.* Whereas the Roman Catholic Church holds marriage to be one of the seven official sacraments, Protestantism has declared that it is not a sacrament in that it was not ordained as such by Christ, that it contains no outward signs of dominical institution which constitute means of grace, that in itself marriage does not bestow a special kind of grace, and that its ratification is not the exclusive property of the church. Article XIV of the Methodist Church denies that marriage is a sacrament as Baptism and Holy Communion are sacraments. However, in Luther's words, marriage is a *"holy* estate." It is sacramental spelled with a small "s," as it were, when the couple accept it as God's will for their lives and when they accept the grace God gives them to live out their relationship in obedience to his will,

80

for such vows as the couple take can never be fulfilled in their own un-aided strength. Further, while marriage may not be a "sacrament" in an ecclesiastical sense, it is sacramental in that the physical relationship of sexuality can express and seal a spiritual relationship. This is to say, the "honor" and "holiness" that pertain to the "estate" of marriage extend to the physical and the sexual, for God himself can consecrate these and make them the means of his grace. He uses an outward sign to communicate a spiritual grace. A moving paradigm of the sacramental nature of marriage in this sense is the action of the couple in taking each other's right hand and pledging their nuptial vows. Actually, at this moment of physical action and speech, the couple marry each other; they are ministers of divine grace to each other, and the clergyman and the congregation only serve as witnesses and as bestower of the church's blessing.

C. *The covenant character of marriage.* Explicitly ("the holy covenant you are about to make") and implicitly, the conception of marriage as a freely chosen, unconditional, lifelong, exclusive covenant the couple make with each other, runs throughout the ceremony. As such, it intimates the same type of covenant relationship God has made with mankind through his church.

1. The marriage covenant has its reality, first, in an *act of the will* on the part of both man and woman in committing themselves to each other. Note that the reply to the betrothal question is: "I will," and that the core of the nuptial pledge is action of the will expressed in the voluntary taking of the right hand of the other and in the verbs of decision and action: "I take thee . . . to have, to hold, to love, to cherish . . . , and thereto I pledge . . . ." This is to say, the marriage covenant does not inhere primarily in feelings of romantic love. To be sure, love is in part feeling, but it is most essentially commitment of the will. The will is the executive agent in human personality, we may say, and commits the selfhood and veracity of a person in a way that the feelings do not.

2. The covenant is enduring and indissoluble: "Whom God hath joined, let not man put asunder." The enduring quality of the covenant relationship extends through *time:* "till death do us part." It also extends through *all the range of human experience:* "for better, for worse, for richer, for poorer, in sickness and in health." The phrases of the Lord's Prayer the couple pray together also mark this: "forgive us our trespasses, deliver us from evil, lead us not into temptation." This grim realism in the marriage ceremony fits our human situation. The covenant relationship between husband and wife is to be understood as

81

enduring amid and through all these—sinfulness, temptation, adversity.

3. The purpose of the covenant is that "the two shall be one flesh" (Matt. 19:4-6; Mark 10:6-8; see also Gen. 2:18). Jesus' use of the term "flesh" means the physical body, but it also means much more, as it does in Hebrew thought: the total being of man and his total existence in the world. Communion between man and woman in this radical sense is thus the culmination of the divine purpose of marriage and its crowning meaning. Church tradition has specified other purposes: the procreation of children, and—as in the thought of Paul and of certain church fathers, chiefly Augustine—provision for the expression of man's sexuality in a morally and socially acceptable way. But these are secondary. The primary purpose of marriage and its fundamental basis are ontological, that is, the union of two beings. The ritual marks this with significant language: "mystical union," "together" (ten uses), "uniting," "join," i.e. "one'd" (six uses), and by the general meaning throughout. Certain actions likewise signify the element of union, most notably the gestures of the man and woman in the nuptial action whereby each reaches out, joins the other to himself by the taking of the hand, and vows his selfhood to the other. The ceremony of the ring also marks this. Union of this kind does not mean that individual identity is suppressed; the "I" of selfhood is preserved. Each remains an individual person as signified by the use of the couple's respective Christian names. But in the covenant of marriage, the being of each becomes complementary to and fulfilled in the other.

4. The marriage covenant by definition is exclusive: "forsaking all others, keep thee only unto . . . ."

D. *The church context of marriage.* The service of marriage is not a private affair between two persons, nor is it to be thought of as conducted only for the family and friends. Rather, it is a liturgical action set within the concern and supervision of the Christian congregation, and the church context of marriage accordingly cannot be ignored nor underestimated. This is true in several senses.

1. The ceremony of marriage is an action executed under the supervision of the church and is normally a public service within the fellowship of the congregation. The rubrics clearly specify the authority of the minister as representative of the congregation and require him to ensure on their behalf that the persons to be married have been qualified according to the standards of the church. The church cares deeply for her

people and reserves the right to decide whether or not her representative shall officiate at any given marriage. The "impediments" and "standards" mentioned earlier affect this decision. The opening charge to the congregation beginning with the phrase, "Dearly beloved," implies and certifies the congregation as "witnesses"; the charge to the couple likewise includes the phrase "this company." Further, the ceremony of the rings significantly concludes with the words: "uniting . . . in holy matrimony, through the Church of Jesus Christ our Lord." The rubric specifying the use of the "Christian name" in the betrothal vows implies the sacrament of baptism previously performed by the church; a "Christian name" is the name given at baptism bestowing theological identity and marking an individual's membership within the Christian community. Likewise the trinitarian formula is a formula of the church, the prayers offered are the prayers of the church, the pronouncement of marriage and the benediction are characteristic acts of the church. This is to say, from the beginning to the end, the church context pervades the entire wedding order.

2. In this emphasis upon the church, the marriage order only reflects the Christian conception of marriage and family life as a vocational emblem of the church. Indeed, a Christian home is an *ecclesiola*, a little church. Luther said that parents are to be as bishops and apostles to their children, and in the love of the home are to make known God's love as revealed in Christ.

3. Christian marriage is to be thought of as a redemptive fellowship in the same sense that the church is a redemptive fellowship. That is, God's law and God's grace operate in both in a saving way. While marriage is part of the created order that is good, it also stands under the sign of the Fall; it is subject to sin; it has laid upon it moral demands and requires obedience to vows. In short, the blessing and fulfillment and peace of marriage are morally conditional, and man's sin in failing to live up to the moral demands of marriage must be expected to be as real here as anywhere. But just as the church is a fellowship of sinners who are yet forgiven, so marriage is to be entered into as an experience of grace known through repentance and faith, of forgiveness and resurrection to new life. Only as husband and wife learn that they cannot of themselves fulfill their obligations, but are forgiven and reconciled to God through his mercy, do they find the barriers of sin and guilt that would otherwise come between them falling away,

and enter into the deepest marital union. Thus it is that marriage is to be understood as a paradigm of Christ's union with his church, and the love between husband and wife as a sign of the love Christ has for his church. In both, Christ is ever the new and living Way.

4. Christian marriage is also a sanctifying fellowship as the church is a sanctifying fellowship. That is, the states of life in both are an experience of growth in love and grace and service. This is perhaps another way of defining marriage as a "holy estate." Growth in married love has been described as growth from *eros* through *philia* into *agape*, that is, from romantic love through fraternal love into divine love (although in another sense the divine *agape* is the prior foundation as well as the consummation of other forms of love). Growth in this profound sense however does not take place without man's most strenuous effort initiated and sustained by God's grace, nor without participation in the means of grace the church alone supplies, such as faithful prayer, the sacraments, public worship. Moreover, while marriage and family are themselves a form of Christian vocation, they are not a refuge from nor a substitute for the ministry in the world which every Christian is charged to perform in his particular calling. Thus while marriage is itself a form of service the couple perform for each other, their growth in service reaches beyond their own life together.

5. Christian marriage bears an eschatological aspect as the church is an eschatological community, that is, each state of life prefigures a still richer life to come. To be sure, Jesus said that in heaven people neither marry nor are given in marriage, and life in neither estate is an end in itself. Christianity, it has been said, affirms marriage and family, but sets limits to their ultimacy. Yet both our life in the church and our life in marriage prefigure the nature of a still richer life bound up with our eternal destiny in God. This aspect of marriage has been described in the words of Rev. 19:6-10. A modern writer has transposed this insight into the following words: "Together they have travelled the road of life, and remembrance holds them close, remembrance of many hours of ineffable felicity, of a sense of union as near to bliss as mortal hearts can realize; of high aspirations pursued in common; of sorrows shared—sacramental sorrows; and now, nearing the end hand in hand, they look forth upon the wide universe, and the love they found in themselves and still find

84

there to the last, becomes to them a pledge of that vaster
love that moves the farther stars and suns."

V.   Liturgical

In light of this understanding of Christian teaching and tradition as
they are embodied in the wedding order, of the standards required by
the church, and of the exalted conception of marriage which Christianity holds, the ceremony describes well the attitude the couple are expected to bring, in the phrases: "advisedly," "reverently, discreetly, and
in the fear of God."

A.   "Advisedly" and "discreetly" mean not merely prudence in making the decision to marry; they also mean becoming informed
about what Christian marriage means and requires. In regard to
the ceremony itself, they mean an appreciation of how the service
is rooted in tradition, how its words and actions have evolved over
many centuries, and how its elements embody universal and time-
less meanings. In its totality as well as in its details, the service
possesses a certain classic shape, dignity, and rhythm which one
cannot alter or adorn without risking injury to its integrity. The
service cannot be freely reshaped to suit individual taste. Innovation may be appropriate to other liturgical occasions in the
church's life, but hardly here. The only permissible additions are
those appropriate to the church's liturgical heritage such as sermon
or homily, biblical lessons, hymns, prayers. Theologically and
liturgically, the burden of proof falls on anyone who wishes to
have the service performed other than in the form in which it has
come down to us from antiquity through Christian history. Here
Wesley's remark concerning the church's worship distinctively
applies: "I love the old wine best."

B.   "In the sight of God," "reverently," "in the fear of God," "in the
presence of God before whom the secrets of all hearts are disclosed"
—this chain of phrases marks the attitude of religious sensitivity
on the part of the couple which alone is appropriate to the
religious meaning of both the ceremony and the estate of marriage.
The phrase "the fear of God" in particular, at one time mistakenly
thought to be too severe, is both biblically sound and liturgically
appropriate. For "fear" before God is a way of expressing one's
awareness of the holy. It denotes the posture of expectancy of
revelation (many theophanies in the Bible characteristically begin:
"fear not") . To fear God also means recognizing the commands he
places upon man; the love of God commanded in the Shema, for
example, is never separated from the fear of God, and it is always
connected with the fact of judgment pronounced upon those who
violate God's commandments. Thus to approach marriage in the
fear of God is a way of acknowledging the moral responsibilities

marriage involves. Lastly, those who "fear God" are precisely those whom the Bible calls "the faithful," and to "fear him" is a way of describing the faith, the obedience, and the service we offer unto him in marriage as everywhere else.

C. The attitude of reverence with which the couple enter upon the holy estate of matrimony comes to focus in the spirit of reverence with which they enter into the ceremony itself. From beginning to end, the ceremony is to be understood and conducted as an act of worship in the same sense that a service of preaching or the celebration of the sacraments of Baptism or Holy Communion are acts of worship. Significantly, the title of the ceremony reads: "The Order for the *Service* of Marriage." Throughout, the ritual is a *service* performed by the people unto God, and everything is to be subordinated to this understanding. Further, it is an *ordered* service whose design embodies an integrity that must not be trifled with. This is underscored in the mandatory grammar of many of the rubrics: "the congregation *shall* stand," "the minister *shall* say," "then *shall* the husband and wife kneel," etc. Etiquette, social convention, individual taste, so-called "mechanics" take second place to religious meaning and liturgical propriety.

Even the wedding rehearsal is to be thought of as more than a rehearsal. It too is a liturgical act and consequently an occasion of reverence as well as of gaiety. It may well be opened with an interpretation of its liturgical meaning by the minister, and a brief scripture reading and prayer.

1. The rubrics specify that the resident minister is in charge of all arrangements, and the couple should not make the mistake of deciding on arrangements before consulting with him. He will always welcome the couple's requests and normally comply with them as far as the provisions of the church allow. Should a couple desire a clergyman other than the resident pastor to conduct or participate in the ceremony, they should discuss their request with the resident pastor. Also, it is appropriate for him to participate in the invitation to another pastor, or to extend it to the other pastor for the couple.

2. As all authentic worship, the wedding service is not performed by the minister alone, as is commonly supposed. Rather, it is a corporate action in which the congregation, the couple, and the minister all participate. The corporate action is executed in words, music, visual symbolism, and ceremonial, and as such these can embody an element of sacred drama as distinguished from theater.

   a. In taking his place before the wedding processional begins, the minister symbolizes the church context in his

86

office as representative of the congregation. Indeed all his actions are to figure this forth. He is not to conceive the service as an occasion to express his individual taste, much less his idiosyncrasy. Rather, he is to function as servant of the church, and his entire conduct of the service is to conform with the church's religious intention.

b. The processional is partly a means of physically providing for the dignified entrance of the wedding party, but it is even more an acting out of the holy joy with which the people of God "ascend unto the hill of the Lord."

c. "The congregation *shall stand* as the wedding procession begins." Note the mandatory character of this rubric. This action is in part one of natural propriety, but it is even more a symbol of the congregation's active, not passive, presence and participation throughout the service. Preferably, the congregation should also remain reverently standing throughout the service, although the minister may, at his discretion, allow the congregation to be seated after the processional or after the opening address. The congregation should also stand for the recessional. It should also participate in the "amens" to the prayers, in the Lord's Prayer, and in any hymns that may be sung. The congregation is not to be thought of as an audience for whom the ceremony is being performed, but as fellow priests, coactors, and witnesses in the service performed unto God.

d. The initial positions prescribed for the man and woman may be held throughout the betrothal, that is, through the action of the giving away of the hand of the bride. Progression into the nuptial part of the service may be legitimately dramatized (if the architecture permits) by movement forward a few paces into the chancel of the minister, bride and groom, and best man and maid of honor (and ring-bearer), perhaps accompanied by a very brief interlude of subdued music whose length the minister should determine, or by a hymn.

e. The rubric providing for the physical action of the man and woman each taking the other's right hand at the direction of the minister, looking at each other and speaking the words of nuptial faith, is extremely important because, as previously noted, this action is the validating action of the entire service and constitutes them husband and wife. The couple are ministers one to the other here. A formula for executing this action is

87

to remember that everything here is done with the right hand: the minister with his right hand receives the woman's right hand from the father's right hand, and causes the man to reach with his right hand and take the woman's right hand. The woman's subsequent action is to be as clearly and autonomously marked, the groom having loosed her hand before she takes his. Preferably, the couple will repeat the words they address to one another as the minister lines them out, phrase by phrase, although they may be repeated from memory if this can be done without undue self-consciousness or any semblance of exhibitionism. The decisive consideration here is: What is most real, sacred, sincere?

f.   The ceremony of the rings is largely self-explanatory. The words spoken by the couple again should be lined out by the minister if so desired. Whoever handles the ring should do it in such a way that the person taking it can do so securely and naturally. A convenient and significant way by which the ring may be given to the minister is to have it placed in his hand over his prayer book. This is according to ancient custom, and the service book symbolizes the church whose representative the minister is and through whom those giving and receiving the ring are blessed.

g.   The pronouncement spoken by the minister is addressed to the congregation as well as to the man and woman. The volume of voice appropriate here and in other passages addressed to the people is to be distinguished from the quieter tone in which the minister addresses portions of the ceremony primarily to the couple, and from the still more quiet tone in which he gives mechanical directions to the couple.

3.   All the music, as noted in the third rubric, is to be "service" music, that is, of a character consonant with worship as service to God. In a word, it is to be liturgical music. (Secular music when desired by a couple is of course often appropriate to their wedding, but it does not qualify as liturgical music and should be performed at the reception or wedding meal.) As part of the "arrangements," the music is to be selected and performed in full consultation with the minister and is subject to his approval and that of the church acting through the minister of music or organist. Suggested texts and settings approved by the church's commission on worship and by the National Fellowship of Methodist Musicians are to be pre-

ferred, and it would be well to have available a prepared list of selections from which the bride and groom may make their choices. "Prelude" music, whether organ, instrumental, or choral, should be selected and performed as an organic part of the service as worship; it is not "incidental" music, much less concert music. The same is true of the postlude. Note that any solo must be sung before the processional; it is impermissible to interrupt the service with a solo after the processional and opening address. Hymns from the Methodist Hymnal mentioned in the footnote are particularly appropriate, more so than solos, in that they directly involve the congregation, voice the Christian faith in which marriage is set, and splendidly express the joy and prayer of the Christian community. Appropriate places for hymns are before or after the processional at the conclusion of the betrothal, that is, after the giving away of the hand of the bride, after the pronouncement and Lord's Prayer, and perhaps after the benediction.

4. The rubrics and ritual do not prescribe but neither do they forbid the use of scripture lessons. Of course much of the text of the service is scriptural or based on scripture, but if lessons are desired, they may include a proper psalm, an epistle, and a gospel reading. Possible selections include: Pss. 23; 37:3-11, 23-28; 67; 91; 96; 103; 111; 113; 121; 128; 139; 145; 150; I Cor. 13; Eph. 3:14-21; 5:15-33; I John 4:7-13; Matt. 19:1-6; John 2:1-11; 15:9-17. Possible Old Testament readings other than the psalms are: Gen. 2:4b-25; Deut. 6:4-9. Lessons are best introduced into the order immediately after the processional and before the address to the congregation, perhaps in conjunction with an opening hymn, brief prayer, and sermon.

VI
The Funeral

H. Grady Hardin

The worship of the church is its celebration of God's good news about life—including death. The community of faith gathers in praise to God for the meaning given to life by the life, death, and resurrection of Jesus Christ. Worship may come from a community stricken with anxiety and grief and sorrow, for Christians are offered a faith that promises joy even in the face of tribulation (John 16:33). This is not an escape from life or death; it is a revelation and insight into being that transcends the changes of time. This is a reason that one of our names for God is the Eternal.

From Paul the Apostle until today, Christians have tried to state clearly how God has revealed in Jesus Christ what happens to us when we die. The mortal nature puts on immortality and the perishable puts on the imperishable (I Cor. 15:33); we are offered "many rooms" (John 14:2); we will enter the "New Jerusalem" (Rev. 21:2). Through the centuries the church has tried to communicate a faith that is founded on the fact that God has shown us in Jesus Christ his care and control of our past, present, and future. He offers us our past in forgiveness and pardon, our present in freedom and power, and our future in promise and hope. To the Christian it is God who is great, and the church gathers to celebrate this fact in every worship service. The funeral of a loved one calls us to stand before the mysteries of life and death in the light of God's greatness. This greatness is manifest in the life we see about us, but it is our sin to permit our grief to cut us off from the greatness and the holiness of the giver and sustainer of life in whose hands we are even in death.

The death of a member of the church, therefore, is a call to worship. Our service for the Burial of the Dead, though not a sacrament, is nevertheless

90

sacramental. This is true in the sense that here is man responding to what God is doing to make himself known at the time of death and within the funeral service. God is offering us his comfort, love, and power, and we offer him ourselves, especially the life which has so recently received death.

The customs of different congregations vary widely in the use of symbols, but the service in our *Book of Worship* can become a vehicle for any congregation to worship God. Most of the directions in the service are permissive precisely because there is so much variety in our funeral customs. Each congregation should find means to examine its own practices to be sure they offer the best means of worship and are in keeping with the Christian faith. The standards of judgment must be considered in terms of our faith in the light of the grief of a family in the congregation and the symbols which have the most meaning for communicating this faith and comfort. Church school classes and special study groups are able to study the message of the church about death and its implications for burial practices. The governing bodies of some charges have encouraged such work and published material about the funeral service and the use of the church building at these times. In many cases this has deepened the faith of the people and led to funeral practices which have more nearly expressed this faith.

Historical Background

Rituals of the church change slowly, yet they are among the clearest reflections of doctrines. The slow but sharp changes in the faith of Christians about death are clearly seen in the funeral services. The fragmentary evidence from the early church indicates services which stood in sharp contrast with pagan practices. Christians wore white at funerals instead of the black worn by non-Christians. Duncan Jones says that "St. Jerome gives the first hint of the form of service when he says that Christians do not use the howling of the heathen but the comfortable words of the Psalter." [1] In those early days of the church when the pressures against the Christians were intense, the day of death was the day of release and triumph. The days of the saints and martyrs which became a large part of the church calendar were usually the day of their death. This is quite in keeping with the centrality of the Cross and Resurrection in the Christian faith. The Orthodox liturgies in particular emphasize the oneness of the fellowship in the church even with those who have died. The church at worship was not confined to the living.

The shape of the early funeral services seem to have included four elements: the funeral procession from the house, the singing of psalms, the reading of scriptures, and Holy Communion. The procession was a practice of many cultures, but the distinctive Christian aspect was the note of triumph shown

---

[1] W. K. L. Clarke, ed., *Liturgy and Worship* (London, S.P.C.K., 1932, 1943). See the chapter on "The Burial of the Dead" by A. S. Duncan-Jones, p. 618.

by the wearing of white, the burning torches, the palm branches, and the shouts of "Alleluia." All this ceremonial ended with prayers at the grave.

From the sixth century, however, there was a sharp departure from the triumphant note of the early church. What happens between death and the final awakening in the Church Triumphant? The doctrine of Purgatory became an emphasis in the Middle Ages based on a theology of the avenging judgment of God. The procession became doleful, the garments were black, and the psalms were penitential. Though it is impossible to eliminate the note of thanksgiving from the Eucharist, *Dies Irae* (day of wrath) is a fearsome note (though some of the greatest music has been written to these words). The prayers for the dead and memorial masses were all influenced by the doctrine of Purgatory. The fears and superstitions of the people were entwined with a faith that had eclipsed much of its triumph and good news with a theology of an angry God.

This complex theological matter became a point of major emphasis in the Reformation. Prayers and masses for the dead were eliminated from the reformed services, and there was an effort to restore the note of triumph at the funeral.

The influence of the Reformation in England retained much of the Catholic tradition, even as it reflected many of the doctrinal emphases of the Reformers on the Continent. *The Book of Common Prayer* is a reflection of both these influences, and the English of Thomas Cranmer became an incomparable vehicle for worship. The funeral service, as did many others, drew heavily upon the old Sarum (Salisbury) services. The rather elaborate and frequent services of the Middle Ages were reduced sharply in the 1549 service. The procession began at the church gate and proceeded to the church or grave. There was a simple service consisting of psalms, lessons, and prayers followed by Holy Communion. The next revision of the service in 1552 reflected more of the Reformation and eliminated the prayers of commendation, the psalms, and the Holy Communion. The revision of 1662 restored the psalms and the general shape of the 1549 service, though without Holy Communion or prayers of commendation.

The 1662 *Book of Common Prayer* used by John Wesley was most influential upon Methodist services. Wesley's *Sunday Service* sent to the young church in America followed the 1662 service very closely except for the committal: "Forasmuch as it hath pleased God of his great mercy, to take unto himself the soul of our dear brother here departed," were strongly objected to by the Puritans and Mr. Wesley alike. The 1549 translation from the Latin of Sarum into English made some changes in this paragraph. Every revision of the *Book of Common Prayer* has made changes. The present committal sentences in the *Book of Worship* reflect the continued effort to say the proper words when returning the body to its burial place.

The changes in the Order for the Burial of the Dead made in American Methodism reflect very little fundamental change in the general pattern of the service. The services included the changes in the English translations of the Bible in the late nineteenth and early twentieth centuries, just as the present service uses the Revised Standard Version. From the 1662 service, Psalms 39 and 90 have been used most frequently. The use of Psalm 23 in the regular service was begun in the ritual of the Methodist Episcopal service in 1916. It had been used for the service of the Burial of a Child earlier.

In 1858 the ritual of the Methodist Episcopal Church, South, added this rubric following the lessons: "Here may follow a suitable hymn, a sermon, or exhortation, and an extemporary prayer." In commenting on this in *The Rites and Ritual of Episcopal Methodism* (1926), Nolan B. Harmon, Jr., says, "The funeral sermon indeed has had a great place in the more evangelical American churches, the Methodist as well as others. Of recent years the former invariable custom of 'remarks by the minister' is going out of favor, being supplanted by the printed form." [2] The changes of the past forty or fifty years since Bishop Harmon's study have made it possible to see the importance of a proclamation of the Word in the funeral worship and at the same time to avoid some of the weaknesses of the "remarks by the minister."

Recent changes in the funeral ritual have been made in the order of worship. The processional anthems have become more often the opening sentences without a processional, and the prayers of invocation follow the sentences or a hymn. The suggestion for the use of the Apostles' Creed (or other affirmation) hymns, and sermon follows more closely the Order of Worship of Methodists in their regular Sunday worship. This structure was introduced first in the ritual of the Methodist Episcopal Church in 1932. It became the basis for the service in the *Discipline* of 1939. Though this was a rather sharp change, it retained strong links with the past and at the same time offered the congregation more opportunities to participate in a more familiar pattern of worship.

For a study of the present service, turn to The Order for the Burial of the Dead in the Methodist *Book of Worship*. (The rubric numbers used in this chapter were determined by numbering consecutively from the beginning.)

The General Rubrics

1. *"The death of a member of the church should be reported to the pastor as soon as possible, and arrangements for the funeral should be made in consultation with him."*

This is a new rubric in the *Book of Worship* which may appear too obvious, yet most ministers can attest to the need of it and wish that it were known among all the members of the church. Pastors can encourage the members of the congregation to see that he is informed of situations that call for his

[2] Nolan B. Harmon, Jr., *The Rites and Ritual of Episcopal Methodism* (Nashville, Publishing House of the M. E. Church, South, 1926), p. 302. This important study is now out of print.

attention. It is better to be called ten times about a death or some other serious matter than not to be informed by those who were assuming he had been called.

The pastoral care of a family at the time of death should call for the minister's most sensitive skills. The pastor and the congregation have both the opportunity and obligation to be a community of comfort, sustenance, encouragement, readjustment, and healing. The subject of this chapter is the funeral service, but it is assumed that the service itself is to be in the context of a larger ministry to those in grief.

The second section of the rubric calls for close cooperation between the pastor and the family and the funeral director. The funeral director has very important work to do in caring for the body of the deceased from the time of death through the disposal of the body. The pastor is in charge of the service of worship at the funeral. The close cooperation of all those involved is required, and both pastor and funeral director should respect each other's prerogatives. The time and place of the services should not be set without consultation with the pastor. When the service is in the church building, the funeral director should be informed in advance about the regulations on the use of the church at funerals.

One of the visits by the pastor with the family should include a discussion about the details of the funeral in order to reach an understanding and agreement about the nature of the service.

2. *"The pastor shall not accept an honorarium for this service when the deceased was a member of his parish."*

The early Methodist *Disciplines* were quite clear in not permitting Methodist ministers to accept honoraria for funerals and weddings. It was the church's way of saying a minister should not be paid for doing what he is expected to do in the normal course of his ministry. In some sections it is still a widespread custom to give a minister an honorarium for conducting a funeral. Methodist ministers should let it be known that no honorarium is to be given for conducting a funeral. When one is given, it should be returned with gratitude or given to some charity in memory of the deceased. It is regrettable that these rubrics are not included in the *Methodist Hymnal* or some other book where large numbers of members could be informed. Some congregations through their commission on worship have prepared pamphlets on the use of the church for various worship services, and in this way this rubric can be known widely.

The wise pastor will be careful not to take the implication here that honorarium may be received for the funeral of non-members. The pastor's service to the people cannot be confined to the members of a particular congregation. Where unusual expenses are incurred in travel, perhaps expenses may be paid, but certainly not an honorarium.

Some funeral directors include a minister's fee in the itemized statement sent to the family. It should be made quite clear to the funeral director and the family that no such fee is to be collected.

3. *"Funeral services of church members should be held in the sanctuary. The casket should be placed before the altar or the Lord's Table and remain closed."*

Many local customs will run counter to these directions. In large urban centers the sanctuary of the church is less frequently used than a funeral chapel. In some sections the casket is often open, and people come to look at the body of the deceased.

Methodism is saying here that this service of worship takes place quite properly in the church sanctuary, and that the altar is a place to which we go in life's great moments. Here we are baptized into the church and given a name. Here we are nutured by the Word of Life by praise and proclamation and Holy Communion. Here we are married and bring our own children. Here we are brought in death in the final act of faith and offertory. The use of the church building for funerals should be encouraged.

Where the community is accustomed to let the congregation view the body, the casket should be opened *before* the service for a suitable time. During and following the service, the casket should be closed. It is in the service of worship where the congregation gathers before God in the reality of death and the reality of a sustaining faith. The closed casket avoids a preoccupation with the dead body.

The rubric is directed to a funeral for a member of the church. It is important to note that the Methodist Church does not list anyone as being unable to be buried from the sanctuary. The pastor and the Official Board should consult when any question arises in this regard. It has been the general practice for Methodist churches to be open to all.

4. *"In the event of cremation the service may be adapted at the discretion of the minister."*

The general order of the service should remain the same. Before the benediction a suitable statement of committal may be made, and the service would end with the benediction. If it is suitable to have a committal service at the crematorium, this is usually done with the family and a small group of friends. In some cases, a brief committal service is held when the ashes are placed in a particular place.

In some areas the service at the church or funeral home is the final service and there is no committal at the grave. Where this is done, the service ends with a suitable statement of committal and benediction.

5. *"The service may begin and end with appropriate music selected in consultation with the minister."*

The implications of the word appropriate in this rubric are as wide as the variety of musicians and listeners. Each pastor should prepare himself to know some of the music which can be widely accepted for a Christian funeral. The topical index in the Methodist Hymnal (Number 851) lists twenty-three hymns under "Funeral" which suggest suitable music. Lists of instrumental music are available from several publishing houses.

It is important to realize that the instrumental music played at a funeral is a part of a service of Christian worship and is to be taken seriously by the pastor and the musician. Consultation between them with the family should recognize the integrity of each ministry, and from this consultation should come a better service of the worship of God. There is a music of faith and a music of shallow sentimentality; the funeral is a service of faith.

The Service

The Order of Worship should be studied to determine its logic and its "shape" in order to plan a service most fitting for Christian worship in a particular circumstance. In very general terms this order is one of proclamation of the gospel and the congregation's response to it. The response is one of supplication, acceptance, affirmation, and dedication. No sharp lines can be drawn between the various movements of the service, for each aspect is present in each part. The Order of Worship is:

Opening Sentences or Call to Worship
Hymn
Prayers of Invocation
Old Testament Lessons
Gloria Patri
Affirmation of Faith; the Apostles' Creed or other
New Testament Lessons
Hymn or Anthem
The Sermon
Pastoral Prayers
The Benediction

6. *"The minister shall begin the service by reading one or more of the following sentences; or the minister, meeting the body, and going before it, shall say one or more of the following sentences"*:

The second part of the rubric which speaks of the minister meeting the body at the entrance of the church comes from the *Book of Common Prayer* and indicates the early practice of the parishes when the body was brought from the home in procession to the parish church by the people. The funeral service began at the gate as the procession moved toward the church or grave. If the body is brought into the church after the congregation is gathered, the minister should read these sentences as he precedes the body moving toward the chancel. If the casket is placed at the chancel before the service, the sentences should be read from the pulpit or lectern.

The first words of the service are those of triumphant faith. During the Reformation, church leaders returned to the note of triumph of the Early Church sounded in the words from John 11:25-26. There is a solemn joy even in the death of those who "die in the Lord." This is reflected in our service of Holy Communion in the last section of the prayer "for the whole state of

Christ's Church: We remember with thanksgiving those who have loved and served thee in thy church on earth, who now rest from their labors. . . . Keep us in fellowship with all thy saints, and bring us at length to the joy of thy heavenly kingdom." The Orthodox liturgies have emphasized the oneness of the membership of the church on either side of the grave, and these sentences make the same affirmation.

7a. *"Here a hymn may be sung . . ."*

Whenever well-chosen hymns are sung by the congregation at a funeral, a sense of community and worship is established. It is little short of tragic that our church has permitted itself to lose the values of great hymns of faith sung by the congregation at funerals. This may be one major reason why large segments of the members have lost a sense of worship at a funeral and are so uncertain of what the Christian faith procaims about life and death.

The opening hymn should be one in which God is praised and our faith in him declared. "O God, our help in ages past" (Number 28) is a good example of a suitable hymn. The very singing of it by the congregation deepens the common triumphant faith which calls the community to worship by engaging the people in a common act of worship and faith.

7b. *". . . and then the minister shall say, Let us pray."*

8. *"Here the minister may offer one or more of the following prayers":*

This first prayer of the service may be read by the minister, or he may prepare a suitable prayer. The four prayers in this section are suggestive of the emphases which should be included in the service at this time. One emphasis is that of invocation, in which we pray for God's presence to be with the people in this particular time. Another emphasis is included in declarations of faith in God's comfort and care in life and death. In the third prayer there is a note of confession.

In any case, this first prayer is quite specific and brief and prayed by the minister on behalf of the people. The Amen is written in bold face and should be said by the people to indicate their participation.

9. *"Here one or more of the following psalms may be read by the minister, or by the minister and people responsively or in unison. If the people participate, they shall stand for the psalm and remain standing for the* GLORIA PATRI."

This rubric is more involved than most because of the variety of ways in which the psalms are used in worship: They are incomparable devotional literature, scripture lessons, and hymns. In the funeral service the psalms are used primarily as Old Testament lessons and therefore should normally be read by the minister. If, however, they are read responsively, as more generally done in regular Methodist worship services, the congregation would stand for the reading. The same procedure would be followed if the psalms were sung. *The Methodist Hymnal* includes each of the suggested psalms in *The Psalter.*

10. *"Then the people shall say or sing,"*

If the congregation participates in the reading of the psalms, the *Gloria Patri* would normally follow. If the psalms are used as Old Testament lessons, the saying or singing of the *Gloria Patri* by the congregation is a proper response to the reading. The wording of the rubrics is not clear as to whether the congregation is encouraged to stand for the *Glory be to the Father* if the psalms are read only by the minister, though there is some question about the value of standing to sing the response only. Perhaps the congregation could participate adequately by saying the response with the minister while remaining seated. The value of the congregational participation in this traditional doxology is great enough to make it general practice, whether standing or seated. If an order of worship is in the hands of the people, they could easily be directed to participate. Where no printed order is provided, the minister need only say an appropriate word to direct the people to participate.

11. *"Here the congregation may confess their faith according to the Apostles' Creed or another affirmation of faith."*

As Methodists are trained more fully in ways to make the funeral a service of Christian worship, they will want to find means of participating in the service. A historic creed is an affirmation by the people gathered which is much more than something for them to do, it is another act of faith by the church. The *Book of Common Prayer* places the Creed in a permissive rubric following the New Testament lessons, but its position is not so important as its use. The use of a creed at a funeral has an important place, just as it does in the regular services. It is much more than a statement of central beliefs; it is a standard of identification raised in the midst of the people. It is a reminder of a faith in which life and death are faced, and a fresh commitment to this faith in a time of sadness.

12. *"Here one or more of the following lessons from the Scriptures shall be read":*

The rubrics of this order of service use the word *may* in the majority of cases. The word *shall* is used unconditionally only four times; this is one of them. Methodist ministers have great freedom in planning an order of worship for a funeral, but they should take the suggestions of the church with great seriousness. This rubric states clearly that the message we proclaim is the message of the New Testament faith. There is a wide variety in interpretations of the Bible, but the foundation of our Christian faith in the New Testament record is not in question. One or more of these six passages *shall* be read. Of course, there are many other passages which may also be read which are fitting for a particular service. Such scripture readings we hold in common with all the services of Christendom. Bible commentaries should be consulted for the meanings of each lesson.

13. *"Here may be sung a hymn or anthem."*

The selection of a proper hymn or anthem will depend to a great extent on the musical tastes of the congregation. In whatever situation, a hymn or anthem which declares the Christian faith in God should be used. Music and words which emphasize sorrow without faith or place faith in man and not God are less than Christian.

14a. *"Then may follow a sermon. . . ."*

The nature of the sermon as a part of a funeral has been a topic of much discussion. *The Book of Common Prayer* from which Methodism drew most of its services does not mention the sermon. Preaching at funerals in some traditions has led to excesses in the use of time, extravagant eulogies to the departed, appeals to emotional outbursts, and narrow evangelistic messages to the assembled crowd. One need not, however, choose between these extremes. The Church of South India includes this rubric following the New Testament lessons: "A short address may be given here." (*The Book of Common Worship* [London: Oxford University Press, 1963], p. 152.) *The Book of Common Worship: Provisional Services and Lectionary for the Christian Year* (Philadelphia: The Westminster Press, 1966), p. 83, is more definite in its direction: "The minister may preach a brief Sermon bearing testimony to the hope and promises set forth in Scripture. . . ." The important thing to note here is that both these new books say the sermon or address should be brief. Studies which inform us about the nature of grief and the care of those who mourn should give a mandate about the length of the service and each of its parts. Each of the fixed parts is short, but the minister is the only one in control of the length of the sermon. Brevity is an important part of witness at a funeral.

The nature of a sermon is not judged by its length. The major demand of a sermon at a funeral is that it be a proclamation of the gospel in one particular setting. The setting is the church gathered at the death of one of its members. The pastor and people are not called to pass God's judgment on him, even if they could. It is a denial of our faith if we feel called upon to list the greatness of the one departed as if we were giving God some basis for mercy. This is equally true for those whose lives have been outstanding in our eyes or for those whose lives have been far from exemplary. The Word which we are called to proclaim is the good news about the greatness of God and the gift of his grace within any given set of circumstances. Perhaps a proper message to the one who prepares the sermon for a funeral would be Romans 14. This speaks a word on our judgment of one another. It also comes to a great declaration of faith: "If we live, we live to the Lord, and if we die, we die to the Lord; so then, whether we live or whether we die, we are the Lord's. For to this end Christ died and lived again, that he might be Lord both of the dead and of the living" (Rom. 14:8-9 RSV). This is the faith we are called to preach no matter what the scripture passage chosen as a text. The life of the one whose death has called the congregation together may have characteristics which proclaim important truths. These may be quite fitting in the sermon. A funeral sermon is not a lecture on a person's life or on theology; but, informed by both, it is a declaration of our faith in the Lord of life and death. A minute is probably too short a time, ten minutes is very close to being too long.

Methodism has been aware of the importance of preaching throughout its history. The valid and vital witness to the Word of God in every worship service is a call to preach when the church worships at a funeral.

14b. ". . . after which the minister may pray as he is moved, or may offer one or more of the following prayers":

The minister will do well to use one or more of these prayers or study each of them for help in the attitudes and language of his own prayer. This is a pastoral prayer which is quite specific in a particular situation. It is fitting that there be praise to God, gratitude to him for the gift of the life of the deceased, petitions of comfort for those who mourn, and dedication of life. For the sake of clarity and time the pastor should prepare this prayer as carefully as he does his sermon. This is a climactic moment when the people are gathered in a community of faith and sorrow to demonstrate their deepest feelings to God.

15. "For a child one or both of the following prayers may be used."

This order of worship is concerned with a particular type of person only at this point. These prayers may be used or may be suggestive to the pastor who prepares the pastoral prayer of a funeral for a child. Each death will face the minister with a particular demand that calls for his very best expression of the people's prayers.

16. "Then the minister shall give this blessing":

As early as the second century the Eucharist was celebrated by the church at the death of a member.[3] It is fitting that the final blessing at the funeral in the church be the benediction most commonly associated by Methodists with the Holy Communion.

The minister will pronounce the blessing and then lead the recessional from the church directly in front of the casket. This practice may vary widely when the service is in a funeral chapel and the casket is not moved until the congregation has withdrawn. However, this benediction so closely associated with the Lord's Supper is highly desirable as a fitting close for this part of the service. This is especially true where many members of the congregation do not go to the grave for the committal.

In some situations the burial comes first with a small group of family and close friends and a memorial service is held in the church at a convenient time. This order of worship may be followed or Holy Communion may be a fitting celebration of the fullness of the gospel and the sustaining fellowship of the church.

Rubrics for the Service at the Grave

17. "At the grave, when the people are assembled, the minister shall say one or more of the following sentences":

Formerly, when the service at the grave was more often near the church

---

[3] Tertullian, De Co., 3. See Liturgy and Worship, ed. by W. K. Lowther Clarke, p. 616.

service in time and space, the committal was a part of the single service. Today the service at the grave is often for a much smaller number of people, because the church is usually a distance from the cemetery. The opening sentences are words of assurance from Scripture which are declarations of trust as the people enter this final rite. The minister usually stands at the head of the grave, and the people are gathered about the grave and the family.

18a, b, c. *"Then the minister may say,"*

This and the following rubrics are concerned with words of committal. It is generally the custom to have the casket placed in the grave but not lowered very far if at all, and flowers are placed about the casket before the family and friends arrive at the site. The words, therefore, are seldom used as the casket is lowered into the ground. There are some who maintain that we do not face the reality of death when we use the machine age to ease the toil of burial, and cover the earth and casket with flowers. The reality of death is stark enough to those who suffer the loss of a loved one, and the agonies of separation are quite real even with the protection the lowering devices and flowers provide.

The minister may wish to insert the name of the deceased in place of "the departed" and thus make this statement more specific. Each of the three statements draws on symbols which point to the difficulty of our day to deal adequately with the Christian message at the time of death. The first statement has a sharp dualism which draws heavily upon our Greek background. The second and third have less of this element. The third is based on the statement made in *The Book of Common Prayer* which directs that this be read "while the earth shall be cast upon the Body by some standing by" (p. 333). Placing earth on the body is an ancient custom which is mentioned as early as Horace's *Odes*, though the Christian practice is quite in keeping with the words "earth to earth, ashes to ashes, dust to dust." This is an act of recognition of the greatness of God's creation of us from dust.

As discussed in the historical treatment, this section of the service has been changed many times. Further efforts will need to be made to give this important part of the service a word and act which expresses the acceptance of the reality of death and the commitment in faith to the Lord of life and death. In this case the Committal is more than the disposition of a body to its grave, it is an act of faith in God's everlasting care.

19. *"Then may be said":*

This is a further word of faith taken from Rev. 14:13 slightly changed from the King James translation. The *Kyrie eleison* or *Lord, have mercy* which follows is a part of a call to prayer in the *Book of Common Prayer*. It is the only use of this ancient prayer in a Methodist service. It has been retained throughout our history, but it is doubtful that many Methodists know the response since it is in no other service.

20. *"Here the minister and people may pray, saying,"*

It is fitting that those gathered about the grave join in the Lord's Prayer.

101

It is an act of common worship which is probably *the* act of common worship in which all gathered can participate without the need of a book or other guide. This is the community at prayer in praise, petition, and faith. At both funerals and weddings people are often uncertain about whether the congregation is to say the Lord's Prayer. In such circumstances the minister may ask the people to join in the prayer in order to avoid uncertainty.

21. *"Then the minister may offer one or more of the following prayers"*: The first two are prayers of offertory and commitment. The third is a prayer of intercession for the family of the deceased. Both these attitudes are proper, and perhaps if the order of the prayers were reversed it would be more in keeping with the traditional form of Christian worship.

22. *"Then the minister may give one of these blessings"*: Either benediction is quite in order. The moments following the benediction are often awkward. Though the benediction is a word of dismissal, the people will look to the pastor for the movement away from the grave. The minister may move to the family and after a brief interval assist them to the automobiles. As in so many aspects of the ceremonial, local customs will direct what is done.

VII

The Ordinal

Albert C. Outler

To bear Christ's name is to share in his ministry to the world. The sacrament of Baptism (and its completion in Confirmation) has been the universal mode of initiation into the "chosen race, royal priesthood, holy nation" (I Peter 2:9) that God calls out of the world (*ekklesia*) in order to send them forth back into the world to be witnesses to his reconciling love in word and work. It is, therefore, an "ordaining" sacrament, by which God's *laos* (laity) are set apart for their ministry in the world—it identifies them as members of Christ's Body, it authorizes their priestly acts of reconciliation in secular society, it defines their obligations and opportunities as commissioned witnesses to God's grace and glory (cf. Acts 1:8). The gospel of God's love incarnated in Jesus Christ is itself incarnated when his love shines forth in the daily lives of God's people:

> Ministry in the Christian church is derived from the ministry of Christ, the ministry of the Father through the Incarnate Son by the Holy Spirit. It is a ministry bestowed upon and required of the entire Church. All Christians are called to ministry, and theirs is a ministry of the people of God within the community of faith and in the world. Members of The United Methodist Church receive this gift of ministry in company with all Christians and sincerely hope to continue and extend it in the world for which Christ lived, died, and lives again. The United Methodist Church believes that Baptism, confirmation, and responsible membership in the Church are visible signs of acceptance of this ministry.[1]

And yet from the beginning, there has been a *cleros* in the church as well: a select company of those who have been called forth by God and authorized

---

[1] *The Discipline of The United Methodist Church, 1968,* ¶ 301.

by the church for those ministries of the church that represent the people of God in a very special way—the ministries of Word, Sacrament, and Order (proclamation and teaching, the regular administrations of "the means of grace," and the direction of the congregation in concord, witness, and service). The distinguishing mark of such ministries is their representative character; they act in the name and on behalf of the whole church. "Ordination is the gift of God, given in answer to the prayers of the church, by which some [duly qualified and authorized persons] are authorized and empowered to be ministers of the Word, Sacrament, and Order." [2]

There is, therefore, an immemorial and valid distinction between the general priesthood (laos) and the representative ministries (cleros) of the church, which has been all too easily misconstrued. The cleros is not superior to the laos, nor yet inferior: their respective offices are both indispensable and mutually interdependent. The laity is the church in the world: they are called and commissioned to body forth the church and make it visible in the secular city, to reveal and commend the Christian life in the daily round of work and play. The clergy are not excluded from this task—they are members of God's laos, too—but they have distinctive clerical functions to perform. These relate chiefly, to those specific acts and processes by which the church is kept in being, as church, those occasions of grace which nourish and guide Christians in their own growth in grace and their own missions in the world. These acts and occasions are by their very nature corporate, liturgical, ecclesial, and for their true signification they require administrants who are truly representative of the entire community of Christ, who act in his name for all his people and who are authorized in such actions by the whole church. The layman's authority is personal: it depends upon the validity of his Christian experience and witness; this, Methodists have held, is fundamental and prerequisite. But by itself it is not enough. The preaching of the Word (as a settled occupation, contrasted with occasional charismatic utterances), the ministrations of the sacraments and the maintenance of effective order within and among the churches—all these offices require an authority that is corporate, conveyed by ecclesial ordination as well as bolstered by the minister's personal gifts and graces. There is, of course, no magic in ordination and none intended. What is intended is a public identification of men and women who are thereby certified as having both the qualities and training for representative action, always to the end that the laos may be the more fruitfully furnished, nurtured, and guided in their mission. When the Word is rightly preached in the Christian congregation it is not, in the first instance, the expression of the preacher's personal opinions (although effective preaching is always deeply personal). It is, rather, the proclamation of a message and a style of life that have been shared by Christ's people through the centuries and around the

[2] Report of the Committee to Study the Ministry to the Uniting Conference, United Methodist Church (1968), p. 4. Cf. Discipline, 1968, ¶ 309.

world. When the sacraments are "duly administered," it is not merely a local group transaction—audio-visual aids to pious reflection. They are, rather, acts of intentional communication, through the Spirit, with the whole church, militant and triumphant. Ministerial authority does not proceed primarily from the charisms of the minister but from his ecclesial authorization (i.e. ordination), whereby he has been identified and endorsed by the church as agent and surrogate. It is, therefore, from the whole church that an ordained minister receives and exercises his authority. It is the whole church that rightly judges his ministerial character and competence. Such a man is "pastor in charge" in the congregation to which he has been appointed by the church, and not the employee of the congregation; he is, however, bound to represent the whole church and the whole gospel in the midst of the congregation and therefore subject to everyone. He must struggle with himself and others to keep clear the distinction between his person and his office, aware that the bishop's "Take thou authority . . . ,"—the hinge of his ordination service— applies then and now to his ministerial *office* and its exercise and not to his person, however charming.

So much, perhaps, is clear and generally consented. But the *history* of the ministerial office with the correlative functions of *laos* and *cleros* through the centuries is a perilous endeavor, partly because the surviving data are not decisive, partly because of the passionate feelings aroused by the tensions of the ecclesial situation, where ministers in the separated churches withhold mutual recognition of valid orders. The evidence for anything resembling a definite pattern of an integrated polity in the New Testament church is sparse and inconclusive. The radical differences between the first-century churches in their historical and sociological milieu and those of succeeding centuries have generated endless confusion ever since whenever rival theologians appeal to *"the* New Testament pattern." The visible distortions of the church in later ages deprive us of any reliable appeal to the *status quo.* What is reasonably clear is that Jesus called, trained, and commissioned "apostles" and "disciples" (at least for that interim period until the Parousia that was expected momentarily). After the great crisis of the second century, there was a double effort to maintain continuity with the apostolic traditions and yet also to preserve the identity of the Christian life in the face of radical cultural change, harsh persecution, and self-confident heresy! It was, therefore, natural that the tasks of Christian teaching, proclamation, and liturgy would be shared by the "elders" (*presbuteroi*) of a congregation and their presiding officers (*episcopoi*). At first the *episcopos* was a presiding elder in a local congregation or city; gradually he became the chief pastor and teacher of a larger region (diocese), chiefly responsible for maintaining the Christian tradition and insuring the supply of qualified *presbyters* (by ordination). Very early (Acts 6:1-6), the policy of mutual assistance between the Christians gave rise to a new ministry of service (*diakonia*), to which men were ordained by prayer and imposition of hands. The deacon was a sort of social case worker, with close links to the other vital functions of the church (*kerygma, leitourgia, didaskalia*). His main job was the church's ministry to the needs, but he also assisted in the instruction of the catechumens and in the conduct of divine worship. Thus, by the end of the second century (e.g., *The Apostolic Tradition* of Hippolytus), there is a comparatively stable pattern for the ordained ministry and definite procedures for their selection, ordination, and appointment.

In every major schism in Christian history the problem of valid ministry has always been somewhere close to the heart of the tragedy. By the same token, in the current ecumenical dialogue, the task of mingling and reconciling separated ministries is far and away the thorniest of all our problems. It is, therefore, important for us to notice, even if cursorily, some of the crucial developments in the doctrines of order and ordination in the Latin West before the Reformation, to identify, even if vaguely, the most obvious differences between Lutherans, Calvinists, Anabaptists, and Anglicans on these points, and to sketch in some needful background material as an aid in understanding and interpreting the ordinal in the current *Book of Worship* of The United Methodist Church.

Three crucial developments in medieval Catholicism lay behind the crisis of the Reformation as far as the issue of ministerial order was concerned. The first was the escalation of ordination to the status of a sacrament and the consequent rise of sacerdotalism and clericalism. This opened a wide gap between *laos* and *cleros*, it reinforced the clerical power of the keys, and it allowed for the conception of the laity as satellite members of the church, solely dependent upon the clergy for the means of grace. A second distortion of patristic polity came with the proliferation of the so-called minor orders ("porters," "lectors," "exorcists," and "acolytes"), thus creating a sort of clerical civil service which depressed still further the ecclesial status of the "mere layman" and added to his burdens in support of the clerical institution. A third factor in aggravation of this laity-clergy split was rooted in the fearfully complex involvement of clerical personnel in the feudal system, where popes and cardinals, bishops and abbots, canons and prebends played double and triple roles as pastors and priests, feudal lords and landlords, and even imperial electors. The life and spirit of medieval Catholicism was far more authentic and vital than Protestants have generally realized or allowed themselves to acknowledge. Nevertheless, despite all formal and official teaching in support of the authentic priesthood of all believers, the Latin church of the late Middle Ages was fatally clericalized and secularized at one and the same time.

Luther's attack on the sacrament of penance was obviously an attack upon the power of the clerical office, and this was what really pinched the nerve of the Roman view of the sacerdotal church as the matrix of salvation. The issues that divided the Protestants and the papists were legion, and most of them were zealously pushed past moderation on both sides. Thus it was that when communion at the Lord's Table was disrupted, ecclesial communication at every other level broke down, and only now are we finding ways to recognize and restore true Christian community. But the crucial issue that has divided us and still does is that of the ministerial status of schismatics—in the eyes of Rome, Constantinople, Canterbury, or wherever.-

The Continental Reformers sought, above all else, to make a radical new beginning in their emphases on the priesthood of all believers, on the right and duty of private judgment instructed by Scripture, on the primacy of faith and, consequently, on the subordination of all ministerial offices (preaching, sacramental ministration, and church government) as only aids to faith, to be judged by fruits rather than form.

The Lutherans laid their chief stress on the heart of the Gospel—justification by faith alone—and then generally sat loose to the issues of polity. Their inclination has been to allow any order and organization in the church that serves to further the preaching and hearing of faith and, conversely, to reject any order that threatened to constrict the freedom of the gospel. Thus Lutherans have employed various modes and patterns of ministry, episcopal, synodical, consistorial, with characteristic tendencies toward regionalism on the one hand and pan-Lutheran denominationalism on the other.

Calvinists (and their "Reformed" cousins) read the New Testament differently and find their own presbyterial patterns of church government as an explicit mandate. For them, therefore, faith and ministerial order have been coordinate concerns, and the remarkable consistency of this conception of the presbyterate has been a prime factor in the vigor and effectiveness of their worldwide outreach past national, regional, and ethnic barriers. In the presbyterian polity, there is a twofold form of the presbyterate. There are the "ruling elders," in charge of the temporal affairs and government of the congregation, and yet also sharing in the sacramental life of the church, and then there are the "teaching elders," responsible for the right preaching of the Word and the due administration of the sacraments. The teaching elder in Calvinist eyes is in all respects the equivalent of an apostolic bishop, an elder who "oversees" the entire life of the congregation and yet also depends on the services and functions of other elders in that congregation.

The Protestant "radicals" began with a deep aversion to the traditional forms of centralized and connectional ministerial order. For them, the local congregation was the microcosm of the whole church and, as such, was autonomous and self-ordering. Only the extreme "spiritualists" ever fully trusted the principle of a charismatic ministry, and even they had finally to develop some kind of authorized and representative ministry. But they held to their conviction that it is always the local congregation ("the gathered church") that is to be represented by a ministry of its own ordering, not the people of God entire. Thus, they fashioned a variety of ministerial offices and functions, consonant with their principles of pluralism. For all their diversity, however, the traditional titles of deacon and elder are used with some regularity. The office and title of bishop occasionally appear, but never in any sacerdotal sense.

As far as conscious intentions went, the Anglican Reformation was more of a break with Rome than with the Catholic tradition. The Anglicans never ceased to stress the link between valid sacraments and validly ordained ministers thereof, and this meant ministers in untainted continuity with the Christian past in direct apostolic succession. After the long struggle of the Tudors for royal supremacy over the church (Henry VIII, Edward VI, and Mary Tudor), Elizabeth I was greatly concerned for an episcopal ministry that stood in avowedly regular and valid apostolic succession. Thus, the controversy over the validity of Anglican orders, in the eyes of the Romans and Orthodox, has turned on the propriety and authenticity of the consecration of the men through whom the Elizabethan clergy received their orders: William Barlow of Chichester (d. 1568), chief consecrator of Matthew Parker (1504-75), and William Laud (1573-1645). This question still continues to be agitated despite the Roman verdict (*Apostolicae Solicitudines*, 1896) that Anglican orders "are absolutely null and utterly void." Anglican orders are currently acknowledged by some of the Orthodox churches, but not to the point of formal intercommunion. The Anglicans, Old Catholics, and the Polish National Catholics are, however, in full communion with one another.

All modern Anglican ordinals are based upon "The Form and Manner of Making and Consecrating Archbishops, Bishops, Priests and Deacons and Other Ministries of the Church" which were authorized by the English Parliament in March, 1550, and designed to replace the various Latin "Pontificals" which had hitherto been in use in the dioceses of England. A slightly revised version of that new ordinal was produced in 1552 and included in the revised ("Second Edwardian") Prayer Book. In Queen Mary's brief reign (1553-58), the Latin rites were restored, but not all of those ordained in the time of Edward VI were reordained. In 1559, the Edwardian ordinal was restored by Elizabeth I and printed as a separate volume. A century later, after the Stuart Restoration, yet another revision of the ordinal was prepared in connection with the new *Book of Common Prayer* (1662). All these ordinals excluded the so-called minor orders and all included an oath of "Royal Supremacy" (perhaps the most consistent motif in the history of the Church of England). It was by this "Form" of 1662 that John Wesley was himself ordained: first deacon (September 19, 1725) and then priest (September 22, 1728).

When Wesley began to organize religious societies and to direct them (in Bristol, London, and then throughout "the three kingdoms"), there was no question of a separate ecclesial ministry. Both in his field preaching and in his pastoral care of his converts, Wesley was acting under the authority of his own ordination as a Fellow of Lincoln College, Oxford, with its *ius praedicandi ubique*,[3] and in consequence of his own self-understanding as an

[3] Cf. "A Library of Protestant Thought," *John Wesley*, Albert C. Outler, ed. (New York: Oxford University Press, 1964), p. 21, n. 72.

"extraordinary minister" of the Church of England called by the Holy Spirit to supplement the ministrations of the *ministerium ordinarium* (i.e., the regular parish clergy). This was the background of his famous aphorism in response to James Hervey's complaints of his irregularities: "I look upon *all the world as my parish.*" [4] There were, of course, other ordained clergy involved in these revival efforts: George Whitefield, Howel Harris, *et al.,*[5] but the question of ministerial order never arose until some of Wesley's "lay helpers" (first John Cennick in Bristol and then Thomas Maxfield in London) began to edge over the line between "expounding" in the societies and "preaching" (1741). Wesley's instinctive impulse was to suppress such an irregular business, but in Maxfield's case he was dissuaded by a prompt warning from his mother (who had heard Maxfield preach) : "John, . . . take care what you do with respect to that young man, for he is as surely called of God to preach, as you are." [6] By 1744, there were enough local societies with such assistants in charge of them that Wesley called them together in a "conference" to consider such questions as "What to *teach*," "*How* to teach," "What to *do;* i.e. how to regulate our doctrine, discipline and practice." [7] Six of those attending this first Conference were ordained priests of the Church of England, and four were lay-preachers.[8] But all of them were Mr. Wesley's personal assistants, answerable to him alone, just as he understood himself as finally answerable to the hierarchy of the Church of England. Here his principle was that any useful form or practice not expressly forbidden was implicitly allowed. Thus, he stoutly defended lay-preaching[9] and his use of lay preachers as subordinate colleagues and personal assistants.[10] Here, he was consistently firm in denying them all ministerial rights, beyond preaching and catechetical instruction. This rigid distinction between what he called the "prophetic" ministry (proclamation and teaching) and the "priestly" ministry (administration of the sacrament and pastoral rule) [11] became a bone of contention at every annual Conference from 1755 onward, provoking a perennial clamor for "separation" from the Church of England and for the establishment of a Dissenting denomination. Wesley stood steadfast against

---

[4] Letter to James Hervey, March 20, 1739, *The Letters of John Wesley,* John Telford, ed. (London: The Epworth Press, 1931) , I, 284-87.

[5] Cf. "Doctrinal Minutes," LPT, *Wesley,* p. 136.

[6] Henry Moore, *The Life of the Rev. John Wesley, A.M.* (New York: Bangs and Emory for the Methodist Episcopal Church, 1826) , I, 293.

[7] LPT, *Wesley,* p. 136; see also *Journal* (Curnock) , III, 143-44, n. 2.

[8] LPT, *Wesley, ibid.*

[9] Cf. his debate with "John Smith" in *Letters,* II, 93-94.

[10] Cf. his letter to Robert Marsden (August 31, 1756) : "These preachers are not *ministers:* none of them undertakes *single* the care of an whole flock, but ten, twenty, or thirty, one following and helping another; and all, under the direction of my brother and me, undertake jointly what (as I judge) no man in England is equal to alone." *Ibid.,* III, 184. See also the letter to Samuel Walker (September 3, 1756) , *ibid.,* III, 192.

[11] Cf. the Korah sermon, "The Ministerial Office," dated Cork, May 4, 1789, *Works,* VII, 273.

this, and in his Deed of Declaration (1784) he tried to insure the continuity of "the Conference of the people called Methodists" as a religious society within the Church of England.

Even so, Wesley's own views of the meaning of ministerial order had been strongly influenced by those of Edward Stillingfleet and Peter King, "latitudinarians" who had argued that, in the primitive church, the office of bishop (*episcopos*) was a functionally superior role within the presbyterate and that the conventional doctrine of apostolic succession through the bishops alone was "a fable." From this he had concluded that, as a validly ordained elder of the Church of England, he was the overseer (*episcopos*) of the Methodist Societies and of his "assistants" who were responsible to him as he was responsible for them to the Church of England. He steadfastly refused to turn "Dissenter" or to let his people go in dissent. For the same reasons, he scrupulously refrained from any bid for power within the Anglican establishment. He forbade his lay preachers to baptize or to administer communion (and dismissed those who defied him). He deliberately designed his preaching services to be liturgically incomplete and urged the Methodists to "go to church" (even when they were denounced), and he scheduled the Methodist preaching services so as not to conflict with "church hours." In every point that affected the essence of ordination, Wesley followed both the theory and practice of the *Book of Common Prayer* (1662) and its ordinal.

With the Methodists in America, however, the case was different. Societies had been formed here, in New York and Maryland, as early as 1766, and Wesley had assumed their supervision in August, 1769,[12] with the appointment of Richard Boardman and Joseph Pilmoor. By the time of the Revolution, there were at least 1,160 Methodists in the colonies[13] and eight personal representatives of Mr. Wesley.[14] But the Revolution ruined this arrangement. Mr. Wesley was an ardent, lifelong royalist, and he felt duty-bound to denounce the American rebels. His preachers readily fell under suspicion as having Tory sympathies, and one by one they fled the scenes of conflict, all save Francis Asbury, who waited out the war in semiseclusion.

[12] The Twenty-sixth Conference at Leeds. *Journal* (Curnock), V, 330-31.

[13] Emory S. Bucke (ed.), *The History of American Methodism* (Nashville: Abingdon Press, 1964), I, 129.

[14] "From 1769 to 1774, twelve British Methodist preachers came to America, either by Wesley's appointment or with his consent but without appointment. . . . The first men sent by Wesley were Joseph Pilmoor and Richard Boardman, who landed in the fall of 1769. About the same time two others arrived, having come without Conference support or appointment: Robert Williams, who may have preceded Boardman and Pilmoor by several weeks, and John King, who followed them sometime before the summer of 1770. In 1771 Francis Asbury and Richard Wright answered Wesley's call to service in America. They were followed in 1773 by Thomas Rankin and George Shadford, who responded to Captain Webb's appeal before the English Conference of 1772, and with whom came an unappointed volunteer, Joseph Yearbry. Finally in 1774 Wesley sent James Dempster and Martin Rodda; they were accompanied by William Glendenning, who like Williams, King, and Yearbry, came on his own responsibility." *Ibid.*, I, 81.

After the Revolution, the religious situation in America was chaotic. Ties with the Church of England had been severed. The few remaining Anglican clergy had no powers to confirm or ordain, and they were as naturally indisposed to receive the Methodist remnant at their altars as the Methodists were to go. And yet, the need for Christian evangelism and nurture had never been greater. There was a new nation to be served, new societies to be linked together, a new frontier opening to zealous Christian endeavor. The American Anglicans and also Mr. Wesley applied to the English hierarchy for orders and authorization. While the American Anglicans were waiting for their eventual approval, Wesley felt compelled to take an initiative to restore his "connection" with the American Methodists. With some practical reservations but no doctrinal misgivings, he convoked a minimum-size "presbytery" [Creighton, Coke and Wesley] in Bristol on September 1, 1784, and ordained two lay preachers (Richard Whatcoat and Thomas Vasey) as "elders for America," and on the day following he "set apart" Dr. Thomas Coke as superintendent for America,[15] with instructions to confer the same office on Francis Asbury as his fellow "superintendent" of the American Methodists. For these "ordinations" he used the *Book of Common Prayer* ordinal.

Two centuries of Anglican criticism and Methodist self-justification have not really settled the question of what was done, or intended, by these ordinations of 1784.[16] At the very least, they were not simply licenses to preach. Whatcoat and Vasey, and the American preachers as well, already had as much license for that as Wesley's other lay assistants. They must therefore have been licensed (1) to administer the sacraments and (2) to ordain and govern those who would in their turn administer the sacraments and serve as "preachers in charge" of the Methodist circuits in America. Already in 1779, the Fluvanna "schism" had defined the issue: the Methodists would have the sacraments with or without Mr. Wesley's authorization.[17] Asbury had suppressed their first bid for self-administered ordinations, but had reported to Wesley that this was only a delaying action. Thus, Wesley proposed to provide the Americans with a sacramental ministry (obviously believing that he had the right and obligation to do so under such wholly exceptional circumstances) through Dr. Coke (*legatus a latere!*) to reestablish his "connection" with the Americans. For these purposes Wesley made a hasty revision of the *Book of Common Prayer* (*The Sunday Service*) which he sent along with Dr. Coke. Its ordinal faithfully followed that of 1662 with minor changes.[18]

If Mr. Wesley's intentions were at all ambiguous, Francis Asbury's were not. He was clear and firm in his conviction that the new nation needed a new

[15] Cf. *Journal* (Curnock), VII, 16.
[16] Cf. Gerald F. Moede, *The Office of the Bishop in Methodism* (Nashville: Abingdon Press, 1964), pp. 34-44.
[17] Cf. Bucke, *The History of American Methodism*, I, 176-80.
[18] See below, p. 113.

church, *self-constituted* and unbeholden to any "foreign succession." It could, and should, be Wesleyan in doctrine and discipline but autonomous in polity and policy. Americans were free to borrow and adapt liturgical texts but bound to use and interpret them in the American context, with its radical separation of church and state and Asbury's "itinerant plan" for exploiting the new frontier. Consequently, Mr. Asbury rejected Coke's authority as legate and declined Mr. Wesley's direct appointment. Instead, he turned to the American preachers (at the Christmas Conference, 1784) and sought their mandate and charter for "The Methodist Episcopal Church," with himself and Dr. Coke its first "superintendents." Mr. Wesley's *spiritual* authority was ungrudgingly affirmed, and his *Notes and Sermons* (together with the Twenty-five Articles of Religion) were stipulated as "standards of doctrine." A crucial distinction was made between the conditions for membership in the Annual Conference on the one hand, and ordination for the ministries of the sacraments and church order on the other. This distinction has remained in force ever since. The former were patterned after Mr. Wesley's practice as recorded in "The Large Minutes" of the Wesleyan Connexion in Britain. The rituals for ordination, however, were taken over verbatim from *The Sunday Service,* with no changes until 1792. This was a quite self-conscious departure in ecclesial order. In his "Notes" appended as commentary to the *Discipline* of 1796, Mr. Asbury makes a special point in defense of the propriety and efficacy of the new polity of the Methodist Episcopal Church.

The only point [in our polity] which can be disputed by any sensible person is the *episcopal* form which we have adopted; and this can be contested by candid men only from their want of acquaintance with the history of the church. The most bigoted devotees to religious establishments (the clergy of the Church of Rome excepted) are now ashamed to support the doctrine of *the apostolic, uninterrupted succession of bishops. . . .*[19] It follows, therefore, indubitably, that every church has a right to *choose,* if it please, the episcopal plan.[20] . . . Mr. Wesley preferred the episcopal form of church government; and God has wonderfully blessed it among us.[21] . . . Nothing has been introduced into Methodism by the present episcopal form of *government* which was not before fully exercised by Mr. Wesley[22]—[save that in America, the bishops] are *entirely dependent* on the General Conference.[23] . . . Our grand plan, in all its parts, leads to an *itinerant* ministry. . . . Every thing is kept moving as far as possible; and we will be bold to say, that, next to the grace of God, there is nothing like this [itinerancy] for keeping the whole body alive from the centre to the circumference and for the continual extension of the circumference on every hand.[24]

[19] Omitted here is Asbury's extended defense of this view of the matter.
[20] David Sherman, *History of the Revisions of the Discipline of the Methodist Episcopal Church* (New York: Nelson and Phillips, 1874) , p. 342.
[21] *Ibid.,* p. 343.
[22] *Ibid.,* p. 347.
[23] *Ibid.,* p. 348.
[24] *Ibid.,* p. 349.

That the polity of the Methodist Episcopal Church was self-constituted with an eye chiefly to effective church government and with no notion of succession, is further confirmed by the action of the General Conference of 1784:

Q. 29. What if there is no Superintendent?
A.   The General Conference shall elect one; and the elders, or any three of them appointed by the General Conference for that purpose, shall ordain him according to our Liturgy [i.e., the ordinal in *The Sunday Service.*].[25]

It was with this basic understanding of ministerial order and ordination that American Methodism adopted Wesley's revision of the Elizabethan ordinal. And when *The Sunday Service* was quickly and quietly jettisoned, the ordinal remained and has continued ever since as, comparatively speaking, the least unaltered block of liturgical material in any of our rituals from the *Book of Common Prayer* of 1662. In this respect, the Methodist ordinals are derivatives from the Anglican ordinal, and this forms one of our most crucial linkages with the Catholic past. The interpretations of the ministerial office, however, have always taken their distinctive flavor from our peculiar polity ("itinerancy," "connectionalism," and the appointive power of the bishops in the stationing of the preachers).

In Mr. Wesley's ordinal (in *The Sunday Service*) there are only three changes of any substantive importance. The first was his choice of the term "superintendent" in place of "bishop," obviously to suggest the administrative aspect of the office rather than anything approaching sacerdotal authority. Second, he simply dropped all references to canon law and to the church as a civil establishment (oaths of allegiance to king, archbishops, etc.). Third, he disengaged the office of deacon from its restricted locus in a single parish and made it a part of the itinerant ministry. He shortened the title "Of the Ordaining and Consecrating Bishops" by dropping "and consecrating," but this carried no implication that he regarded the episcopacy as a "third order." In his consistent usage, "ordain" meant "authorize," no more, no less. Other alterations—and they are very few—are merely rhetorical.[26]

In 1792, this first ordinal of the new church underwent its first revision. The changes were minimal; the only major one was the substitution of "bishop" for "superintendent." This was Asbury's doing, and he had been berated for it by Mr. Wesley.[27] Nothing is clearer, however, than that Mr. Asbury's preference for "bishop" was based on his theory of centralized church government. He made no claims for his sacerdotal authority, ever.

From 1792 to 1844, the ordinal of the Methodist Episcopal Church continued unchanged, even in the turmoil of the Methodist Protestant schism in

---

[25] *Ibid.*, p. 165.
[26] Cf. Nolan B. Harmon, *The Rites and Ritual of Episcopal Methodism* (Nashville: Publishing House of the Methodist Episcopal Church, South, 1926), pp. 378-98.
[27] Cf. *Letters*, VIII, 91. See below, p. 129, n. 1.

1828. Here the issue turned on "lay representation" in church government. This was stoutly resisted by the Methodist Episcopal leaders, not because of any doctrine of clerical superiority but because, in their view, lay representation posed a mortal threat to "the itinerant plan," a point which Asbury stressed from the beginning:

We have a great respect for trustees [i.e., who might be lay delegates to a Conference]. We consider them as men to whom the connection is greatly obliged. They fill up an important province in our church and have a claim to a high rank among us. Humanly speaking, the work could not be carried on without them to any extent in the cities and towns. . . . But still they are *located* men. They cannot be expected to act impartially for the whole. They will think it their duty, and perhaps it is their duty, to prefer the interest of their own congregation to any other.[28]

The schism of 1844 left the ordinal intact in the *Disciplines* of both the Methodist Episcopal Church and the Methodist Episcopal Church, South, a noteworthy fact since the key constitutional issue in that rupture had been the status of the episcopal office in relation to the General Conference. After the break, the ordinal of the Methodist Episcopal Church, South, continued for nearly a century (till 1939) with no substantive revision.[29] The Methodist Episcopal ordinal, however, underwent a series of revisions, most of them with the evident intention of pruning its Elizabethan rhetoric and of purging the residues of suspected sacerdotalism. In the revision of 1864, there were several alterations that amounted to doctrinal changes as well. In the order for deacons, his authority to baptize was made unconditional, and the Communion service was omitted. In the elders' ordinal, the charge to the ordinands was abridged and redrafted, and the formulas for "the imposition of hands" were changed to emphasize the thought that the elder's authority comes directly from the church herself, *through* the symbolic acts of the ordainers. In the ordinal for bishops, "ordaining" is changed to "consecrating," the opening collect is revised so as to rank "elders" and "evangelists" alongside "apostles," the Exhortation to Prayer has an added phrase ("on their [Paul and Barnabas] first mission to the Gentiles"), the examination itself is abridged, the original phrase "perfect and irreprehensible" becomes "blameless," and the formula for the imposition of hands is altered from: "And remember that thou stir up the grace of God *which is given thee by this imposition of our hands*" (an obvious echo of II Tim. 1:6) to "And remember that thou stir up the grace of God *which is in thee.*" In 1916, the "final prayers" gained a new phrase (and accent!) : "and exercising authority in Thy church. . . ."[30]

In 1884 a new first rubric was added to the bishop's ordinal, presumably to dispel any notion that the episcopate amounted to a "third order":

[28] Cf. Sherman, *History* . . . , p. 348.
[29] Cf. Harmon, *The Rites* . . . .
[30] This maintained itself until 1932, when a new prayer was substituted for a quadrennium [see below pp. 122-23] and did not reappear in 1939.

This service is not to be understood as an ordination to a higher order in the Christian ministry, beyond and above that of elders or presbyters, but as a solemn and fitting Consecration for the special and most sacred duties of Superintendency in the Church.

An even more extensive revision was proposed and adopted in 1916. In this, the "challenge for impediment" in the "Form of Ordaining Deacons" was changed to suggest a closer parity between deacons' and elders' orders. The word "office" [of deacon] was expanded to the phrase "this holy ministry," and a new preface was added to the elders' ritual, both suggesting that the diaconate shares the fullness of ministerial order. "Objected" became "alleged"; "surcease" became "desist." Throughout the entire ritual, "Holy Ghost" was changed to "Holy Spirit." In the post-Communion collects, the traditional text was abridged, with "inferior" dropped from the phrase "inferior office." The "Form of Ordaining Elders" was shortened with two verses dropped from the Epistle text and three from the Gospel. Both the charge to the ordinands and their examination were abridged and revised so as to reflect the newly ascendant liberal theology of the period. The bishop's prayer was cut by more than half and the final collects pared down. In the *Book of Common Prayer* the bishop-elect was presented to his consecrator as "this godly and well-learned man." Wesley shortened this to "this godly man." The revision of 1805 [31] altered it to "this holy man." The 1916 revisers settled for a neutral phrase, "this elder chosen." In the Exhortation to Prayer, "move" becomes "call upon," and the double reference to the sole authority of Holy Scriptures in the bishop's examination was decisively weakened. A mitigating nuance is added to the question about the new bishop's faithfulness in office: ". . . and will you ever seek to deal justly and kindly with your brethren of the ministry over whom you are placed as chief pastor?" The traditional first Communion with the newly consecrated bishop was omitted and the "final prayers" still further abridged.

One might think that revisions past those of 1916 might more readily produce new texts rather than further abridgments and reabridgments. And yet the 1932 revisers continue to rely more heavily on their blue pencils than to risk original formulations of their own. In the ordinal for deacons, "mercifully" turns into "graciously"; the Epistle is changed from I Timothy 3 to Ephesians 5; "trust" becomes "believe"; the ordinand is asked to "accept" the Scriptures of the Old and New Testaments [with the adjective "canonical" omitted—to signify that the Apocrypha was a dead issue?]; "Holy Scriptures" become "Scriptures"; the ordinand is asked to "heed" rather than "obey" "them to whom the charge over you is committed," and the definition of the

[31] *The Doctrines and Discipline of the Methodist Episcopal Church.* The Thirteenth Edition (New York: Ezekiel Cooper and John Wilson for The Methodist Connection, 1805) , p. 193. Robert Emory, *History of the Discipline of the Methodist Episcopal Church* (New York: Carlton and Porter, 1843) , p. 245, Sherman, *History* . . . , p. 323, and Harmon, *The Rites* . . . , pp. 385, 403, all say 1808, but the *Discipline* of 1805 is quite clear on the point.

duties and rights of the deacon's office is considerably enlarged. In the closing collects the Elizabethan phrase, "Prevent us, O Lord" is mistranslated, "Direct us, O Lord." "Prevent" is simply the transliteration of the ancient Latin *praevenire* and means to "go before," which is to say, we pray God that he will graciously anticipate our ordeals and ventures. "Direct us," on the other hand, is rather more a petition for executive control. Alterations in the elders' ordinal were minor: the selection for the Epistle is changed; the charge to the ordinands is revised yet once more; "humbly kneeling" is reduced to "kneeling." There is one original touch: the closing collect is new; it appears in the *Discipline* of 1936 with no indicated "source," and then, in 1939, quickly disappears.

Holy Spirit of God, may thy celestial fire that came upon the Apostles in Pentecostal power, so baptize these elders into a true apostolic ministry that they may kindle in many hearts conviction of sin, desire for new life, and longing for perfect love. Grant this, we pray thee, in the name of the Risen Christ, our Lord and Saviour. Amen.

The bishop's ordinal for 1932 was shortened, but its sense was left essentially unaltered. "Divers offices in the church" became "offices" and the revised "examination of the bishop-elect" of 1924 was rephrased yet once again, as also the prayer of the consecrator. The order of the questions was shifted, perhaps in the interest of a more climactic buildup. In the original text there had been an intriguing pastoral admonition to the newly consecrated bishop: "Be to the flock of Christ a shepherd, not a wolf; feed them, devour them not." This was shortened—and flattened—to: "Be to the flock of Christ a shepherd."

Once again, for the last collect, the revisers of 1932 produced a new prayer in place of the original collect of 1662 ("Most merciful Father, we beseech thee to send down upon this thy servant thy heavenly blessing, etc.") :

Send, O Lord, on these thy servants, bishops of the Church, the Holy Spirit, the spirit of wisdom and understanding, the spirit of counsel and might, the spirit of knowledge and the fear of the Lord, that through their sacred service the devotion of all our ministers and members may increase and that the salvation of the flock may be the joy and crown of all thy shepherds, through Jesus Christ our Lord. Amen.

This essay in pneumatological immanence was also short-lived. It disappeared in 1939.

When the Methodist Episcopal Church, the Methodist Episcopal Church, South, and the Methodist Protestant Church merged in 1939, the rule was followed that the most recently revised ritual should be preferred above the others. Thus, in the ordinal of the new Methodist Church (1940), the text of 1932 is followed in almost every instance, despite the fact (or perhaps because of it) that the ritual of the Methodist Episcopal Church, South, had remained closer to the Wesleyan prototype for a long time. Only two changes are worth noticing, but one of these amounts to an unobtrusive mutation in ecclesiology.

116

The first is simply a swap: both the "final collects" of 1932, mentioned above, were dropped and the old ones reinstated. In the "Examination" of the elders, one of the questions has its meaning altered. From 1662 to 1932, it had read invariably as follows:

Will you then give your faithful diligence always so to minister the doctrines and sacraments and discipline of Christ, as the Lord hath commanded?

In the 1940 version, this became:

Will you give your faithful diligence duly to minister the doctrine of Christ, the sacraments and the discipline of the Church . . . ?

In this way, both sacraments and Christian discipline are assimilated to the church, in a context where "church" has already been defined largely in "functional," human, historical terms. There is no public record of this revision being discussed in the General Conference. Presumably, it was received and adopted as a vote of confidence in the revisers.

The editors of our present ordinal (1964-) seem to have intended to pick and choose from almost every one of the previous revisions, with very few original touches of their own. On the question of whether there "may" or "shall" be a sermon or exhortation, they go back to the mandatory "shall be" of The Sunday Service. But they decline to follow the sermon with the traditional service of Holy Communion. In the opening collect, they restore the reference to "Divine Providence" (1662; changed to "Holy Spirit" in 1940) and replace "advancement of thy church" (1932, 1940) with the old word "edification." But in the choice of the Epistle, they stay with 1932 and 1940. They go back to "trust" (1662) for "believe" (1932) and "believe" (1662) for "accept" (1932), but they leave the weakened "heed" (1932) in place of "obey" (1662). All the deacon's ordinals from the beginning had specified that "it appertaineth to the office of a deacon to assist the Elder in divine service, etc." The 1964 ordinal changes this to read: "It appertains to the office of a deacon to conduct divine worship . . . ," thus "settling" a vexed question by a liturgical formulation. In the formula for the imposition of hands, however, 1964 goes back to The Sunday Service: "Take thou authority to execute the office of a deacon, etc."

The Communion Collect in the elders' ordinal gets a slight addition, evidently in the interest of Christian monotheism. Since 1662, the trinitarian climax of the prayer had read: ". . . through the merits of our Saviour Jesus Christ, who liveth and reigneth with thee and the Holy Ghost [Spirit after 1916], world without end." 1964 inserts "one God" after "Holy Spirit." In the charge to the candidates for elders' orders, 1964 reverts generally to the text in The Sunday Service, but then in the conclusion, we find a rare example where 1964 actually shortens the 1932 abridgment: from "We have good hope

. . . [where 1932 follows *The Sunday Service*] to "We hope . . . ." And it follows the revision of 1940 that distinguished "the doctrine of Christ" from "the sacraments and discipline of the Church." The bishops' ordinal has no noteworthy change, unless "ministration" (1662) in place of "administration" (1932) be noteworthy, or the added adjective, "officiating," in the rubric for the imposition of hands.

It is worth remarking, however, that the ordinal of 1964 was presented and adopted by The Methodist Church at a time when negotiations for union with the EUB Church were very far advanced, and there is no evidence that the EUB ordinal was ever seriously considered as a "source" for a revised ordinal for the new church. Thus, the ordination ritual of The United Methodist Church continues to follow the line set by *The Sunday Service,* and its successive abridgments, rather than reflect the complexity of the rather different liturgical traditions of Otterbein and Albright. Perhaps the *next* revision will take this heritage, with its vital rootage in Reformed pietism, into serious account.

One might also mention that the 1964 ordinal was being prepared and was adopted at the very same time that the *Constitution on the Sacred Liturgy* of Vatican II was being debated and promulgated. This *Constitution* did not deal specifically with the Roman ordinals, but it did give explicit encouragement to vernacular translations of liturgical texts and the updating of the rhetoric of corporate prayer. By now it is a commonplace in Roman Catholic churches, and increasingly in ecumenical gatherings, to hear the once-familiar "thees" and "thys," "hasts" and "didsts," in liturgical address to God, changed to "you" and "your," "have" and "did." Thus, even when they declined to restore the liturgical richness of Wesley's *Sunday Service,* the 1964 revisers committed the new church to a thoroughly conservative principle of liturgical language. This, too, is a matter for reconsideration when yet another revision becomes feasible, and as the harvest of the liturgical renewal and innovation in all the churches becomes increasingly available for experiment and use.

The Methodist Ordinal

1) *The Order for the Ordination of Deacons*[32]

The simplest, literal translation of the term "deacon" is "servant" and the origin of the office, as described in Acts 6:2-8 stresses the distinction in the minds of the Jerusalem Christians between those chores of mutual service necessary in a community of outcasts in a hostile environment and those apostolic tasks of proclamation and teaching appropriate in a community of "the end-time." It is interesting, though, that we have no record of Stephen's social casework, but we do have a reported *sermon* of his—actually the longest single speech recorded in Acts. In any case, the deacon's office was rather

---

[32] In *The Sunday Service* (and *Book of Common Prayer*): "The Form and Manner of Making Deacons."

118

quickly sub-joined to the presbyterate, especially in the West, until finally it came to be little other than the probationary status for men on their way to the priesthood. In the East, however, the office of "permanent deacon" was retained and something of the sort has been restored in the Roman Catholic Church by Vatican II.[33] A new definition of the deacon's office, as something more distinctive in itself, not a way station to "the higher ministry of the Church," is being sought by many churches and ecumenical groups (e.g., WCC and COCU). As it stands here, however, the term "deacon" signifies merely the initial stage of the representative ministry of The United Methodist Church.

2) *"When the day appointed by the bishop is come . . . ."*
Before this service, the ordinands have already passed through a demanding process of licensing and examination (first Charge and District Conferences, the district superintendent and bishop, and the Annual Conference Board of the Ministry). Here are the prescribed qualifications for deacon[34]:

A deacon is a minister who has been received by an Annual Conference either as a probationary member or as an associate member and has been ordained deacon. A deacon has authority to conduct divine worship, to preach the Word, to perform the marriage ceremony where the laws of the state or province permit, and to bury the dead. When invited to do so by an elder, he may assist in the administration of the Sacraments. When serving as a regularly appointed pastor of a charge, he shall be granted authority to administer the Sacraments on the charge to which he is appointed.
Persons of the following classes are eligible for the order of deacon:
1. Lay pastors who have been received into associate membership after having met the requirements of ¶ 323.
2. Theological students who have been received into probationary membership after having met the requirements of ¶ 327 or ¶ 328.1.

3) *The Sermon*
In the Latin pontificals a sermon was optional and was expected to be addressed chiefly to the ordinands. The Reformers had a dual purpose in making such a sermon mandatory: to signify the close correlation between Word and Order and to explain the distinction between the general priesthood and the representative ministry. This was continued in Methodist ordinals generally, save for the interim 1916-1939 in the Methodist Episcopal Church. Since 1940 it has been restored and is a useful occasion for stressing the positive importance of the ordained ministry in the minds and hearts of the people.

4) *Presentation and Charge*
The challenge for impediment reflects a time when bishops had to deal with ordinands presented to them with little or no previous acquaintance; the prior assessment of their qualifications was largely the business of the archdeacon.

[33] Cf. *Lumen Gentium*, ¶ 29.
[34] *The Discipline of The United Methodist Church, 1968*, ¶¶ 311, 312.

The *Book of Common Prayer* (1662) prescribes for a monitory address by the bishop to the archdeacon:

Take heed that the persons whom ye present us be apt and meet, for their learning and godly conversation, to exercise their ministry duly, to the honour of God and the edifying of his Church.

The archdeacon's stipulated answer was: "I have enquired of them, and also examined them; and think them so to be."

The examination then went on to involve the congregation—a ward against the scandals of unworthy ordinations: "If there be any of you who knoweth any impediment or notable crime . . . ."

"Impediment" would include all legal disabilities, "crime" all moral barriers. Wesley reduced the phrase "notable crime" to "crime" (1784), but it was only in 1932 that the whole phrase was reduced to its present "valid reason." The change is significant: it reflects the fact that a Methodist bishop is acting as agent of the Annual Conference and Church, and may ordain only those who are duly presented to him as approved and elected to deacon's order, according to the conditions stipulated by *The Discipline.*

In the *Book of Common Prayer* (1662) and *The Sunday Service,* it was directed that the Litany should proceed only after the clearance of the ordinand's character. This was then to be followed by Communion, so as to set the event of ordination within its appropriate eucharistic framework. The Litany was omitted by the Americans in 1792; the Communion was dropped by the Methodist Episcopal Church, South, in 1858, by the Methodist Episcopal Church in 1864. The revisers of 1964 did not see fit to restore either.

5) *Collect*

The first Collect ("Almighty God, who by thy divine providence . . .") derives from the Sarum Pontifical and appears in the 1550 ordinal as an appendage to the Litany. In 1662 it was made the proper Collect for Communion. It summarizes two main points: the divine origin of the orders of ministry in the church and the apostolic institution of the order of *deacon* as one of those essential ministries. This was an indirect answer to those who argued for *one order* (the presbyterate) as sufficient for all the offices of the representative ministry.

6) *The Epistle*

In the *Book of Common Prayer* (1662), two alternate selections were given: I Tim. 3:8-13 (which describes the deacon's character) and Acts 6:2-7 (which relates the appointment of "the Seven" by the apostles as a division of ministerial labor in the Jerusalem church). Wesley dropped the passage from Acts; the revisers of 1932 substituted a cento of verses from Ephesians 5 and 6 in place of I Tim. 3:8-13, presumably to provide a broader ecclesiological context for the diaconal ministry. 1964 restored three snippets from I Timothy 3 and added to them the 1932 selections from Ephesians.

7) Examination by the Bishop

The first question here comes quickly to grips with the most crucial of all the motives involved in "the call to the ministry": the ordinand's self-understanding of his vocation, moved thereunto by the inner stirrings of the Holy Spirit. It is this "inner call," professed by the man himself, that must precede and be matched by the "outer call," i.e., the church's judgment that he is fully qualified for the tasks and expectations of his ministry. Together, these constitute the twin sign of a genuine ministerial vocation. Either without the other is insufficient and invalid.

In the *Book of Common Prayer* (1662) and *The Sunday Service,* there was a second and specific question regarding this "outer call." It was dropped in 1792, as being already covered by the previous question. What are now the second and third questions call for a profession of "unfeigned" belief in the Holy Scriptures and a promise to read and expound them to the people. This emphasis Martin Bucer supplied the to 1550 ordinal, and it takes the place of more explicit tests of doctrinal orthodoxy (e.g., the Articles of Religion). The fourth question carries with it an implied definition of the office of deacon, and this has evolved in The United Methodist Church from a mere assistant-to-the-elder to something more comprehensive: "to conduct divine worship . . . and to baptize." Note the parallel description of the rights and duties of a "probationary member of the Annual Conference" (i.e., a deacon) [35]:

A probationary member is on trial in preparation for a membership in full connection with his Annual Conference. He is on probation as to his character, preaching, and effectiveness as a pastor. The Annual Conference has jurisdiction over a probationary member. Annually the Board of the Ministry shall review and evaluate his relationship and make recommendation to the Annual Conference regarding his continuance. His continuance as a probationary member shall be equivalent to the renewal of his license to preach. A probationary member may request discontinuance of this relationship or may be discontinued by the Annual Conference, upon recommendation of the Board of the Ministry, without reflection upon his character.

Questions 5 and 6 concern the ordinand's personal life (and that of his family) and his willingness to conform to lawful church government. It is arguable whether a man's commitment "reverently to *heed*" his ecclesiastical superiors amounts to a flat promise to *obey* them, and it has never been altogether clear as to how "their *godly* admonitions" are to be distinguished from their less awesome opinions.

8) The Imposition of Hands

The formula here has remained unchanged from 1662, save for the switch from "Holy Ghost" to "Holy Spirit." This suggests that manual imposition

---

[35] *The Discipline of The United Methodist Church, 1968,* ¶ 325.

has been understood by Methodists as the essential outward act in the ordination ritual. It symbolizes the conferring of the authority to represent the whole church *ex officio,* by a man who is hereby designated as qualified to do so. The investment of such an authority adds no increment of grace or virtue nor is it intended to. But it does convey delegated authority *and* responsibility. It is then followed by a similar symbolic act: the delivery of a Bible to each ordinand with an authorizing formula, "to read the Holy Scriptures in the Church of God and to preach the Word." This is all that now remains of the medieval *porrectio (traditio) instrumentorum*—"the traditioning of the instruments" (i.e., supplying him with the necessary "tools" of his profession). Once ordination became a sacrament, the question as to what constituted its "matter" became a topic for earnest debate. Many theologians, including Thomas Aquinas, concluded that the "instruments" (i.e., the Bible for the deacon, the paten and chalice for the priest) were the essential "matter" of the sacrament. Hence, their "traditioning" (handing over) was the crucial sacramental sign of ordination. The English Reformers denied this and put their stress equally upon the conveyance of general authority and the traditioning of the Holy Bible. This became an issue in the conflict between Anglicans and Roman Catholics; it was a prominent item in the condemnation of Anglican orders by Rome in 1896.

9) *The Gospel*

In a service climaxed by Holy Communion, the Gospel naturally falls between the ordination and consecration of the elements. In a non-eucharistic service it would more properly come *before* the ordination. The selection here (Luke 12:35-38) is one of the very few items in the whole ritual that has stood unchanged (save for successive translations) since 1662.

10) *Final Collects*

The first of these is based upon its equivalent in the Sarum Pontifical and was the original "ordination prayer." If we believed that it is the Holy Spirit who actually ordains, this would be the prayer that marked the decisive point of the church's action: her invocation of the Spirit and her petition that her ministers act validly on her behalf. This was probably the primitive understanding of ordination, as we can see from the oldest ordinal for deacons that we know: the *Apostolic Tradition* of Hippolytus, *Deus, qui omnia creasti et verbo praeordinasti:*[36]

O God, who hast created all things and hast ordered them by thy Word; O Father of our Lord Jesus Christ, whom thou didst send to minister thy will and reveal unto us thy purpose; bestow the Holy Spirit of grace and zeal and diligence upon this thy servant, whom thou hast chosen to minister to thy Church and to bring forth the

[36] Cf. H. B. Porter, *The Ordination Prayers of the Ancient Western Churches* (London: S.P.C.K., 1967), pp. 10-11. See also Gregory Dix, *The Treatise on the Apostolic Tradition of St. Hippolytus of Rome* (London, S.P.C.K., 1937), pp. 17-18.

holy things which are offered to thee by thine ordained high-priests to the glory of thy Name: that, having ministered to them blamelessly and purely, he may by thy goodwill be found worthy of this exalted office, praising thee; through thy servant (son) Jesus Christ our Lord . . . . Amen.

The second collect is a general petition, seeking God's prevenient grace for the sustaining and upholding of all his faithful children, assembled here and elsewhere. Its Latin prototype was the Collect for Saturday in the fourth week of Lent in the Gregorian Sacramentary and in the Sarum Missal. It was translated by Cranmer and placed here by the revisers of 1662. In the *Book of Common Prayer* of the Protestant Episcopal Church (1790), it was dropped from the ordinal and relocated among the collects "to be used after the collects of Morning or Evening Prayer, or Communion, at the discretion of the Minister." [37]

The benediction here is the remnant of the primitive Blessing of the People and, probably, the Giving of the Peace. Thomas Cranmer rephrased it and placed it at the close of the Communion in the form of 1548, and it has since remained the most usual of all the communion benedictions. Here it serves to remind us once again of the original integration of the rite of ordination within a service of Holy Communion.

1) *The Order for the Ordination of Elders*

The title for this service in the *Book of Common Prayer* (1662) is "The Form and Manner of Ordering Priests." Wesley changed "Priests" to "Elders," "Bishop" to "Superintendent," and left the rest of the service relatively untouched. In the New Testament the term "priest" (in the singular) is applied only to Jesus Christ (e.g., Hebrews 9–10); as a plural or common noun, it signifies the entire *koinonia* of Christ (e.g., I Peter 2:5, 9). The word *presbyteros* (literally "old man": "elder") is the normal reference in the New Testament and patristic documents for indicating the mature or experienced men, with evident spiritual gifts and wisdom, who have appeared as congregational leaders and rulers. By the time of Clement of Rome and Ignatius of Antioch, the chief elder in a given locality is called *episcopos*, the symbol and agent of the unity of the churches and their catholicity. In the second-century chuch, the term "priest" applies only to the bishops.[38] It was not until the Middle Ages that the terms "presbyter" and "priest" became interchangeable. This is why Wesley, along with his mentor Richard Hooker, believed that "priest" was an inappropriate title for the pastor and teacher in a congregation[39] and that, save for the functions of overall church government (superintendency!) "elder" was the equivalent of "bishop." It has long been an open question among Anglicans as to whether there are two or three orders

---

[37] See above.

[38] Cf. Hippolytus, *The Apostolic Tradition*, in Porter, *The Ordination Prayers* . . . , p. 7.

[39] Richard Hooker, *Of the Laws of Ecclesiastical Polity*, Book V, lxxviii, 2-3.

of the ministry. Wesley and the Methodists settled for two. Hence, ordination as an elder represents the highest level of *ministerial* authority and responsibility. It is conferred by the bishop, together with other elders, but only after examination by the Annual Conference Board of the Ministry and election by the Conference members.

2) *Sermon*

"When the day appointed by the bishop is come . . . ." What matters most is that, before this day, two concurrent though separate processes of examination have been completed. First, the ordinand has been adjudged to have met the qualifications for "full connection" in the Conference and has given it positive answers to the following deeply probing, personal questions, first propounded by John Wesley to those prepared to serve him as his assistants[40]:

1. Have you faith in Christ?
2. Are you going on to perfection?
3. Do you expect to be made perfect in love in this life?
4. Are you earnestly striving after it?
5. Are you resolved to devote yourself wholly to God and his work?
6. Do you know the General Rules of our Church?
7. Will you keep them?
8. Have you studied the doctrines of The United Methodist Church?
9. After full examination do you believe that our doctrines are in harmony with the Holy Scriptures?
10. Will you preach and maintain them?
11. Have you studied our form of church discipline and polity?
12. Do you approve our church government and policy?
13. Will you support and maintain them?
14. Will you diligently instruct the children in every place?
15. Will you visit from house to house?
16. Will you recommend fasting or abstinence, both by precept and example?
17. Are you determined to employ all your time in the work of God?
18. Are you in debt so as to embarass you in your work?
19. Will you observe the following directions?
    a) Be diligent. Never be unemployed. Never be triflingly employed. Never trifle away time; neither spend any more time at any one place than is strictly necessary.
    b) Be punctual. Do everything exactly at the time. And do not mend our rules, but keep them; not for wrath, but for conscience' sake.

A satisfactory response to this interrogatory becomes the basis for his admission into the Annual Conference, in "full connection," *before ordination.*

Concurrently, he has been elected to the order of elder, on the basis of the following qualifications[41]:

---

[40] *The Discipline of The United Methodist Church, 1968,* ¶ 334.
[41] *Ibid.,* ¶ 333.

(1) served full-time under episcopal appointment under the supervision of a district superintendent satisfactorily to the Board of the Ministry in one of the positions specified in ¶ 391.1-.6 for one year following the completion of the educational requirements specified in #3 below;

(2) been previously ordained deacon; *provided* that until July 1, 1971, §§ 1 and 2 above shall not apply to seminary students who have completed one fourth of the work required for the Bachelor of Divinity or the equivalent first professional degree by July 1, 1968;

(3) met educational requirements . . . in either of the following ways: (a) graduation with a Bachelor of Divinity or equivalent degree from a school of theology accredited or approved by the University Senate or (b) graduation with a Bachelor of Arts or equivalent degree from a college or university approved by the University Senate and completion of two years of advanced study beyond the requirements for probationary membership (¶ 328.2d) under the supervision of the Department of the Ministry;

(4) satisfied the board regarding his physical, mental, and emotional health;

(5) prepared at least one written sermon on a specified biblical passage and given satisfactory answers in a written doctrinal examination administered by the Board of the Ministry.

His presentation to the bishop by an elder is, therefore, symbolic of all these prior approvals.

The direction for a mandatory "sermon or exhortation" ["the sermon *of* exhortation" is an obvious misprint] represents a return by he 1964 revisers to the original rubric of *The Sunday Service.*

3) *Challenge for Impediment*

This is practically identical with the challenge in the deacon's ordinal. Indeed, that formula was first designed for *this* ordination and not for deacons. It was supposed to be followed by the Litany and Communion. Both of these were dropped in 1792, probably in reaction to the new text of the American Episcopal *Book of Common Prayer* (1790) which had continued the older tradition of integrating ordination with communion.

4) *Collect*

This collect is similar to that in the deacon's ordinal, save for the obvious differences in the specific references, and the citation of "the Holy Spirit" here instead of "divine providence," as above (p. 120). The revisers of 1964 have restored "mercifully" in place of "graciously" (1932) but continue "the *advancement* of thy Church" in the place of the traditional term "edification." The overall effect is to narrow, by nuance, the gap between elders' and deacons' orders and at least to countenance the question as to whether or not the two orders might be merged.

5) *The Epistle*

In the ordinal of 1550, there was a choice of readings: Acts 20:17-35 or I Tim. 3:1-16. In 1662 these were dropped in favor of Eph. 4:7-13, partly because the Dissenters had interpreted the 1550 selections as supporting the theory of elders and bishops as constituting a single order. Wesley followed 1662 and so did all subsequent revisions until 1932 (Methodist Episcopal Church), when Eph. 3:7-9 was added, 4:7-13 shortened to 11-13, and 3:14-21 added. The present revision has followed 1932, minus 3:14-21.

6) *The Gospel*

Here again, the first ordinal (1550) specified Matt. 27:18-20, but 1662 moved this over to the bishop's ordinal and substituted Matthew 9:36-38, plus John 10:1-16. Wesley omitted the Matthew passage, and the revisers of 1916 abridged the Johannine passage by dropping out vss. 3-6. Our text is further reduced to 9-16.

7) *The Episcopal Charge*

Originally, this was a splendid short homily, modeled on Bucer's *De Ordinatione Legitima* (1549), in exposition of the Gospel metaphor of the Good Shepherd (cf. John 10). Wesley, who had a hearty taste for good preaching, took it over intact and was followed in this (with minor retouchings, like "evil world" for "naughty world" [1816]) until 1870 when the Methodist Episcopal Church, South, first abridged it. Another relatively mild abridgment followed in 1916 and then a more drastic one in 1932. Our current version follows the 1932 abridgment, with one original touch: the "We have good hope" is flattened to "We hope." In the sparse remainder, three basic points are made: (1) the importance of the pastoral office; (2) the consequently grievous fault of dereliction; (3) the never-ending need for continued prayer, study, discipline, and aspiration in the responsible exercise of the office.

8) *The Examination of the Ordinand*

This begins with the prime question about the ordinand's "inner call"; in the *Book of Common Prayer* (1662) this was linked to a twin query about the "outer call" as well. The original text was: "Do you think in your heart . . . ?" This was changed (1932) to "Do you believe . . . ?"

The second question concerns the persuasion of the candidate as to the authority of the Holy Scriptures. In the original, the accent upon *sola Scriptura* was loud and clear. Our revision, following the pruners of 1932, has weakened this emphasis.

The present text of the third question affects the substance of ecclesiology and not merely the matter of liturgical rhetoric. The original put "the doctrine *and* sacraments *and* discipline of Christ," thus implying that theology, liturgy, and ethics are *all* equally rooted in the revelation of God in Christ. This was taken for granted by all subsequent revisers (even those of 1932! except for their substitution of "truth" for "doctrine"). The Ritual of 1939 (the first in the new Methodist Church), however, turned the phrase in a way that amounts to a change in meaning. Now, only "doctrine" is "of Christ";

liturgy and ethics are shifted to the jurisdiction of the church. The 1964 revision approved this ecclesiological mutation, with no public discussion recorded. Also, in the original there was a separate third question about the pastor's word against "all erroneous and strange doctrine," and this was linked to the charge to care for the sick as diligently as for "the whole." A pastor's defense against "all doctrine contrary to God's Word" has been combined above in question two, and the reference to the sick dropped altogether.

The fourth question relates to the prayer life and study habits of the ordinand. This, too, was abridged, in 1916, and our version follows that. Question five suggests the crucial exemplary influence of the preacher's family upon his ministry and reflects the assumption (already firm by 1662) of a married clergy as the rule rather than the exception. Question six identifies the pastor as peacemaker in his flock and community. Question seven returns to the matter of church discipline and demands that the elder "reverently *heed*" and gladly follow the "godly admonitions" of his rulers. Before 1932, the answer was contingent: "I will so do, the Lord being my helper." Now it is categorical: "I will so do." What more than overconfidence is implied by this is not clear.

At the conclusion of the examination, the bishop prays a suffrage that is obviously directed to the ordinand, as if it were a blessing. Then follows a rubrical stipulation for silent prayer, the only one of its kind in the *Book of Common Prayer* or *The Sunday Service*. It is repeated again in our bishop's ordinal.

9) *Veni, Creator Spiritus*

This is a translation of a famous medieval Latin hymn, set as a poetic bridge between the examination of the ordinand and the ordination prayer. Its authorship is ascribed, without certain proof, to the great ninth-century theologian Hrabanus Maurus (*ca.* 784-856), Abbot of Fulda and Archbishop of Mainz. It appears in the Sarum Missal as an item in the priest's preparation for celebrating the Mass. Cranmer produced a somewhat hapless verse translation of it which appeared in the first Edwardian Prayer Book, one of the few times his liturgical muse failed him. The Cranmer version was retained in the 1662 *Book of Common Prayer* (perhaps out of reverence), but a happier alternative provided: the metrical translation of John Cosin (1594-1672), royalist bishop of Durham, composed for the coronation of Charles I (1625), and published in Cosin's *Collection of Private Devotions* in 1627. Wesley kept Cosin and dropped Cranmer, and all subsequent Methodist versions have followed suit.

The *Veni* is a hymn to the Holy Spirit, a lacework of pneumatological metaphors (Fount of Life, Fire of Love, Heavenly Unction, Finger of the Hand of God) and a petition for the Spirit's gifts most needed in the pastoral office. Here it serves to define the spirit and temper in which the ordinand

127

is expected to accept his ministerial authorization and to enter upon his sacred calling.

10) Ordination Prayer

This text appears first in the 1550 ordinal, with echoes from Bucer's *De Ordine*. It stresses the ways in which the ministry of Christ is to be shared and extended in and through the ministries of the church; it confesses that the goal of all ministry is the glory of God and the enlargement of *his* Kingdom. The original text was heavily abridged in 1916; the 1964 revisers preferred that abridgment.

11) The Imposition of Hands

Here again we have nearly the same formulas of transmission of authority and the "traditioning of the instruments" as in the deacon's ordinal.[42] It is essential to the service that both bishops and elders join (to form "a presbytery"!) in the imposition of hands and that equal stress be placed on the preaching of the Word *and* the administration of the sacraments as the twin prototypes of the entire round of the minister's tasks: prophetic *and* priestly. In the *Book of Common Prayer* (1662 and thereafter) the prayer begins: "Receive thou the Holy Ghost . . . ," and Wesley kept this in *The Sunday Service*. The revisers of 1792 presumably regarded this as too explicitly sacerdotal (they could have seen it in the new ordinal of the Protestant Episcopal Church, U.S.A., 1790) and altered it to "The Lord pour upon thee the Holy Ghost . . . ." In 1864, the Methodist Episcopal Church qualified the traditional meaning of imposition by explaining that the authority being conveyed comes from and is lodged in the church and not in any of its office-bearers. A reference to the power of the keys (cf. Matt. 16:19), which was standard in all medieval pontificals and retained in the 1662 *Book of Common Prayer,* was omitted by Mr. Wesley, and it never occurred to the American Methodists to restore it.

In the medieval rituals, the "instruments" delivered to the new-made priest included both chalice and paten, and this practice was retained in the first English ordinal of 1550. In the second (1552), however, it was dropped, and only the Bible remains as the sole and sufficient "tool of the trade" for a well-furnished minister. All the rubrics before 1932 specify that the elders shall be "kneeling." Since then, the custom has continued generally but without a specific direction.

In both the English rite and Bucer's the ceremony of imposition was followed by a recitation of the Nicene Creed, as if a priest's proper first act after ordination was to stand up and, with the congregation, confess the faith of the Catholic Church. Next after this came Communion, concelebrated by ordinand, ordaining bishop, and elders. Wesley proposed a service of Communion, but the 1792 revisers shelved it.

12) Closing Collects

The first of these is the bishop's blessing upon the new elder and a petitionary prayer, as by the congregation, for their genuine receptivity to his faithful proclamation of the Gospel. The second collect is the same here as in the deacon's ordinal. The third is the common eucharistic benediction.[43]

13) A Final Rubric

This makes provision for what has long been the common practice: the combining of the ordinations of deacons and elders in a single service. The Epistle is to be read only once, in the service for the deacons; and the Gospel once, in the service for elders. Otherwise, the rubrics and text are to be the same as if there were separate services. In the *Discipline* of 1944 a curious innovation appears: "the order *for* deacons." displaces the traditional (and grammatical) "order *of* deacons." If this was a misprint, it has been faithfully repeated in all the succeeding *Disciplines* from 1948 to 1962, and it now appears in our text of 1964.

1) The Order for the Consecration of Bishops

The Latin title in the Sarum Pontifical for bishops speaks only of their "consecration" (*consecratio*) and specifies that the act is to be performed "upon some Sunday or Holy Day," always together with the Eucharist. In the *Book of Common Prayer* (1662) the title for the ceremony was enlarged: "The Form of Ordaining or Consecrating of an Arch-bishop or Bishop Which Is Always to Be Performed Upon Some Sunday or Holy-Day." Wesley (*The Sunday Service*) shortened this to: "The Form of Ordaining of a Superintendent." This can scarcely mean that he thought of episcopal "ordination" as constituting a third order. Other evidence suggests that he understood the word "ordain" to mean "authorize," and this was all he ever intended for Francis Asbury to understand by it. The revisers of 1792 retained the term "ordaining" but changed "Superintendent" to "Bishop." [44] In 1864 the Methodist Episcopal Church changed "ordaining" to "consecrating" and in 1884 added the deprecatory rubric quoted above, p. 115. Since 1940, this rubric has been omitted.

---

[43] See above, p. 123.

[44] Mr. Wesley had died the year before, much outraged by Mr. Asbury's quick translation of "superintendent" to "bishop." Cf. his letter of 20 September, 1788: "How can you, how dare you suffer yourself to be called Bishop? I shudder, I start at the very thought. . . . For my sake, for God's sake, for Christ's sake, put a full end to this . . . ." Telford, VIII, 91. But the Americans had already decided upon an "episcopal" polity; "bishop" seemed shorter and more straightforward than "superintendent." Besides, it referred only to the power to govern, not to any increment of ministerial status or authority. Thus, on this point, Mr. Wesley was quickly set aside, and as soon as he was dead the ritual form followed the fact.

2) *In Lieu of an Examination*

"When the time appointed . . . ." Unlike the case with bishops and deacons, there is no prior examination of the bishop-elect as to his qualifications and disposition; these are presumed to be established by the fact of his election by the Jurisdictional Conference. Thus the examination by "the officiating bishop" is the only public test provided. Originally, this, too, was set in the context of a service of Holy Communion.

3) *The Collect*

This is an ante-Communion prayer, derived from the somewhat simpler "proper" for St. Peter's Day [29 June]. It echoes John 21:15-17 and calls upon God not only to bless his ministers but to confirm the especial importance of such ministry in the church, thus looking to the climax of the present service when a new Chief Pastor will be set in office among God's people. Note here that "Word" and "godly discipline" are correlated.

4) *The Epistle*

In the *Book of Common Prayer* (1662) the first Epistle was I Timothy 3:1-7. Mr. Wesley dropped it but retained the second reading, from Acts 20:17-35, which earlier (1550) was in the *priest's* ordinal. The Prayer Book rubric directed this to be read by "another bishop"; Wesley changed it to "one of the elders," possibly to recall the practice in second-century Alexandria of episcopal consecration by the presbytery, a tradition by which he set great store. Such a direction has been retained in all Methodist "episcopal" churches. The selection from Acts was abridged in 1916 and again in 1932. 1964 follows 1932, except that our translation is from the RSV in place of the ARV of 1932 and also that the 1964 citation corrects the misprint of 1932 *et seq.*: "Acts 20:17-24, 28-32" instead of 35. This valedictory of Paul serves as an appropriate initiation for a new "apostle."

5) *The Gospel*

Three choices were given in the 1662 *Book of Common Prayer:* John 21:15-17; 20:19-23; Matthew 28:18-20. Wesley reduced these to two, omitting any reference to the powers of absolution and anathema in John 20:19-23. The revisers of 1932 combined the two remaining passages. 1964 divided them once more.

6) *The Presentation*

Originally there followed here the Creed and a sermon. Mr. Wesley dropped the Creed and kept the sermon. Since 1932, even the sermon has been dropped from the rubrical directions, though it remains the usual custom. In the *Book of Common Prayer,* the presentation of the consecrand is made by two bishops; in *The Sunday Service* and thereafter, it is made by two elders. The original formula spoke of a "godly and well-learned man"; Mr. Wesley reduced this to "godly man"; it was escalated in 1805 [45] to "holy man"; in 1916 the

---

[45] See above.

bare fact is cited: "this elder chosen . . . ." In 1864 "ordained" was changed to "consecrated," and this has remained in force ever since.

The call to prayer enlists the congregation in the rite, inviting them to join in the deliberation and invocation of the Holy Spirit's guidance that has traditionally attended the election of bishops since apostolic times. The prayer itself reiterates most of the first collect in the elder's ordinal. One noteworthy point is that the perennial argument about "orders" and "offices" continues to be reflected here. The *Book of Common Prayer* (1662), *The Sunday Service*, and all Rituals until 1864 read "divers orders." 1864 changed this to "offices"; 1920 opted for "officers" [a misprint?], 1932 went back to "offices," which remains in our present version.

7) *The Examination*

The questions here are both like and unlike their equivalents in the service for elders. They cover the same ground, but there are more of them. What is less obvious is that, in addition to having their texts abridged by successive Methodist revisers, the order of the last three has been inverted.

We begin with the crux of the matter: the inner call to the heart that matches the outer call of the church expressed in the election. The second question establishes the Scripture as the decisive norm for all doctrine relevant to the knowledge of our salvation. This leads into a charge (question three) that the bishop-elect immerse himself in Scripture and specifies his allegiance to it as the vital ground of his authority as teacher and ruler in the church. One might remark in passing that this is one of the rare instances where the 1964 revisers abridged the abridgment of 1932 still further.

Question four is a faint echo of the ancient conviction that the bishop's office makes him the chief warden of the People of God, "to banish and drive away from the church all erroneous and strange doctrine contrary to God's Word, etc." Question five is an even paler shadow of the original demand that the bishop set the standard for personal self-discipline: "Will you deny all ungodliness and worldly lusts . . . that the adversary may be ashamed, having nothing to say against you?"

Question six (from 1784 to 1932) concerned the duty of the bishop to maintain and promote "quietness, love and peace. . . ." The present question six was then the last question in the series. The revisers of 1662 apparently wanted to end with an appeal to episcopal clemency; those of 1932 wanted to conclude with a reference to episcopal authority. Note that the reference to the appointive power of the bishop appears in none of the older versions. 1932 added it and all subsequent revisions have retained it. Along with this, however, they added the exhortation that he exercise this power "justly and kindly"—a note that the earlier revisers might have thought gratuitous.

After the examination comes a suffrage addressed to God as if in dialogue with the bishop-elect standing here before God and God's people. Then (since 1916) comes a "space" for silent prayer (as in the elder's ordinal) followed by the *Veni, Creator Spiritus* which is here designed to perform a similar function as in the elder's ordinal, a transition from the interrogation to the ordination prayer. Indeed, it concludes with a call to prayer:

Versicle: Lord, hear our prayer
Response: And let our cry come unto thee

The *Discipline* of 1944 let this versicle drop, without explanation.

8) *The Consecration Prayer*
The original of this is much longer than our present text—apparently a composite from Bucer, Cranmer (probably the preamble) and the Sarum Pontifical. Curiously enough, more of the medieval material has been retained here than the sentences supplied by the sixteenth-century Reformers. It is, thus, a curious link with our longer Catholic past of which most of us are not always conscious.

9) *The Consecration*
The standard Catholic formula, since the earliest Latin pontificals, began with a hortative: *Accipe Spiritum Sanctum.* All versions of the *Book of Common Prayer* follow this form, translating it "Receive the Holy Ghost." The Methodist Episcopal Church, South (1854), and the Methodist Episcopal Church (1864) changed this to the petitionary prayer that we now have. 1864 also interposed the authority of the church in the conveyance: "Now committed unto thee by the authority of the Church, etc." For good measure, they abridged the Scripture quotation from II Tim. 1:6-7, canceling the reference to the imposition of hands. Those who check the AV reading of II Tim. 1:6 will notice the phrase "the *gift* of God"; but all our texts, from 1550 until now, read "*grace* of God." The warrant for this was the Vulgate text that Cranmer had before him: *admoneo te ut resuscites* GRATIAM *Dei quae est in te per impositionem manuum mearum.*

In the medieval rites, the "tradition of the instruments" included the laying of the Bible on the neck of the prostrated bishop and then handing him a pastoral staff. Now only the Bible is "delivered" and is meant to symbolize all else that may be included in the warrant for episcopal authority. The accompanying exhortation has been shortened and softened.

Originally this service was designed to proceed from the act of consecration to the concelebration of Communion, and this was Methodist custom as late as 1858 in the Methodist Episcopal Church, South, and 1916 in the Methodist Episcopal Church: "Then the bishop shall administer the Lord's Supper, with whom the newly-ordained bishop, and other persons present, shall communicate (1792)." The revisers of 1964 declined to restore this ancient collegial practice, although it has been the nearly universal custom in all "episcopally" ordered churches.

10) Closing Prayers

The first one is a clutch of phrases from the Pastoral Epistles: II Tim. 4:2; I Tim. 4:12; II Tim. 4:7. Its prototype is in the Sarum Pontifical for "the Enthronement of a Bishop." Its translation in the 1550 ordinal is especially fine, a fitting climax to the ritual by which a chief pastor in the church is authorized and commissioned for his career of service.

The second collect is our old friend, "Prevent us, O Lord . . . ." [46] And the final Benediction is familiar to us from the Communion Service, even though that has been dispensed with. In some future revision one might hope that the ancient linkage between ordination and Eucharist will be restored, as we come to understand their quintessential connection of ministry and sacraments both in the life of the church and in her ministry in Christ's name.

[46] See above.

VIII

The Lectionary

William F. Dunkle, Jr.

Lectionaries and calendars are twin developments. Both undoubtedly have Jewish origins long prior to Christian usage. The reading of selections from the Law and the Prophets as well as the use of the Psalter almost surely followed some sequence or plan in synagogue meetings in very ancient times, even as in Jewish worship today. Days of fast and feast were Levitical and Deuteronomic institutions, and it seems sure that the biblical materials establishing them would be reviewed at each recurring observance. The Sabbath was the fixed factor in Jewish worship, thus providing the weekly foundation for a calendar-oriented worship. The seasons of Pasch and Pentecost, for example, were Hebrew occasions.

Established liturgical readings among the earliest Christians may be found within the New Testament itself, some scholars believe, as in Col. 4:16 or Rev. 1:3. Such verses refer to *pericopes,* which in Greek meant literally only "short passages." Not until the Protestant Reformation did the word *pericope* come to mean a Scripture lesson prescribed for a certain calendar event. Very early collections of pericopes from the Gospels have been found which predate the fourth century. In the West they were called *evangeliarium* and in the East, *evangelistarion.* Justin Martyr (c. 114-165) and Clement of Alexandria (c. 160-215) cited Isa. 43:5-13 and Jer. 11:19 as pericopes for liturgical use, though they did not assign them to calendar dates. Origen (c. 182-251) also seems to have known such usages. By the time of Augustine (354-430) it was possible for Christian writers to speak of "the order of lections" in general use among the churches. Latin Christians referred to readings from Scripture as *lectiones,* and Greeks called them *anagnoseis.* Rubrical references to "readings from Paul and the Gospels" may be found in early editions of the Syrian Liturgy of St. James, as well as Armenian, Coptic Jacobite, Nestorian, and Ethiopic liturgies.

Meanwhile the fixity of Sunday, the Lord's Day or weekly commemoration of the Resurrection, as a Christian calendar factor extended from New Testament times firmly into succeeding centuries. The influence of Christian observances may be noted in Roman calendars dating as early as the reign of Constantine II in the middle of the fourth century and in a calendar authorized by Emperor Valentinian III in 448, obviously reflecting far earlier and generally observed Christian anniversaries. A fourth-century Gothic fragment found in Thrace is a calendar for October and November listing several festivals and saints' days.

By the middle of the fifth century the parallels of lectionary and calendar development began to coincide. Dioceses in Gaul, Burgundy, and Marseilles left to history lists of suggested pericopes for full yearly calendars. A Nestorian liturgy of the same period in the East mentions lections from II Corinthians, Acts, I Timothy, and Luke as appropriate for the observance of Ascension Day.

But neither lectionaries nor calendars ever achieved exact conformity. They do not conform even today. Eastern calendars usually begin September 1, for example, while Western calendars begin four Sundays before Christmas Day. Dioceses and provinces within liturgical or language groupings have provided varied pericopes or lections for calendar observances. In general, the Latin calendar sequence from Advent through post-Pentecost has obtained in Western communions, though not always with the same seasonal names. The Roman Catholic Church numbers summer and autumn Sundays "after Pentecost" and Anglican churches, "after Trinity," as an example. The Protestant Reformation in sixteenth-century Germany and its later spread into other countries and cultures particularly interrupted the establishment of calendar and lectionary uniformity as many saints' days, occasions associated with Mariology, and certain other observances were arbitrarily dropped from the calendar, hence withdrawing from liturgical use various pericopes of Scripture previously related to these anniversaries.

Two fundamental principles, closely related, have arisen out of the development of lectionaries and calendars across all the centuries, however variously arranged. The purpose of the Christian calendar is to insure that the whole sequence of God's mighty acts revealed in Christ shall be remembered in the churches annually. The use of a lectionary likewise provides that the whole range of biblical revelation is read in public worship within a prescribed period—if not in one year, then in not more than four. Both calendar and lectionary are the guarantors of wholeness.

As such they are returning to wider acceptance in the twentieth century than has been true for a very long time. An important aspect of the liturgical reform and renewal which is current in many communions has been the restoration of lectionaries and calendars, both much revised, to Christian usage.

Some resistance to the use of lectionaries, or even calendars, seems to stem from mistaken suppositions that freedom in worship, especially in preaching, may be jeopardized by prescribed biblical readings or observances. It may be quite sufficient to *read* the Bible in an ordered sequence without preaching on each passage. There is nothing wrong if a preacher adds another, even extended, biblical passage to a service of worship at the time he enters the pulpit, if he does not feel led to use one of the lections for preaching purposes. It is hoped, indeed, that the comparative lectionaries listed in this chapter may help to serve such a purpose. A lectionary has only the purpose of offering guidance in the public *reading* of Scripture and is not necessarily a homiletical program. On the other hand, many preachers have found that a lectionary provides wholesome discipline to their homiletical study and may be very useful indeed in guiding a year's preaching. It should be emphasized, however, that there is no *necessary* relationship between preaching and either lectionaries or calendars.

Although the lectionaries of the different churches are not always the same, there are two major principles common to most. The first is the thematic relationship between lessons and observances. For instance, Luke 2 is obviously associated with Christmas and Acts 2 with Pentecost. Thematic considerations govern the selection of lectionary pericopes for almost a third of the calendar, though different lectionaries may not use the same lessons for each occasion. Another principle provides for "readings in course," when possible, between thematic lessons. For various successions of Sundays or during some whole liturgical season, lectionaries often provide for the reading of biblical books chapter by chapter or section by section. More recent lectionary revisions tend to depart somewhat from this earlier practice.

Some form of lectionary has been available in Methodism from John Wesley's day, though it is clear that both the Christian calendar and any formal lectionary fell into general disuse, especially in America. It is probable that Mr. Wesley assumed that Methodists would continue to observe the Anglican calendar and the Prayer Book table of lessons. This seems to have been the case more in British Methodism than in American. At least the Psalter appears to have remained in general use in American Methodist worship. In the 1935 edition of *The Methodist Hymnal* an Old Testament lectionary was provided, though it is doubtful that its use was widespread. For each Sunday in a year and for some special occasions the Psalter was exchanged for a sequence of responsive readings compiled from the Psalms and both Testaments. In *The Book of Worship for Church and Home* which was published in 1944 lectionary elements included a month of daily readings for devotional purposes, a table of two lessons for all Sundays of the traditional Christian year, and another table of Epistles and Gospels for Holy Communion arranged in a truncated Christian year calendar.

When the Commission on Worship of The Methodist Church began its work on the complete revision of *The Book of Worship* (1964 edition) and *The Methodist Hymnal* (1965 edition), Charles S. Hempstead was appointed to compile tables for the use of the Psalms, canticles, and other acts of corporate worship. William F. Dunkle, Jr., was appointed to develop a complete lectionary of Old Testament, Epistle, and Gospel lessons.

Several guidelines were given. The traditional Christian year was to be followed, except that the three pre-Lenten Sundays (Septuagesima, Sexagesima, and Quinquagesima) were to be absorbed in the season of Epiphany, and the designation *Kingdomtide* was to be retained as first developed by a Committee on Worship of the Federal Council of Churches in 1937, mainly under the leadership of the late Fred Winslow Adams, a New England Methodist pastor.

Moreover, it was agreed that a lectionary for only one year's sequence (or for morning services only) was most likely to be used by Methodists in America in the latter decades of the twentieth century. It was argued that Sunday evening services were not regularly conducted in a majority of American Methodist churches, and that complete lectionaries for either both morning and evening service or a two-year cycle might prove only confusing. The Commission further expressed the hope that lessons would be about ten Scripture verses in length, though this was not a mandatory directive. Various tentative lectionaries were tested in many Methodist churches for most of a year.

All of this greatly restricted the *amount* of biblical material which could be included in the new lectionary. Many "favorite passages" had to be passed over. Nevertheless, all of the major meaning and message of the Bible found its place in the lectionary, and all but Esther and Song of Solomon were used.

Old Testament lessons in the Methodist lectionary are in two major sequences: the Folklore of the Hebrew People and the Word of God's Prophets. Epistle readings offer the beginnings of the church and the teaching of the apostles. Gospels are also in two principal sections: the teachings of Christ and the mighty works of Christ. Into all of these sequences, however, traditional thematic lessons are inserted for certain seasons and occasions. Relationships between the Old Testament lessons and the New Testament lessons are not likely to be as close as those between the Epistle lessons and Gospel lessons, since the latter are to be read together in services of Holy Communion. Where possible, the Old Testament lesson bears some relationship to *either* the Epistle or Gospel lesson.

The following table of books in their biblical order indicates the amount of each used in the Methodist lectionary:

Genesis

1:1-3, 26-31, Race Relations Sunday	22:1-2, 9-13, Passion Sunday
3:1-6, 22-23, First Sunday after Pentecost	28:10-22, Third Sunday after Pentecost
9:8-15, Second Sunday after Pentecost	45:4-11, Fourth Sunday after Pentecost

Exodus

3:1-8b, 10-15, Trinity Sunday
12:1, 3, 6-8, 11, 14, 25-27, Maundy Thursday
20:1-20, Fifth Sunday after Pentecost
33:18-23, Second Sunday in Lent

Leviticus

19:1-2, 15-18, Eighth Sunday after Epiphany

Numbers

27:12-14a, 15-20, 22-23, Sixth Sunday after Pentecost

Deuteronomy

1:5, 8-18, Independence Day
7:6-11, Fourth Sunday after Easter Day
8:7-18, Thanksgiving Day
10:12-15, 20–11:1, Fifth Sunday after Easter Day
30:8-20, Universal Bible Sunday

Joshua

24:1-15, 24, Seventh Sunday after Pentecost

Judges

7:2-7, 19-22, Eighth Sunday after Pentecost

Ruth

1:1, 4-9, 16, 19a, Ninth Sunday after Pentecost

I Samuel

1:19c-28, Third Sunday after Epiphany
9:15-17; 10:1, Tenth Sunday after Pentecost
16:1-13, Eleventh Sunday after Pentecost

II Samuel

12:1-10, 13a, Twelfth Sunday after Pentecost

I Kings

18:21-39, Second Sunday in Kingdomtide

II Kings

17:5-14, 18-23, Fifteenth Sunday after Pentecost

I Chronicles

28:1-3, 5-10, Thirteenth Sunday after Pentecost

Ezra

1:2-4; 3:10-13, Thirteenth Sunday in Kingdomtide

Nehemiah

8:1-3, 5-8, Reformation Day

Job

19:1, 23-27, First Sunday after Easter Day

Proverbs

4:10-18, Ninth Sunday after Epiphany
31:10-31, Festival of the Christian Home

Ecclesiastes

11:6-9; 12:13, New Year's Day or Watch Night

Isaiah

5:11-12, 20-24, Commitment Day
6:1-8, Third Sunday in Kingdomtide
7:10-14, Fourth Sunday in Advent
9:2, 6-7, Christmas Day
11:1-10, Second Sunday in Advent
12:1-6, Second Sunday after Easter Day
25:1, 7-9, Easter Day
40:1-5, Fourteenth Sunday in Kingdomtide
42:1-9, First Sunday after Christmas Day
49:8-13, Second Sunday after Epiphany
51:11-16, All Saints Day
52:1-2, 7-12, Aldersgate Sunday
52:13–53:12, Good Friday
60:1-3, 6b, First Sunday after Epiphany
62:10-12, Third Sunday in Advent

Jeremiah

10:1-7, Sixth Sunday after Epiphany
31:31-34, Pentecost Sunday

Lamentations

3:22-26, 31-33, Fourth Sunday in Lent

Ezekiel

18:23-32, Seventh Sunday in Kingdomtide
33:7-16, First Sunday in Lent

34:11-16, 30-31, Third Sunday after Easter Day

37:1-6, 11-14, Tenth Sunday in Kingdomtide

Daniel

7:9-10, 34-14, Ascension Day

Hosea

6:1-3, Fifth Sunday after Epiphany

Joel

2:12, 15-17, Ash Wednesday

Amos

5:11-15, Labor Day

5:18-24, Eighth Sunday in Kingdomtide

7:7-10, 14-16a, Third Sunday in Lent

Obadiah

1:1-4, 15-17a, 21, Fourth Sunday in Kingdomtide

Jonah

3:1-5, Fourth Sunday after Epiphany

Micah

4:1-5, World Order Sunday

6:1-4, 5d-8, Sixth Sunday in Kingdomtide

Nahum

1:1-8, Fifth Sunday in Kingdomtide

Habakkuk

2:18-20; 3:2-4, Seventh Sunday after Epiphany

Zephaniah

3:8-13, Eleventh Sunday in Kingdomtide

Haggai

1:3-9; 2:2-3, Twelfth Sunday in Kingdomtide

Zechariah

2:10-13, Second Sunday after Christmas Day

9:9-12, Palm Sunday

Malachi

3:1-7b, First Sunday in Advent

Matthew

1:18-25, Fourth Sunday in Advent

2:1-12, First Sunday after Epiphany

5:1-12, All Saints Day

5:14-20, Second Sunday after Epiphany

5:43-48, World Order Sunday

6:16-21, Ash Wednesday

7:15-23, Fourth Sunday in Kingdomtide

7:24-29, Twelfth Sunday in Kingdomtide

8:23-27, Sixth Sunday in Kingdomtide

10:16-23, Eighth Sunday after Pentecost

11:2-6, First Sunday after Pentecost

11:25-30, Twelfth Sunday after Pentecost

16:13-19, Fourth Sunday after Pentecost

17:1-9, Second Sunday in Lent

18:15-22, Fifth Sunday in Kingdomtide

19:1-5, 10-14, Festival of the Christian Home

20:20-28, Thirteenth Sunday after Pentecost

25:14-30, Eighth Sunday in Kingdomtide

25:31-40, First Sunday in Kingdomtide

28:16-20, Trinity Sunday

Mark

1:9-12, First Sunday in Lent

1:14-22, Ninth Sunday after Epiphany

3:31-35, Race Relations Sunday

6:31-44, Eleventh Sunday in Kingdomtide

10:17-27, Third Sunday in Lent

10:28-31, Third Sunday in Kingdomtide

12:28-34a, Aldersgate Sunday

13:33-37, First Sunday in Advent

14:3-9, Fifteenth Sunday after Pentecost

14:17-25, Maundy Thursday

16:1-7, Easter Day

Luke

1:26-35, Second Sunday in Advent

2:1-20, Christmas Day

2:21-32, Second Sunday after Christmas Day

2:39-52, Third Sunday after Epiphany

3:2b-6, Third Sunday in Advent

4:16-21, Universal Bible Sunday
8:4-15, Seventh Sunday after Pentecost
9:57-62, New Year's Day or Watch Night
10:1-11, Second Sunday after Pentecost
10:25-37, Eighth Sunday after Epiphany
11:1-4, 9-13, Eleventh Sunday after Pentecost
12:16-31, Thanksgiving Day
13:22-24, 34-35, Thirteenth Sunday in Kingdomtide
15:1-10, Ninth Sunday after Pentecost
15:11-32, Ninth Sunday in Kingdomtide
16:10-15, Second Sunday in Kingdomtide
17:20-25, Fourteenth Sunday in Kingdomtide
18:1-14, Fourth Sunday in Lent
18:18-30, Tenth Sunday after Pentecost
19:1-10, Fifth Sunday after Pentecost
21:1-4, Seventh Sunday in Kingdomtide
21:23-26, Commitment Day
23:33-38, 44-46, Good Friday
24:44-53, Ascension Day

John

1:1-14, First Sunday after Christmas Day
1:19-30, Fifth Sunday after Epiphany
1:35-51, Seventh Sunday after Epiphany
2:1-11, Fourteenth Sunday after Pentecost
2:13-16, Reformation Day
3:4-17, Third Sunday after Pentecost
4:7-26, Sixth Sunday after Epiphany
6:5-14, 26-27, Labor Day
6:37-40, Second Sunday after Easter Day
8:1-11, Tenth Sunday in Kingdomtide
8:31-36, Independence Day
10:1-10, Sixth Sunday after Pentecost
10:11-16, Third Sunday after Easter Day
11:47-53, Passion Sunday
12:20-36a, Fourth Sunday after Epiphany
14:15-17, 25-27, Pentecost Sunday
16:16-22, Fourth Sunday after Easter Day
17:1-5, Fifth Sunday after Easter Day
20:19-31, First Sunday after Easter Day

The Acts

2:1-8, 12-21, Pentecost Sunday
3:1-7, 11-21, First Sunday after Pentecost
4:8, 10-13, 18-20, Second Sunday after Pentecost

8:26-35, Sixth Sunday in Epiphany
9:22, 26-31, Third Sunday after Pentecost
10:9-15, 34, Race Relations Sunday
13:26-33, Easter Day
15:1, 6-11, Fourth Sunday after Pentecost
16:1-10, Fifth Sunday after Pentecost
17:21-31, Seventh Sunday after Pentecost
18:24–19:6, Sixth Sunday after Pentecost
20:17-28, 32, Eighth Sunday after Pentecost
28:16-20, 23-24, 30-31, Ninth Sunday after Pentecost

Romans

5:1-11, Aldersgate Sunday
6:3-11, Second Sunday after Easter Day
6:15-23, Third Sunday in Lent
8:14-39, Tenth Sunday after Pentecost
11:33-36, Trinity Sunday
13:8-14, First Sunday in Advent
15:4-13, Universal Bible Sunday

I Corinthians

1:18-31, Fourth Sunday after Epiphany
2:1-16, Ninth Sunday after Epiphany
3:16-17, Commitment Day
4:1-5, Third Sunday in Advent
9:24-27, Ash Wednesday
11:23-26, Maundy Thursday
15:12-22, First Sunday after Easter Day

II Corinthians

3:4-11, 17-18, Eleventh Sunday after Pentecost
4:1-6, Third Sunday after Epiphany
5:1-10, Fourth Sunday after Easter Day
5:17–6:2, Third Sunday in Kingdomtide
6:1-10, Fourth Sunday in Lent
9:6-12, Thanksgiving Day

Galatians

3:23-26, Reformation Day
4:1-7, Christmas Day
5:13-15, Independence Day

Ephesians

1:15-23, Ascension Day
2:11-18, Second Sunday after Epiphany

3:1-12, First Sunday after Epiphany
3:13-21, Twelfth Sunday after Pentecost
4:1-8, Fourteenth Sunday after Pentecost
4:17-32, Eighth Sunday after Epiphany
5:25–6:4, Festival of the Christian Home
6:10-20, Thirteenth Sunday after Pentecost

Philippians
2:5-11, Palm Sunday
4:4-9, 19-20, Fifteenth Sunday after Pentecost

Colossians
1:21-29, Fifth Sunday after Epiphany
3:1-15, Fourth Sunday in Kingdomtide
3:23-25, Labor Day

I Thessalonians
5:1-11, Second Sunday in Advent

II Thessalonians
1:3-5, 11-12; 2:1-2,13-15, Fourteenth Sunday in Kingdomtide

I Timothy
6:6-19, Second Sunday in Kingdomtide

II Timothy
2:1-13, Eighth Sunday in Kingdomtide

Titus
2:11–3:7, Fourth Sunday in Advent

Philemon
1:1-3, 10-16, Ninth Sunday in Kingdomtide

Hebrews
1:1-12, Second Sunday after Christmas Day
9:11-14, Passion Sunday

10:4-7, 10-23, Good Friday
11:1-3, 6, Sixth Sunday in Kingdomtide
12:18-29, Second Sunday in Lent
13:1-6, Fifth Sunday in Kingdomtide

James
1:17-27, Seventh Sunday in Kingdomtide
4:1-12, World Order Sunday

I Peter
2:4-10, Seventh Sunday after Epiphany
2:19-25, Third Sunday after Easter Day

II Peter
3:8-14, Twelfth Sunday in Kingdomtide

I John
2:1-3, 15-17, First Sunday in Lent
2:24-25, 28-29; 3:1-2, Eleventh Sunday in Kingdomtide
4:9-16, First Sunday after Christmas Day
5:1-5, 11, Fifth Sunday after Easter Day

II John
1:3-4, 6, Tenth Sunday in Kingdomtide

III John
1:11, Tenth Sunday in Kingdomtide

Jude
1:17-21, 24-25, Thirteenth Sunday in Kingdomtide

Revelation
7:9-17, All Saints Day
19:1, 4, 6-8, First Sunday in Kingdomtide
21:1-6a, New Year's Day or Watch Night

Lectionaries from all over the world, from both ancient and modern branches of Christianity, those still in use and several being proposed, were studied. On color-coded cards all the lectionaries used in English-language worship were arranged in files of complete word-texts.

Almost universally, lectionaries direct that lessons be read from the Old Testament and from either the Epistles or Gospels at all services of worship, except that when Holy Communion is celebrated the Old Testament lesson may be omitted and both Epistle and Gospel shall be read. Sometimes readings from Acts or very occasionally from the Psalms (British Methodist lec-

141

tionary) are substituted for Old Testament lessons. The United Church of Canada lectionary does not always provide an Old Testament lesson; the Anglican lectionary suggests an Old Testament lesson for optional use at Holy Communion; and the revised lectionary being proposed for Roman Catholic use includes an Old Testament lesson for Mass. The Church of Scotland provides "propers" for four Communion services each year, but also includes Epistles and Gospels in its lectionary for every Sunday.

In several lectionaries the paucity of biblical materials thought to be suitable for Advent and Christmastide has led to use of the same lessons more than once in these seasons. For some occasions the Church of Scotland repeats the same Epistle and Gospel lessons in both the first and second year lectionaries. For Lent the Scottish lectionary offers two Gospels for the same Sundays. The Roman Catholic lectionary lists the same Gospels for all three Masses on Lenten Sundays.

There is considerable variance between lectionaries about the three pre-Lenten Sundays. The Church of South India lists them as "Sundays before Easter." Other lectionaries combine them with Epiphany, as does American Methodism. Others direct that though the Sundays after Epiphany may vary in number, the three pre-Lenten Sundays shall always be observed intact.

Other comparisons may be observed in the following lectionaries of denominations which worship in the English language.

Readers should be aware that Christian lectionaries as a whole are in constant revision. American Presbyterians are still working on their provisional lectionary, and further revisions are almost sure. In 1967 the Joint Liturgical Group in England published a proposed calendar and lectionary and in 1969 an additional lectionary, both of which are being used experimentally by Anglicans and are expected to be used by British Methodists beginning in January, 1971.

First Sunday in Advent

Roman Catholic Traditional
Rom. 13:11-14; Lk. 21:25-33

Roman Catholic Revised

First Year:	Is. 2:1-5; Rom. 13:11-14; Mt. 24:37-44
Second Year:	Is. 63:16b-17; 64:1, 3b-8; I Cor. 1:3-9; Mk. 13:33-37
Third Year:	Jer. 33:14-16; I Thess. 3:12-4:2; Lk. 21:25-28, 34-36

Anglican (Protestant Episcopal, 1945 Revision)

| Morning Prayer: | Mal. 3:1-6; 4:4-6 or *Is. 28:14-22; Lk. 1:5-25 or Heb. 12:14-29 |

| Evening Prayer: | Is. 62 or Is. 13:6-13; Mt. 25:1-13 or I Thess. 5:1-11 |
| Holy Communion: | Rom. 13:8-14; Mt. 21:1-13 |

Lutheran Churches in America

Matins:	Is. 28:14-22; Lk. 1:1-25
Vespers:	Is. 62:1-12; Col. 1:9-23
Holy Communion:	Jer. 31:31-34; Rom. 13:11-14; Mt. 21:1-9 or Lk. 3:1-6

*British Methodist**

| First Year, Morning: | Is. 1:1-4, 11-20; I Thess. 4:13-5:11 |
| First Year, Evening: | Mal. 1:1-14; Lk. 1:5-25 |

* Morning and Evening Lessons for British Methodists are from the 1958 lectionary; Communion Lessons are from the 1936 *Book of Offices.*

142

Second Year, Morning: Zeph. 3:1-8, 12-15; Mt. 25:1-13
Second Year, Evening: Is. 5:1-7; Rev. 1:1-20
Holy Communion: Rom. 13:8-14; Mt. 21:1-13

Church of Scotland
First Year, Morning: Is. 1:1-20; Rom. 13:8-14; Mk. 13:1-13
First Year, Evening: Is. 2:1-17; Lk. 1:1-17
Second Year, Morning: Is. 43:1-13; Rom. 13:8-14; Mt. 21:1-9
Second Year, Evening: Is. 44:6-23; Rev. 14:31-15:4

American Presbyterians (Provisional)
First Year: Zech. 10:6-12; Rom. 13:8-10; Mt. 21:1-13
Second Year: Gen. 12:1-9; Heb. 11:8-16; Lk. 1:26-33

United Church of Canada
Is. 60:1-11; Rom. 13:8-14; Mt. 21:1-9 or Mt. 21:1-13

Church of South India
Morning: Is. 40:1-5; Rom. 13:11-14; Jn. 3:16-21
Evening: Is. 26:1-9; Jn. 3:1-15

Second Sunday in Advent

Roman Catholic Traditional
Rom. 15:4-13; Mt. 11:2-10
Roman Catholic Revised
First Year: Is. 11:1-10; Rom. 15:4-9; Mt. 3:1-12
Second Year: Is. 40:1-5, 9-11; II Pet. 3:8-14; Lk. 1:1-8
Third Year: Bar. 5:1-9; Phil. 1:4-6, 8-11; Lk. 3:1-6

Anglican (Protestant Episcopal, 1945 Revision)
Morning Prayer: Is. 52:1-10 or *Is. 55; Lk. 1:26-56 or II Tim. 3
Evening Prayer: Amos 3:1-8 or Is. 11:1-10; I Thess. 2:1-13 or Jn. 5:30-40
Holy Communion: Rom. 15:4-13; Lk. 21:25-33

Lutheran Churches in America
Matins: Is. 52:1-10; Lk. 1:26-38
Vespers: Amos 3:1-8; Rom. 2:1-16
Holy Communion: Mal. 4:1-6; Rom. 15:4-13; Lk. 21:25-33

British Methodist
First Year, Morning: Is. 2:1-4; Rom. 15:4-13
First Year, Evening: Mal. 2:17-3:12; Lk. 1:26-38

Second Year, Morning: Is. 11:1-10; Lk. 4:16-30
Second Year, Evening: Ps. 119:105-12, 129-36; Rev. 20:11-21:8
Holy Communion: Rom. 15:4-13; Lk. 21:25-33

Church of Scotland
First Year, Morning: Is. 5:1-16; Rom. 15:4-13; Mk. 13:24-37
First Year, Evening: Is. 12; Lk. 1:18-35
Second Year, Morning: Is. 45:1-19; Rom. 15:4-13; Mt. 25:1-13
Second Year, Evening: Is. 46; Rev. 19:1-16

American Presbyterians (Provisional)
First Year: Is. 33:17-22; Rom. 13:11-14; Mt. 25:14-29
Second Year: Gen. 15:1-15; Rom. 9:1-8; Jn. 3:1-17

United Church of Canada
Is. 35 or Is. 32:1-4, 16-18; Rom. 15:4-13; Lk. 21:25-31 or Mt. 25:1-13
Church of South India
Morning: Is. 11:1-10; Rom. 15:4-13; Lk. 24:13-27
Evening: Deut. 18:9-19; Acts 8:26-40

Third Sunday in Advent

Roman Catholic Traditional
Phil. 4:4-7; John 1:19-28
Roman Catholic Revised
First Year: Is. 35:1-6a, 10; Jas. 5:7-10; Mt. 11:2-11
Second Year: Is. 61:1-2a, 10-11; I Thess. 5:16-24; Jn. 1:6-8, 19-28
Third Year: Wis. 3:14-18a; Phil. 4:4-7; Lk. 3:10-18

Anglican (Protestant Episcopal, 1945 Revision)
Morning Prayer: Jer. 1:4-10, 17-19 or *Is. 35; Lk. 1:57-80 or I Thess. 5:12-23

Evening Prayer: Nah. 1:3-8, 15 or Is. 26:1-11; I Cor. 9:7-23 or Mt. 9:35-10:15
Holy Communion: I Cor. 4:1-5; Mt. 11:2-10
Lutheran Churches in America
Matins: Jer. 1:4-10, 17-19; Lk. 1:39-56
Vespers: Nah. 1:3-8, 15; Rom. 1:16-25
Holy Communion: Is. 40:1-8; I Cor. 4:1-5; Mt. 11:2-10

British Methodist
First Year, Morning: Is. 25:1-9; II Tim. 3:1-7, 14-17

First Year, Evening: Mal. 3:13–4:6; Lk. 1:39-56

Second Year, Morning: Ezek. 34:1-12; Mt. 25:14-30

Second Year, Evening: Is. 26:1-9; Rev. 21:9-16, 22–22:5

Holy Communion: I Cor. 4:1-5; Mt. 11:2-10

Church of Scotland

First Year, Morning: Is. 25; I Cor. 3:16–4:5; Mt. 11:2-11

First Year, Evening: Is. 26:1-15; Lk. 1:39-56

Second Year, Morning: Is. 51:1-16; I Cor. 3:16–4:5; Mt. 13:14-52

Second Year, Evening: Is. 52:1-12; Rev. 21

American Presbyterians (Provisional)

First Year: Jer. 33:14-16; I Cor. 3:18–4:5; Mt. 3:1-11

Second Year: Gen. 28:10-22; I Jn. 5:1-5; Mt. 11:2-10

United Church of Canada

Is. 62:10-12; I Cor. 4:1-5; Mt. 11:2-15

Church of South India

Morning: Mal. 3:1-5; Rev. 3:14-22; Lk. 3:2-17

Evening: Is. 40:6-11; Mt. 11:2-15

Fourth Sunday in Advent

Roman Catholic Traditional
I Cor. 4:1-5; Lk. 3:1-6

Roman Catholic Revised

First Year: Is. 7:10-14; Rom. 1:1-7; Mt. 1:18-24

Second Year: II Sam. 7:1-5, 8b-11, 16; Rom. 16:25-27; Lk. 1:26-38

Third Year: Mic. 5:2-5a; Heb. 10:5-10; Lk. 1:39-45

Anglican (Protestant Episcopal, 1945 Revision)

Morning Prayer: *Is. 40:1-11 or Jer. 33:7-16; Lk. 3:1-17 or I Thess. 1

Evening Prayer: Is. 40:12-18, 21-31 or Is. 42:1-16; I Thess. 3:7-13 or Mt. 11:11-24

Holy Communion: Phil. 4:4-7; Jn. 1:19-28

Lutheran Churches in America

Matins: Jer. 33:7-16; Lk. 1:67-80

Vespers: Is. 40:12-26; Heb. 12:11-29

Holy Communion: Deut. 18:15-19 or Is. 40:9-11; Phil. 4:4-7; Jn. 1:19-28

British Methodist

First Year, Morning: Is. 35:1-10; Mt. 3:1-17

First Year, Evening: Zech. 2:1-5, 10-13; Lk. 1:57-80 or Titus 2:11–3:7

Second Year, Morning: Ezek. 34:20-31; Mt. 25:31-46

Second Year, Evening: Is. 29:9-19; Rev. 22:8-17, 20-21 or Titus 2:11–3:7

Holy Communion: Phil. 4:4-7; Jn. 1:19-28

Church of Scotland

First Year, Morning: Is. 32; Phil. 4:4-9; Jn. 1:19-28 or Mt. 3:1-12

First Year, Evening: Is. 35; Lk. 1:59-80

Second Year, Morning: Is. 54; Phil. 4:4-9; Lk. 1:68-79 or Lk. 3:1-14

Second Year, Evening: Is. 64; Rev. 22

American Presbyterians (Provisional)

First Year: Jer. 23:3-8; Phil. 4:4-7; Lk. 1:26-38

Second Year: I Sam. 1:21-28; Gal. 3:23-29; Lk. 1:39-56

United Church of Canada

Is. 40:1-11; Phil. 4:4-7; Jn. 1:19-28 or Lk. 3:3-14

Church of South India

Morning: Zech. 2:10-13; Phil. 4:4-7; Lk. 15:1-10

Evening: Is. 64:1-8; Rev. 1:1-8

Christmas Eve

Anglican (Protestant Episcopal, 1945 Revision)

Morning Prayer: Bar. 4:36–5:9; Lk. 1:67-80

Evening Prayer: Zech. 2:10-13; Mt. 1:18-25

British Methodist
Is. 35:1-10 or Ezek. 34:20-31; Titus 2:11–3:7

Church of South India
Mic. 5:2-4; Titus 3:3-7; Lk. 2:1-20

Christmas Day

Roman Catholic Traditional

First Mass: Titus 2:11-15; Lk. 2:1-14

Second Mass: Titus 3:4-7; Lk. 2:15-20

Third Mass: Heb. 1:1-12; Jn. 1:1-14

Roman Catholic Revised

First Mass: Is. 9:2-7; Titus 2:11-14; Lk. 2:1-14

Second Mass:	Is. 62:11-12a; Titus 3:4-7; Lk. 2:15-20
Third Mass:	Is. 52:7-10; Heb. 1:1-5a; Jn. 1:1-18

Anglican (Protestant Episcopal, 1945 Revision)

Morning Prayer:	Is. 9:2-7; Lk. 2:1-20
Evening Prayer:	Mic. 4:1-5; 5:2-4; I Jn. 4:7-14
Holy Communion:	Heb. 1:1-12 or Titus 2:11-15; Jn. 1:1-14 or Lk. 2:1-14

Lutheran Churches in America

Matins:	Is. 9:2-7; Jn. 1:1-14
Vespers:	Mic. 4:1-5, 5:2-4; Lk. 2:15-20
Holy Communion:	Is. 9:2-7 or Is. 45:1-8; Titus 2:11-14 or I Jn. 4:7-16 or Heb. 1:1-2; Lk. 2:1-14 or Jn. 1:1-14

British Methodist

First Year, Morning:	Is. 9:2, 6, 7; Lk. 2:1-20
First Year, Evening:	Is. 7:10-14; Mt. 1:18-25
Second Year, Morning:	Is. 7:10-14; Mt. 1:18-25
Second Year, Evening:	Is. 9:2, 6, 7; Lk. 2:1-20
Holy Communion:	Heb. 1:1-12; Jn. 1:1-14

Church of Scotland

First Year, Morning:	Is. 9:2-7; Titus 2:11–3:7; Lk. 2:1-20
First Year, Evening:	Is. 11:1-13; Mt. 1:18-25
Second Year, Morning:	Is. 9:2-7; Gal. 4:1-7; Mt. 1:18-25
Second Year, Evening:	Mic. 4:1-7; I Jn. 4:7-21

American Presbyterians (Provisional)

First Year:	Is. 40:25-31 or Is. 52:7-10; Gal. 4:1-7 or I Tim. 3:14-16; Lk. 2:1-14 or Jn. 1:1-18
Second Year:	Is. 9:2-7 or Is. 60:1-6; Heb. 1:1-12 or II Tim. 1:8-12; Mt. 1:18-25 or Mt. 2:1-12

United Church of Canada
Mic. 4:2, 4, 5a; Titus 2:11-14; Lk. 2:1-14

Church of South India

Morning:	Is. 9:2-7; Heb. 1:1-12; Jn. 1:1-14
Evening:	Is. 7:10-14; Mt. 1:18-25

First Sunday after Christmas

Roman Catholic Traditional
Gal. 4:1-7; Lk. 2:33-40

Roman Catholic Revised

First Year:	Ecclus. 3:3-7, 14-17a; Col. 3:12-21; Mt. 2:13-15
Second Year:	Prov. 23:19, 22-25; Col. 3:12-21; Mt. 2:19-23
Third Year:	Prov. 23:19, 22-25; Col. 3:12-21; Lk. 2:25-35, 39-40

Anglican (Protestant Episcopal, 1945 Revision)

Morning Prayer:	*Is. 9:2-7 or Is. 49:8-13; Lk. 2:1-20 or Heb. 2
Evening Prayer:	Is. 63:7-16 or Job 28:12-28; II Pet. 1:1-12 or Mt. 11:25-30
Holy Communion:	Gal. 4:1-7; Mt. 1:18-25

Lutheran Churches in America

Morning:	Is. 49:8-13; Lk. 2:22-32
Vespers:	Job 28:12-28; Heb. 2:9-16
Holy Communion:	Is. 63:7-16; Gal. 4:1-7; Lk. 2:33-40

British Methodist

First Year, Morning:	Is. 40:1-11; Lk. 2:21-40
First Year, Evening:	Josh. 1:1-11, 16-17; I Jn. 4:7-21
Second Year, Morning:	Is. 40:12-31; Phil. 2:1-18
Second Year, Evening:	Is. 42:10-17; Jn. 1:1-18
Holy Communion:	Gal. 4:1-7; Mt. 1:18-25

Church of Scotland

First Year, Morning:	Is. 40:1-11; Heb. 1:1-12; Jn. 1:1-18
First Year, Evening:	Is. 40:12-31; Lk. 2:1-20
Second Year, Morning:	Is. 40:1-11; I Jn. 4:9-16; Jn. 1:1-18
Second Year, Evening:	Is. 40:12-31; Heb. 1

American Presbyterians (Provisional)

First Year:	Is. 62:10-12; Titus 2:11-14; Lk. 2:36-40
Second Year:	Is. 11:1-9; Col. 1:9-20; Jn. 1:1-18

United Church of Canada
Is. 9:2-7 or Is. 11:1-9; Heb. 1:1-12 or II Cor. 8:9; Jn. 1:1-14

Church of South India

Morning:	Jer. 31:10-13; Heb. 2:10-18; Jn. 1:14-18
Matins:	Is. 45:18-25; Rom. 11:25-36

Second Sunday after Christmas

Roman Catholic Traditional
Acts 4:8-12; Lk. 2:21

Roman Catholic Revised
Ecclus. 24:1-4, 12-16; Eph. 1:3-6, 15-18; Jn. 1:1-18

Anglican (Protestant Episcopal, 1945 Revision)

Morning Prayer:	*Mic. 4:1-5; 5:2-4 or Is. 44:1-8, 21-23; Lk. 2:21-32 or Col. 2:6-17

Evening Prayer: Prov. 9:1-6, 10 or Hag. 2:1-9; II Cor. 4:1-6 or Lk. 2:34-40
Holy Communion: Is. 61:1-3; Mt. 2:19-23

Lutheran Churches in America
Matins: Is. 44:1-8, 21-23; Mt. 3: 1-12
Vespers: Hag. 2:1-9; Rom. 3:23-31
Holy Communion: I Sam. 2:1-10; Titus 3:4-7; Jn. 1:14-18

British Methodist
First Year, Morning: Is. 40:12-31; Phil. 2:1-18
First Year, Evening: Is. 42:10-17; Jn. 1:1-18
Second Year, Morning: Is. 40:1-11; Lk. 2:21-40
Second Year, Evening: Josh. 1:1-11, 16-17; I Jn. 4:7-21

Church of Scotland
First Year, Morning: Deut. 11:1-17; I Jn. 4:9-16; Lk. 1:46-55

First Year, Evening: Deut. 30; Lk. 2:21-38
Second Year, Morning: Josh. 1:1-9; I Thess. 5; Lk. 2:21-32
Second Year, Evening: Eccles. 3:1-15; Phil. 2:1-11

American Presbyterians (Provisional)
First Year: Mic. 4:1-4; I Pet. 2:1-10; Lk. 3:4-17
Second Year: Is. 40:1-11; II Cor. 4:1-6; Lk. 2:25-35

United Church of Canada
Epiphany: Isa. 60:1-6; Eph. 3:1-12; Mt. 2:1-12

Church of South India
Morning: Is. 60:1-7; Rev. 21:22–22: 2; Mt. 2:1-12
Evening: Job 28; I Cor. 1:18-25

Epiphany Day

Roman Catholic Traditional
Isa. 60:1-6; Matt. 2:1-12

Roman Catholic Revised
Is. 60:1-6; Eph. 3:2-3a, 5-6; Mt. 2:1-12

Anglican (Protestant Episcopal, 1945 Revision)
Morning Prayer: Is. 60:1-9; II Cor. 4:1-6
Evening Prayer: Is. 61; Rom. 15:8-21
Holy Communion: Eph. 3:1-12; Mt. 2:1-12

Lutheran Churches in America
Matins: Is. 2:2-5; Mt. 3:13-17
Vespers: Is. 61:1-11; Rom. 3:23-31
Holy Communion: Is. 60:1-6; Col. 1:23-27 or Eph. 3:1-12; Mt. 2:1-12

British Methodist
First Year, Morning: Is. 60:1-9, 18-22; Mt. 2: 1-12
First Year, Evening: Is. 44:6-20; Jn. 1:35-51
Second Year, Morning: Is. 61:1-11; Mt. 2:1-12

Second Year, Evening: Is. 49:1-13; Eph. 2:1-22
Holy Communion: Eph. 3:1-12; Mt. 2:1-12

Church of Scotland
First Year, Morning: Is. 60; Eph. 2:11-18; Mt. 2:1-12
First Year, Evening: Is. 49:5-23; Mt. 2:13-23
Second Year, Morning: I Kings 10:1-13; Eph. 2: 11-18; Mt. 2:1-12
Second Year, Evening: I Chron. 29:10-19; Eph. 3

American Presbyterians (Provisional)
Is. 60:1-6; II Cor. 4:3-6; Mt. 2:1-12

United Church of Canada
Is. 60:1-6; Eph. 3:1-12; Mt. 2:1-12

Church of South India
Morning: Is. 60:1-7; Rev. 21:22–22: 2; Mt. 2:1-12
Evening: Job 28; I Cor. 1:18-25

First Sunday after Epiphany

Roman Catholic Traditional
Rom. 12:1-5; Lk. 2:42-52

Roman Catholic Revised
First Year: Is. 42:1-7; Acts 10:36-43; Mt. 3:13-17
Second Year: Is. 42:1-7; Acts 10:36-43; Mk. 1:6b-11
Third Year: Is. 42:1-7; Acts 10:36-43; Lk. 3:15-18, 21-22

Anglican (Protestant Episcopal, 1945 Revision)
Morning Prayer: Is. 60:1-9 or *Prov. 8:22-35; Mt. 2:1-12 or Col. 1:9-29
Evening Prayer: I Sam. 1:21-28 or Is. 49: 1-7; Mt. 18:1-14 or I Jn. 1:1-9

Holy Communion: Rom. 12:1-9; Lk. 2:41-52

Lutheran Churches in America
Matins: Prov. 8:22-35; Mk. 10: 13-16
Vespers: Is. 49:1-7; Eph. 6:1-4
Holy Communion: Eccles. 12:1-7; Rom. 12: 1-5; Lk. 2:41-52

British Methodist
First Year, Morning: Is. 61:1-11; Mt. 2:1-12 or Mt. 2:13-23
First Year, Evening: Is. 49:1-13; Eph. 2:1-22
Second Year, Morning: Is. 60:1-9, 18-22; Mt. 2: 1-12 or Mt. 2:13-23
Second Year, Evening: Is. 44:6-20; Jn. 1:35-51
Holy Communion: Rom. 12:1-5; Lk. 2:41-52

Church of Scotland
First Year, Morning: Is. 55; Rom. 12:1-9; Lk. 2:39-52
First Year, Evening: Is. 60; Mk. 1:1-11
Second Year, Morning: Is. 60; Rom. 12:1-9; Lk. 2:40-52
Second Year, Evening: Is. 49:5-23; Col. 1:21-2:7
American Presbyterians (Provisional)
First Year: Mic. 7:18-20; Eph. 3:1-12; Mt. 2:1-12

Second Year: Is. 61:1-3; I Jn. 1:1-2:2; Lk. 2:41-52
United Church of Canada
Is. 60:1-6; Eph. 3:1-12; Mt. 2:1-12
Church of South India
Morning: Is. 60:1-7; Rev. 21:22-22:2; Mt. 2:1-12
Evening: Job 28; I Cor. 1:18-25

Second Sunday after Epiphany

Roman Catholic Traditional
Rom. 12:6-16; John 2:1-11
Roman Catholic Revised*
Anglican (Protestant Episcopal, 1945 Revision)
Morning Prayer: *Zech. 8:1-8, 20-23 or Ex. 34:29-35; I Cor. 12:12-31a or Mk. 9:2-13
Evening Prayer: Is. 45:1-15 or Is. 54:11-17; Rom. 9:14-26 or Jn. 1:35-51
Holy Communion: Rom. 12:6-16; Mk. 1:1-11
Lutheran Churches in America
Matins: Is. 41:8-10, 17-20; Lk. 19:1-10
Vespers: Num. 20:1-11; Eph. 5:22-33
Holy Communion: Is. 61:1-6; Rom. 12:6-16a; Jn. 2:1-11
British Methodist
First Year, Morning: Jon. 1:1-17; I Thess. 1:1-10
First Year, Evening: Gen. 37:3-14, 18-28; Jn. 2:1-12

Second Year, Morning: Gen. 42:1-20; Mt. 16:13-28
Second Year, Evening: Is. 49:14-16, 22-26; I Cor. 1:1-17
Holy Communion: Rom. 12:6-16; Jn. 2:1-11
Church of Scotland
First Year, Morning: Is. 41:1-20; Rom. 12:10-21; Jn. 2:1-11
First Year, Evening: Is. 42:1-12; Lk. 3:1-22
Second Year, Morning: Is. 62; Rom. 12:10-21; Mk. 1:14-28 or Mt. 3:13-17
Second Year, Evening: Is. 63:7-19; I Cor. 1:1-17
American Presbyterians (Provisional)
First Year: Ezek. 34:11-16; Eph. 4:17-24; Mt. 2:16-23
Second Year: Mic. 5:2-4; Phil. 2:3-11; Mk. 1:1-11
United Church of Canada
Mic. 4:1-4; Eph. 2:11-18; Lk. 2:25-35
Church of South India
Morning: I Sam. 1:20-28; Rom. 11:33–12:2; Lk. 2:22-40
Evening: Mic. 4:1-5; Lk. 2:41-52

Third Sunday after Epiphany

Roman Catholic Traditional
Rom. 12:16-21; Matt. 8:1-13
Anglican (Protestant Episcopal, 1945 Revision)
Morning Prayer: *Is. 41:8-10, 17-20 or Deut. 16:18-20, 17:8-11; Jn. 4:1-14 or Jas. 2:1-13
Evening Prayer: Is. 56:1-8 or Is. 54:1-8; Jn. 2:13-25 or Rom. 14:1-15:3
Holy Communion: Rom. 12:16-21; Jn. 2:1-11
Lutheran Churches in America
Matins: Deut. 4:5-13, 32-40; Lk. 17:5-10
Vespers: Dan. 10:10-19; Heb. 11:1-16

Holy Communion: II Kings 5:1-15b; Rom. 12:16b-21; Mt. 8:1-13 or Jn. 1:29-34
British Methodist
First Year, Morning: Jon. 2:10–3:10; I Thess. 5:12-24
First Year, Evening: Gen. 39:20–40:22; Jn. 3:22-36
Second Year, Morning: Gen. 45:1-15; Mt. 17:1-13
Second Year, Evening: Is. 50:4-10; I Cor. 1:18-31
Holy Communion: Rom. 12:16-21; Mt. 8:1-13

---

* At this point the Roman Catholic Revised lectionary begins lessons from a table also used for the Sundays after the Second Sunday after Pentecost. See page 162.

Church of Scotland
First Year, Morning: Prov. 2; I Jn. 3:1-8; Mt. 8:1-13
First Year, Evening: Job 1; Mk. 1:14-28
Second Year, Morning: Job 37:1-19; Rom. 8:1-9, 12-17; Mt. 9:9-17
Second Year, Evening: Prov. 9; I Cor. 3
American Presbyterians (Provisional)
First Year: Ezek. 34:25-31; Rom. 14: 1-9; Mk. 1:14-22

Second Year: Jer. 1:4-12; Rom. 12:1-13; Lk. 5:1-11
United Church of Canada
Rom. 12:1-5; Lk. 2:41-52
Church of South India
Morning: Is. 42:1-7; Gal. 3:23-29; Mk. 1:1-11
Evening: Is. 49:1-6; Col. 2:8-15

Fourth Sunday after Epiphany

Roman Catholic Traditional
Rom. 13:8-10; Mt. 8:23-27
Anglican (Protestant Episcopal, 1945 Revision)
Morning Prayer: Is. 61 or *Deut. 4:5-13, 32-40; Lk. 4:16-32 or Eph. 2
Evening Prayer: Is. 45:20-25 or Dan. 10: 10-19; Rom. 10 or Mk. 6:45-56
Holy Communion: Rom. 13:1-7; Mt. 8:1-13
Lutheran Churches in America
Matins: Josh. 3:14-17; Mt. 14:22-33
Vespers: Job 38:1-11; Rom. 4:16-25
Holy Communion: Ex. 14:21-31; Rom. 13:8-10; Mt. 8:23-27
British Methodist
First Year, Morning: Jon. 4:1-11; Gal. 1:1-12
First Year, Evening: Gen. 41:14-15, 25-41; Jn. 4:43-54
Second Year, Morning: Gen. 45:16–46:7; Mk. 9: 14-29

Second Year, Evening: Is. 54:1-10; I Cor. 3:1-13, 16-23
Holy Communion: Rom. 13:1-7; Mt. 8:23-34
Church of Scotland
First Year, Morning: Prov. 3; Rom. 3:21-26, 5:18-21; Mk. 4:35-41
First Year, Evening: Job 2; Mk. 1:29-45
Second Year, Morning: Job 38:1-21; Rom. 8:18-25; Lk. 14:25-35
Second Year, Evening: Prov. 22; I Cor. 4:1-16
American Presbyterians (Provisional)
First Year: Gen. 18:22-33; I Cor. 6: 12-20; Mt. 8:23-27
Second Year: II Kings 5:1-14; Rom. 1: 8-17; Jn. 2:1-11
United Church of Canada
Rom. 12:6-16a; Jn. 2:1-11
Church of South India
Morning: Is. 8:11-18; Phil. 2:12-18; Mk. 1:16-20
Evening: Jer. 1:4-10; Mt. 10:1-16

Fifth Sunday after Epiphany

Roman Catholic Traditional
Col. 3:12-17; Mt. 13:24-30
Anglican (Protestant Episcopal, 1945 Revision)
Morning Prayer: Ruth 1:1-17 or *Hab. 1: 12–2:4, 9-14; Col. 3:5-11 or Lk. 12:35-48
Evening Prayer: Joel 3:9-17 or Amos 5:14-24; Mt. 13:36-52 or Gal. 6:1-10
Holy Communion: Col. 3:12-17; Mt. 13:24-30
Lutheran Churches in America
Matins: Joel 3:9-17; Mt. 13:44-52
Vespers: Amos 5:14-24; I Cor. 3: 3-23
Holy Communion: Ezek. 33:10-16; Col. 3:12-17; Mt. 13:24-30
British Methodist
First Year, Morning: Is. 64:1-12; Gal. 5:16–6:5
First Year, Evening: Jer. 23:1-8; Jn. 9:1-12

Second Year, Morning: Gen. 48:1-21; Mt. 17:22-27
Second Year, Evening: Is. 57:15-21; Heb. 12:14-29
Holy Communion: Col. 3:12-17; Mt. 13:24-30
Church of Scotland
First Year, Morning: Prov. 4; Col. 3:12-17; Mt. 13:24-30
First Year, Evening: Job 14; Lk. 4:16-32
Second Year, Morning: Job 38:22-41; Col. 3:12-17; Mt. 13:24-30
Second Year, Evening: Prov. 25:1-22; I Cor. 9
American Presbyterians (Provisional)
First Year: Ezek. 33:10-16; Gal. 6:1-5; Mt. 13:24-30
Second Year: Jer. 7:1-7; Col. 3:12-17; Mk. 2:1-17
United Church of Canada
Rom. 12:16b-21; Mt. 8:1-13

Church of South India
Morning: I Kings 17:8-16; II Pet. 1:3-8; Jn. 2:1-11

Evening:

Ezek. 47:1-12; I Cor. 15: 35-45

Sixth Sunday after Epiphany

Roman Catholic Traditional
I Thess. 1:2-10; Mt. 13:31-35

Anglican (Protestant Episcopal, 1945 Revision)
Morning Prayer: Is. 2:6-19 or *Is. 66:1-2, 10, 12-16, 18-23; Mt. 25:14-29 or II Thess. 1

Evening Prayer: Gen. 19:1-3, 12-17, 24-28 or II Es. 8:63–9:13; Lk. 17:20-37 or II Pet. 3:1-14, 17-18

Holy Communion: I Jn. 3:1-8; Mt. 24:23-31

Lutheran Churches in America
Matins: Ex. 3:1-6; Mt. 11:25-30
Vespers: Ex. 24:12-18; II Cor. 4:5-6
Holy Communion: Ex. 34:29-35; II Pet. 1: 16-21; Mt. 17:1-9

British Methodist
First Year, Morning: Zech. 13:1-9; Gal. 6:6-18
First Year, Evening: Mic. 4:1-8; Jn. 9:13-16, 24-25, 34-41
Second Year, Morning: Gen. 50:15-26; Mt. 15:1-20

Second Year, Evening: Ex. 35:30-35; Jude 1-4, 11-25
Holy Communion: I Jn. 3:1-8; Mt. 24:23-31

Church of Scotland
First Year, Morning: Prov. 8:12-36; I Jn. 1:1-9; Mt. 24:23-31
First Year, Evening: Job 28; Lk. 5:1-15
Second Year, Morning: Job 42; I Jn. 1:1-9; Mt. 24:23-31
Second Year, Evening: Prov. 31:10-31; I Cor. 10:1-14

American Presbyterians (Provisional)
First Year: Deut. 34:1-8; Eph. 4:10-16; Mt. 17:1-8
Second Year: Jer. 18:1-11; I Cor. 9:24-27; Mk. 4:1-20

United Church of Canada
Rom. 13:8-10; Mt. 8:23-27

Church of South India
Morning: Is. 61:1-4; I Pet. 3:8-18; Mt. 5:1-12
Evening: Deut. 11:26-32; Lk. 10: 17-24

Seventh Sunday after Epiphany
Septuagesima

Roman Catholic Traditional
I Cor. 9:24–10:5; Mt. 20:1-16

Anglican (Protestant Episcopal, 1945 Revision)
Morning Prayer: *Josh. 1:1-9 or Ezek. 3:4-11; II Tim. 2:1-13 or Mt. 5:1-16 1-16

Evening Prayer: I Macc. 2:49-64 or Is. 5: 1-7; I Tim. 6:11-19; Mt. 21:23-32

Holy Communion: I Cor. 9:24-27; Mt. 20:1-16

Lutheran Churches in America
Matins: Josh. 1:1-9; Mt. 25:14-30
Vespers: Is. 5:1-7; Acts 17:22-34
Holy Communion: Jer. 9:23-24; I Cor. 9:24–10:5; Mt. 20:1-16

British Methodist
First Year, Morning: Prov. 8:1-4, 22-36; Mt. 5:1-16
First Year, Evening: Gen. 2:4-9, 15-25; I Jn. 1:1-9
Second Year, Morning: Gen. 1:1–2:3; Jn. 1:1-18
Second Year, Evening: Gen. 12:1-9; Mt. 6:1-15

Holy Communion: I Cor. 9:24-27; Mt. 20:1-16

Church of Scotland
First Year, Morning: Gen. 1:1-19; I Cor. 9:24–10:6; Mt. 11:28-30
First Year, Evening: Gen. 1:20–2:3; Mk. 2:1-17
Second Year, Morning: Gen. 22:1-18; I Cor. 9: 24–10:6; Mt. 20:1-16
Second Year, Evening: Gen. 27:6-40; I Cor. 11: 17-34

American Presbyterians (Provisional)
First Year: Jer. 9:23-24; II Pet. 1:16-21; Mt. 20:1-16
Second Year: Jer. 23:23-29; II Cor. 11: 16-31; Mt. 5:38-48

United Church of Canada
Col. 2:12-17; Mt. 13:24-30

Church of South India
Morning: Gen. 1:1-5, 26-31; Rev. 21:1-17; Jn. 5:1-18
Evening: Job 38:1-11; Col. 1:9-20

149

Eighth Sunday after Epiphany
Sexagesima

Roman Catholic Traditional
II Cor. 11:19–12:9; Lk. 8:4-15

Anglican (Protestant Episcopal, 1945 Revision)

Morning Prayer: *Is. 50:4-10 or Is. 30:8-21; II Cor. 12:1-12 or Mk. 4:26-34

Evening Prayer: Eccles. 11:1-6 or Dan. 3:1-26; Jn. 4:31-38 or Mt. 10:16-23, 40-42

Holy Communion: II Cor. 11:19-31; Lk. 8:4-15

Lutheran Churches in America

Matins: Is. 50:4-10; Mk. 4:26-32

Vespers: Eccles. 11:1-6; II Tim. 3:10–4:5

Holy Communion: Amos 8:11-12; II Cor. 11:19–12:9; Lk. 8:4-15

British Methodist

First Year, Morning: Ex. 20:1-17; Mt. 5:17-32

First Year, Evening: Gen. 3:1-21; Rev. 12:7-12

Second Year, Morning: Ex. 17:1-16; Mt. 7:1-14

Second Year, Evening: Gen. 13:1-18; Mt. 7:15-29

Holy Communion: II Cor. 11:19-31; Lk. 8:4-15

Church of Scotland

First Year, Morning: Gen. 2:4-17; II Cor. 11:19-31; Lk. 8:4-15

First Year, Evening: Gen. 3; Lk. 6:27-49

Second Year, Morning: Gen. 28:10-22; II Cor. 11:19-41; Jn. 12:20-32

Second Year, Evening: Gen. 32:1-12, 24-31; I Cor. 12:1-11

American Presbyterians (Provisional)

First Year: Amos 8:11-12; I Pet. 2:1-6; Lk. 8:4-15

Second Year: Gen. 45:1-15; I Cor. 12:27–13:13; Lk. 18:18-30

United Church of Canada
I Cor. 9:24-27; Mt. 20:1-16 †

Church of South India

Morning: Gen. 3:1-19; Rom. 5:12-19; Jn. 8:39-47

Evening: Jer. 17:9-17; Rom. 3:21-30

Ninth Sunday after Epiphany
Quinquagesima

Roman Catholic Traditional
I Cor. 13; Lk. 18:31-43

Anglican (Protestant Episcopal, 1945 Revision)

Morning Prayer: Wis. 7:7-14 or *Deut. 10:12-15, 17–11:1; Jn. 15:1-17 or I Jn. 2:1-17

Evening Prayer: Lev. 19:1-2, 9-18 or Is. 51:1-8; I Jn. 4 or Mk. 9:14-32

Holy Communion: I Cor. 13; Lk. 18:31-43

Lutheran Churches in America

Matins: Deut. 10:12–11:1; Jn. 12:23-36

Vespers: Lev. 19:1-2, 9-18; I Pet. 3:18-22

Holy Communion: Jer. 8:4-9; I Cor. 13:1-13; Lk. 18:31-43

British Methodist

First Year, Morning: Lev. 19:1-4, 9-18; Mt. 5:33-48

First Year, Evening: Gen. 3:22–4:13; I Jn. 3:1-12

Second Year, Morning: II Chron. 28:8-15; I Jn. 3:13-24

Second Year, Evening: Gen. 18:20-33; Lk. 10:25-42

Holy Communion: I Cor. 13:1-13; Lk. 18:31-43

Church of Scotland

First Year, Morning: Gen. 4:1-16; I Cor. 13; Lk. 18:18-31

First Year, Evening: Gen. 6; Lk. 7:1-16

Second Year, Morning: Gen. 37:1-22; I Cor. 13; Lk. 18:18-31

Second Year, Evening: Gen. 37:23-36; I Cor. 12:12-31

American Presbyterians (Provisional)

First Year: Jer. 8:4-7; I Pet. 2:7-10; Lk. 18:31-43

Second Year: Gen. 45:16-28; I Cor. 10:1-12; Mk. 7:24-37

United Church of Canada
II Cor. 11:19-31; Lk. 8:4-15

† A note to the reader: For the purpose of this comparative study the author of this chapter has edited the lectionary of the United Church of Canada to make it conform to other contemporary lectionaries of English-speaking churches. Since the Eighth Sunday after Epiphany is the First Sunday in Lent for the United Church of Canada, the lessons for the Sundays following do not conform to those called for in the *Book of Common Order of the United Church of Canada.*

Church of South India
Morning: Ex. 6:2-9; Titus 2:11-14; Lk. 19:1-10

Evening: Is. 44:21-28; Rom. 8:26-39

Ash Wednesday

Roman Catholic Traditional
Joel 2:12-19; Mt. 6:16-21

Roman Catholic Revised
Joel 2:12-18; II Cor. 5:20–6:2; Mt. 6:1-6, 16-18

Anglican (Protestant Episcopal, 1945 Revision)
Morning Prayer: Is. 58:1-12; Heb. 12:1-14
Evening Prayer: Jon. 3, 4; Lk. 15:10-32
Holy Communion: Joel 2:12-17; Mt. 6:16-21

Lutheran Churches in America
Matins: Is. 59:12-21; Lk. 6:20-36
Vespers: Jon. 3:1–4:11; I Jn. 1:5-10

Holy Communion: Joel 2:12-19; I Jn. 1:5-9 or Phil. 3:7-14; Mt. 6:16-21

American Presbyterians (Provisional)
First Year: II Cor. 7:2-10; Mt. 6:16-21
Second Year: I John 1:5-9; Mk. 7:14-23

Church of South India
Morning: Is. 58:1-8; II Cor. 7:2-10; Mt. 6:16-21
Evening: Joel 2:12-17; I Cor. 9:19-27

First Sunday in Lent

Roman Catholic Traditional
II Cor. 6:1-10; Mt. 4:1-11

Roman Catholic Revised
First Year: Gen. 2:7-9; 3:1-7; Rom. 5:12-19; Mt. 4:1-11
Second Year: Gen. 9:8-15; I Pet. 3:18-22; Mk. 1:12-15
Third Year: Deut. 26:4-10; Rom. 10:8-13; Lk. 4:1-13

Anglican (Protestant Episcopal, 1945 Revision)
Morning Prayer: *Is. 58 or Ecclus. 2; Mt. 6:1-18 or Rom. 7:14-25
Evening Prayer: Jer. 17:5-14 or Dan. 9:3-10; I Cor. 10:1-13 or Lk. 5:33–6:10
Holy Communion: II Cor. 6:1-10; Mt. 4:1-11

Lutheran Churches in America
Matins: Is. 58:1-12; Lk. 22:24-32
Vespers: Jer. 17:5-14; Jas. 1:2-15
Holy Communion: Gen. 22:1-14; II Cor. 6:1-10; Mt. 4:1-11

British Methodist
First Year, Morning: Is. 58:1-12; Mt. 4:1-11
First Year, Evening: Gen. 6:5-8, 13-22; Mt. 26:1-16

Second Year, Morning: Joel 2:12-17; Lk. 22:1-23
Second Year, Evening: Gen. 21:9-20; Heb. 4:14–5:9
Holy Communion: II Cor. 6:1-10; Mt. 4:1-11

Church of Scotland
First Year, Morning: Is. 58; I Jn. 2:7-17; Mt. 4:1-11
First Year, Evening: Jon. 3; Lk. 4:1-13
Second Year, Morning: Is. 1:1-20; II Tim. 3:14–4:8; Lk. 4:1-13
Second Year, Evening: Ezek. 33:1-16; II Cor. 1:1-20

American Presbyterians (Provisional)
First Year: Gen. 22:1-8; II Cor. 6:1-10; Mt. 4:1-11
Second Year: Is. 42:1-9; Heb. 2:9-18; Lk. 9:14-29

United Church of Canada
Joel 2:12-19; Mt. 6:16-21

Church of South India
Morning: Ex. 17:1-7; Jas. 1:12-18; Mt. 4:1-11
Evening: Ex. 32:1-14; I Cor. 10:1-13

Second Sunday in Lent

Roman Catholic Traditional
I Thess. 4:1-7; Mt. 17:1-9

Roman Catholic Revised
First Year: Gen. 12:1-4a; II Tim. 1:8b-10; Mt. 17:1-9
Second Year: Gen. 22:1-2, 9a, 10-13, 15-18; Rom. 8:31b-34; Mk. 9:1-9

Third Year: Gen. 15:5-12; Phil. 3:17–4:1; 20-21 Lk. 9:28-36

Anglican (Protestant Episcopal, 1945 Revision)
Morning Prayer: *I Kings 8:37-43 or Ezek. 18:1-4, 25-32; Col. 3:12-17 or Mt. 5:27-37
Evening Prayer: II Sam. 12:1-10, 13-14 or Ecclus. 51:1-12; I

151

Cor. 6:9-20 or Lk. 18:
1-8

Holy Communion: I Thess. 4:1-8; Mt. 15:
21-28

Lutheran Churches in America
Matins: I Kings 8:37-43; Mk. 9:
17-29

Vespers: II Sam. 12:1-10, 13-14;
Jas. 5:13-20

Holy Communion: Ex. 33:12-23; I Thess.
4:1-7; Mt. 15:21-28

British Methodist
First Year, Morning: Job 1:6-22; Phil. 1:1-21
First Year, Evening: Gen. 7:24–8:13; Mt. 26:
17-35

Second Year, Morning: Amos 7:7-16a; Lk. 22:24-
46

Second Year, Evening: Gen. 22:1-18; Rom. 6:
15-23

Holy Communion: I Thess. 4:1-8; Mt. 15:21-
28

Church of Scotland
First Year, Morning: Gen. 8; I Thess. 4:1-8;
Mt. 15:21-28

First Year, Evening: Gen. 9:1-17; Lk. 15:1-10
Second Year, Morning: Gen. 40; Rom. 2:1-10;
Mt. 16:21-28 or Mt.
17:1-9

Second Year, Evening: Gen. 41:15-36; II Cor. 3

American Presbyterians (Provisional)
First Year: Ex. 34:1-9; I Thess. 4:
1-8; Mt. 7:24-29

Second Year: Ex. 1:1-14; Rom. 3:19-
31; Mk. 9:30-37

United Church of Canada
II Cor. 6:1-10; Mt. 4:1-11

Church of South India
Morning: II Sam. 12:1-13; I Jn.
1:5–2:2; Lk. 15:11-32

Evening: Jer. 7:1-15; Lk. 11:24-
36

Third Sunday in Lent

Roman Catholic Traditional
Eph. 5:1-9; Lk. 11:14-20

Roman Catholic Revised
First Year: Ex. 17:3-7; Rom. 5:1-2,
5-8; Jn. 4:5-42

Second Year: Ex. 20:1-17; I Cor. 1:22-
25; Jn. 2:13-25

Third Year: Ex. 3:1-8a, 13-15; I Cor.
10:1-6, 10-12; Lk. 13:
1-9

Anglican (Protestant Episcopal, 1945 Revision)
Morning Prayer: *Deut. 6:1-9, 20-25 or
Zech. 1:1-6, 12-17; I
Cor. 3 or Mk. 8:27–
9:1

Evening Prayer: Amos 5:4-15; Gal. 5:16-
24

Holy Communion: Eph. 5:1-14; Lk. 11:14-28

Lutheran Churches in America
Matins: Zech. 1:1-6, 12-17; Jn. 8:
42-51

Vespers: Amos 4:4-13; Rev. 2:1-7
Holy Communion: Jer. 26:1-15; Eph. 5:1-9;
Lk. 11:14-28

British Methodist
First Year, Morning: Job 2:1-13; Phil. 3:1-16
First Year, Evening: Gen. 11:1-9; Mt. 26:36-56

Second Year, Morning: Amos 3:1-6, 8-12; Lk.
22:47-71

Second Year, Evening: Gen. 25:19-34; Rom. 12:
1-21

Holy Communion: Eph. 5:1-14; Lk. 11:14-28

Church of Scotland
First Year, Morning: Gen. 11:1-9; Eph. 5:1-14;
Lk. 11:14-28 or Mt. 20:
17-28

First Year, Evening: Gen. 11:31–12:7; Lk. 15:
11-32

Second Year, Morning: Gen. 42:1-21; Acts 12:1-
11; Mt. 1:33-46 or
Lk. 13:31-35

Second Year, Evening: Gen. 43:1-14; II Cor. 4

American Presbyterians (Provisional)
First Year: Jer. 23:1-4; Eph. 5:1-10;
Mk. 10:17-22

Second Year: Ex. 2:1-15; Rom. 5:1-11;
Lk. 9:51-62

United Church of Canada
I Thess. 4:1-8; Mt. 15:21-28

Church of South India
Morning: Gen. 50:15-21; Col. 3:
12-17; Mt. 18:21-35

Evening: I Sam. 24; Mk. 11:19-26

Fourth Sunday in Lent

Roman Catholic Traditional
Gal. 4:22-31; Jn. 6:1-15

Roman Catholic Revised
First Year: I Sam. 16:1b, 6-7, 10-
13a; Eph. 5:8-14; Jn.
9:1-41

Second Year: II Chron. 36:14-16, 19-
23; Eph. 2:4-10; Jn. 3:
14-21

Third Year: Josh. 5:9a, 10-12; II Cor.
5:17-21; Lk. 15:1-3, 11-
32

THE LECTIONARY

Anglican (Protestant Episcopal, 1945 Revision)
Morning Prayer: Ex. 16:4-15 or *Ezek. 39: 21-29; Jn. 6:27-40 or II Cor. 3:12-18
Evening Prayer: Is. 55 or II Es. 2:15-32; Jn. 6:41-51 or Rev. 3: 1-12
Holy Communion: Gal. 4:21-31; Jn. 6:1-14

Lutheran Churches in America
Matins: Ex. 16:4-15; Jn. 6:35-51
Vespers: Is. 52:7-10; II Pet. 1:2-11
Holy Communion: Is. 55:1-7; Gal. 4:21-5: 1a; Jn. 6:1-15

British Methodist
First Year, Morning: Job 29:1-18, 30:1; Phil. 3:17-4:1, 4-9
First Year, Evening: Mic. 6:1-8; Mt. 26:57-75
Second Year, Morning: Amos 5:18-24; Lk. 23:1-25
Second Year, Evening: Gen. 29:1-20; I Pet. 2:11-25
Holy Communion: Gal. 4:21-31; Jn. 6:1-14

Church of Scotland
First Year, Morning: Gen. 13; Heb. 12:22-29; Jn. 6:1-14 or Mt. 18: 15-22
First Year, Evening: Gen. 18:16-33; Lk. 18:1-17
Second Year, Morning: Gen. 45; Phil. 3:7-15; Jn. 8:1-11 or Jn. 2:13-22
Second Year, Evening: Gen. 48; II Cor. 5:14-6: 10

American Presbyterians (Provisional)
First Year: Is. 51:4-6; I Jn. 3:7-14; Jn. 6:1-14
Second Year: Ex. 2:23-3:12; Rom. 6: 1-11; Lk. 13:10-21

United Church of Canada
Eph. 5:1-14; Lk. 11:14-28
Church of South India
Morning: Ex. 24:12-18; II Pet. 1: 16-19; Lk. 9:28-36
Evening: Ex. 34:29-35; II Cor. 3: 4-18

Passion Sunday

Roman Catholic Traditional
Heb. 9:11-15; Jn. 8:46-59
Roman Catholic Revised
First Year: Ez. 37:12-14; Rom. 8:8-11; Jn. 11:1-45
Second Year: Jer. 31:31-34; Heb. 5:7-9; Jn. 12:20-33
Third Year: Js. 43:16-21; Phil. 3:8-14; Jn. 8:1-11

Anglican (Protestant Episcopal, 1945 Revision)
Morning Prayer: *Is. 1:10-20 or Deut. 18:15-22; I Pet. 4:12-19 or Lk. 20:9-18
Evening Prayer: Hos. 6:1-6 or Jer. 14:7-21; Heb. 10:1-25 or Jn. 10:17-38
Holy Communion: Heb. 9:11-15; Jn. 8:46-59

Lutheran Churches in America
Matins: Is. 1:10-20; Mt. 10:32-42
Vespers: Hos. 6:1-6; I Cor. 1:21-31
Holy Communion: Num. 21:4-9; Heb. 9:11-15; Jn. 8:46-59

British Methodist
First Year, Morning: Job. 38:1-11, 31-36, 40: 2-4; II Cor. 5:1-19

First Year, Evening: Mic. 7:1-9, 18-19; Mt. 27:1-2, 11-31
Second Year, Morning: Amos 8:1-12; Lk. 23:26-49
Second Year, Evening: Gen. 32:22-32; I Pet. 3: 8-22
Holy Communion: Heb. 9:11-15; Jn. 8:46-59
Church of Scotland
First Year, Morning: Ex. 2:1-22; Heb. 9:11-22; Jn. 6:27-35 or Jn. 10:7-18
First Year, Evening: Ex. 6:1-13; Lk. 13:22-35
Second Year, Morning: Ex. 19:1-13; Heb. 9:11-22; Jn. 8:46-59 or Mt. 12:14-21
Second Year, Evening: Ex. 20:1-17; II Cor. 11: 22-12:11

American Presbyterians (Provisional)
First Year: Deut. 8:1-10; Heb. 9:11-14; Jn. 12:20-33
Second Year: Ex. 5:1-9; Rom. 8:28-39; Mk. 10:32-45

United Church of Canada
Heb. 12:22-24; Jn. 6:1-14
Church of South India
Morning: Job 19:21-27; Heb. 9:11-15; Mk. 10:35-45
Evening: Is. 44:1-8; Mt. 11:20-30

Palm Sunday

Roman Catholic Traditional
Phil. 2:5-11; Mt. 26—27
Roman Catholic Revised
Each Year: Is. 50:4-7

Each Year: Phil. 2:5-11
First Year: Mt. 26:14—27:66
Second Year: Mk. 14:1—15:47
Third Year: Lk. 22:14—23:56

153

Anglican (Protestant Episcopal, 1945 Revision)
Morning Prayer: *Zech. 9:9-12 or Is. 52:
13–53:12; Mk. 11:1-11
or Mt. 26

Evening Prayer: Jer. 8:9-15, 18–9:1 or
Is. 59:1-3, 9-11; I Cor.
1:17-31 or Jn. 12:20-
36

Holy Communion: Phil. 2:5-11; Mt. 27:1-54

Lutheran Churches in America
Matins: Is. 59:1-3, 9-16; Mk. 14:
3-9

Vespers: Jer. 8:9-15, 18-22; Heb.
12:1-11

Holy Communion: Zech. 9:9-12; Phil. 2:5-
11; Mt. 21:1-9 or Mt.
26:1–27:66

British Methodist
First Year, Morning: Zech. 9:9-12, 16; Mk. 11:
1-11
First Year, Evening: Ex. 11:1-8; Mt. 27:32-56
Second Year, Morning: Is. 59:12-20; Mt. 21:1-17
Second Year, Evening: Is. 52:13–53:12; Jn. 12:
20-36
Holy Communion: Phil. 2:5-11; Mt. 27:1-54

Church of Scotland
First Year, Morning: Zech. 9:9-14; Phil. 2:5-
11; Jn. 12:1-16 or Mt.
27:1-54
First Year, Evening: Mal. 3:1-12; Mk. 11:1-11
Second Year, Morning: Jer. 7:1-11; Phil. 2:5-11;
Mt. 21:1-11 or Mt. 27:
1-54
Second Year, Evening: Is. 59:1-2, 12-21; Lk. 19:
29-44

American Presbyterians (Provisional)
First Year: Is. 59:14-21; I Tim. 1:
12-17; Mk. 11:1-11
Second Year: Zech. 9:8-10; Heb. 12:1-
6; Lk. 19:29-44

United Church of Canada
Phil. 2:5-11; Mt. 26:1-27 or 27:1-54 or 21:1-9

Church of South India
Morning: Zech. 9:9-12; Phil. 2:5-
11; Mk. 15 or Jn. 12:
12-19
Evening: Gen. 22:1-14; Mk. 11:1-
11

Maundy Thursday

Roman Catholic Traditional
I Cor. 11:20-32; Jn. 13:1-15
Roman Catholic Revised
Each Year: Ex. 12:1-14; I Cor. 11:
23-29; Jn. 13:1-15
Anglican (Protestant Episcopal, 1945 Revision)
Morning Prayer: Jer. 31:31-34; Jn. 13:18-
38
Evening Prayer: Lam. 3:40-58; Jn. 17
Holy Communion: I Cor. 11:23-26; Lk. 23:
1-49 or Jn. 13:1-15

Lutheran Churches in America
Matins: Jer. 31:31-34; Lk. 22:14-
20
Vespers: Lam. 3:40-58; I Cor. 10:
16-17
Holy Communion: Ex. 12:1-14; I Cor. 11:
20-32; Jn. 13:1-15 or
Jn. 6:28-37

British Methodist
Morning: Ex. 16:2-15; Jn. 19:1-16a
Evening: Lev. 16:3-10, 20-22; Jn.
13:1-20

Church of Scotland
First Year, Morning: Is. 50:4-11; I Cor. 11:17-
34; Jn. 13:1-17 or Lk.
23:1-49
First Year, Evening: Ex. 24:1-11; Mt. 26:36-46
Second Year, Morning: Is. 50:4-11; I Cor. 11:17-
34; Mt. 26:17-30 or
Lk. 23:1-49
Second Year, Evening: Ex. 24:1-11; Jn. 17

American Presbyterians (Provisional)
First Year: Heb. 8:1-6; Jn. 13:1-17
Second Year: I Cor. 11:23-32; Jn. 13:
21-35

United Church of Canada
I Jn. 4:7-19 or I Cor. 11:23-28; Lk. 23 or 23:1-47
or Jn. 13:1-15 or Jn. 6:53-63

Church of South India
Morning: Jer. 31:31-34; Heb. 8:1-6;
Mk. 14:12-72
Evening: Is. 63:7-9; Jn. 13

Good Friday

Roman Catholic Traditional
Hos. 6:1-6; Ex. 12:1-11; Jn. 18:1–19:42
Roman Catholic Revised
Each Year: Is. 52:13–53:12; Heb. 4:
14-16; 5:7-9; Jn. 1–19:
42

Anglican (Protestant Episcopal, 1945 Revision)
Morning Prayer: Gen. 22:1-18 or Wis. 2:1,
12-24; Jn. 18
Evening Prayer: Is. 52:13–53:12; I Pet.
2:11-25

Holy Communion: Heb. 10:1-25; Jn. 19:1-37

Lutheran Churches in America
Matins: Gen. 22:1-18; Mt. 27:33-54
Vespers: Is. 52:13–53:12; Rev. 5:6-10
Holy Communion: Is. 53:4-12 or Hos. 6:1-6; Rev. 5:1-14; Jn. 18:1–19:42

British Methodist
First Year, Morning: Is. 52:13–53:12; Jn. 19:16b-37
First Year, Evening: Gen. 22:1-18; Lk. 23:26-49
Second Year, Morning: Num. 21:4-9; Mk. 15:16-41
Second Year, Evening: Ps. 22:1-8, 15-18, 22-24; Mt. 27:32-56
Holy Communion: Heb. 10:1-25; Jn. 19:1-37

Church of Scotland
First and Second Years, Morning: Is. 52:13–53:5; Heb. 10:1-25; Mt. 27:33-50 or Jn. 19:1-37
First Year, Evening: Gen. 22:1-19; Mk. 15:15-39
Second Year, Evening: Gen. 22:1-19; Lk. 23:33-46

American Presbyterians (Provisional)
First Year: Heb. 10:4-18; Jn. 19:17-42
Second Year: Rev. 5; Lk. 23:32-43

United Church of Canada
Is. 53; Heb. 10:4-25; Jn. 18, 19 or Jn. 19:1-37

Church of South India
Morning: Is. 52:13–53:12; Heb. 10:4-18; Jn. 18:1–19:16
Evening: Lam. 1:7-12; Jn. 19:17-42

Easter Day

Roman Catholic Traditional
First Mass: Col. 3:1-4; Mt. 28:1-7
Second Mass: I Cor. 5:7-8; Mk. 16:1-7

Roman Catholic Revised
Each Year: Acts 10:34a, 37-43; Col. 3:1-4; Jn. 20:1-9

Anglican (Protestant Episcopal, 1945 Revision)
Morning Prayer: *Is. 25:1-9 or Ex. 12:1-14; Mt. 28:1-10, 16-20 or Rev. 14:1-7, 12-13
Evening Prayer: Is. 51:9-16 or Is. 12; Lk. 24:13-35 or Jn. 20:11-18
Holy Communion: Col. 3:1-4 or I Cor. 5:6-8; Jn. 20:1-10 or Mk. 16:1-8

Lutheran Churches in America
Matins: Is. 25:1-9; Mt. 28:1-8
Vespers: Is. 51:9-16; Lk. 24:13-35
Holy Communion: Dan. 3:8-25 or Is. 25:6-9; I Cor. 5:7-8 or I Cor. 15:20-26; Mk. 16:1-7

British Methodist
First Year, Morning: Ex. 15:1-5, 10-13, 17-19; Lk. 23:50–24:12
First Year, Evening: Ex. 12:21-36; Lk. 24:13-35
Second Year, Morning: Ex. 12:1-14; Mt. 28:1-15

Second Year, Evening: Ex. 14:5-16, 21-27, 31; Mk. 15:42–16:8
Holy Communion: Col. 3:1-7; Jn. 20:1-10

Church of Scotland
First Year, Morning: Ex. 12:1-14; Col. 3:1-11; Jn. 20:1-10
First Year, Evening: Ex. 12:21-28, 40-42; Lk. 24:13-49
Second Year, Morning: Is. 25:1-9; Rev. 1:10-18; Lk. 24:1-12
Second Year, Evening: Ex. 15:1-18; Lk. 24:13-35

American Presbyterians (Provisional)
First Year: Is. 26:1-8 or Dan. 3:13-25; Col. 3:1-4 or Acts 1:1-5; Mk. 16:1-8 or Lk. 24:13-32
Second Year: Ex. 14:15-29 or Ex. 16:4-17; I Cor. 15:1-11 or Rev. 1:1-8; Mt. 28:1-20 or Jn. 20:1-18

United Church of Canada
Col. 3:1-11 or Rev. 1:10-18; Jn. 20:1-10 or Lk. 24:1-12

Church of South India
Morning: Ex. 15:1-11; Col. 3:1-4; Jn. 20:1-18
Evening: Is. 12; Lk. 24:13-35

First Sunday after Easter Day

Roman Catholic Traditional
I Jn. 5:4-10; Jn. 20:19-31

Roman Catholic Revised
First Year: Acts 2:42-47; I Pet. 1:3-9; Jn. 20:19-31
Second Year: Acts 4:32-35; I Jn. 5:1-6; Jn. 20:19-31

Third Year: Acts 5:12-16; Rev. 1:4-8; Jn. 20:19-31

Anglican (Protestant Episcopal, 1945 Revision)
Morning Prayer: Wis. 2:23–3:9 or *Is. 43:1-12; Rom. 1:1-12 or Lk. 24:36-49
Evening Prayer: Zeph. 3:14-20 or II Es.

2:33-48; Jn. 20:19-23 or
Rev. 1:4-18

Holy Communion: I Jn. 5:4-12; Jn. 20:19-23

Lutheran Churches in America
Matins: Is. 43:1-12; Jn. 21:15-19
Vespers: Zeph. 3:14-20; I Pet. 1: 17-2:3
Holy Communion: Gen. 32:22-30; I Jn. 5:4-12; Jn. 20:19-31

British Methodist
First Year, Morning: I Kings 17:8-24; Jn. 20: 19-31
First Year, Evening: Ex. 13:3-16; Jn. 14:1-14
Second Year, Morning: Lev. 23:1-14; Rev. 5:1-14
Second Year, Evening: Job 19:1-9, 21-29; Jn. 21: 1-19
Holy Communion: I Jn. 5:4-12; Jn. 20:19-23

Church of Scotland
First Year, Morning: Ex. 14:1-22; Rom. 6:1-14; Jn. 20:19-31

First Year, Evening: Ex. 16:1-15; Jn. 41:1-14
Second Year, Morning: Ex. 32:1-20; Acts 13:26-33a; Lk. 24:36-49
Second Year, Evening: Ex. 33; Rev. 1

American Presbyterians (Provisional)
First Year: Ex. 17:1-6; I Jn. 5:1-12; Jn. 21:1-12
Second Year: Ex. 15:1-13; I Cor. 15:12-20; Jn. 20:19-31

United Church of Canada
Acts 10:34-43 or 13:26-33a or Rom. 6:2-11; Lk. 24:13-35 or 24:36-49

Church of South India
Morning: Zeph. 3:14-20; I Jn. 5:1-12; Jn. 20:19-31
Evening: II Kings 6:8-23; Jn. 11: 17-44

Second Sunday after Easter Day

Roman Catholic Traditional
I Pet. 2:21-25; Jn. 10:11-16

Roman Catholic Revised
First Year: Acts 2:14, 22-28; I Pet. 1:17-21; Lk. 24:13-35
Second Year: Acts 3:13-15, 17-19; I Jn. 2:1-5a; Lk. 24:35-48
Third Year: Acts 5:27-32; Rev. 5:11-14; Jn. 21:1-19

Anglican (Protestant Episcopal, 1945 Revision)
Morning Prayer: *Is. 50:1-11 or Bar. 4:21-30; Jn. 10:1-10 or Phil. 3:7-16
Evening Prayer: Ezek. 34:11-16, 30-31 or II Es. 8:20-30, 46, 51-54; Jn. 21:1-19 or I Cor. 15:12-23
Holy Communion: I Pet. 2:19-25; Jn. 10:11-16

Lutheran Churches in America
Matins: Is. 40:1-11; Jn. 10:22-30
Vespers: Ezek. 34:24-31; Heb. 13: 20-21
Holy Communion: Ezek. 34:11-16; I Pet. 2: 21b-25; Jn. 10:11-16

British Methodist
First Year, Morning: Deut. 4:1, 23-35; Lk. 7:1-17

First Year, Evening: Ex. 13:17-22; Jn. 15:1-11
Second Year, Morning: Ex. 19:1-11, 16-20; I Cor. 15:1-11
Second Year, Evening: Lam. 3:22-33; Jn. 11:1-16
Holy Communion: I Pet. 2:19-25; Jn. 10:11-16

Church of Scotland
First Year, Morning: Lev. 6:1-13; I Pet. 2:11-25; Jn. 10:1-10
First Year, Evening: Deut. 6:1-15; Jn. 21:15-25
Second Year, Morning: Num. 13:1-3, 17-33; Rev. 21:10-14, 21-27; Jn. 10: 11-16
Second Year, Evening: Num. 14:1-24; I Cor. 15: 1-22

American Presbyterians (Provisional)
First Year: Is. 26:16-19; I Pet. 2: 21-25; Jn. 21:13-19
Second Year: Is. 25:1-9; I Cor. 15:21-28; Jn. 14:1-14

United Church of Canada
I Jn. 5:4-12; Jn. 20:19-31

Church of South India
Morning: Ezek. 34:11-16; I Pet. 2: 18-25; Jn. 10:7-18
Evening: Jer. 23:1-8; Lk. 15:1-7

Third Sunday after Easter Day

Roman Catholic Traditional
I Pet. 2:11-19; Jn. 16:16-22

Roman Catholic Revised
First Year: Acts 2:36-41; I Pet. 2: 20b-25; Jn. 10:1-10

Second Year: Acts 4:8-12; I Jn. 1:5-9; Lk. 24:36-43
Third Year: Acts 13:16, 26-33; I Jn. 3:1-2; Jn. 10:11-18

Anglican (Protestant Episcopal, 1945 Revision)
Morning Prayer: II Sam. 12:15b-23 or *I Sam. 2:1b-10; Jn. 14:1-14 or Acts 2:22-36
Evening Prayer: Is. 26:12-16, 19 or Wis. 5:1-6, 14-16; II Cor. 5 or Lk. 20:27-39
Holy Communion: I Pet. 2:11-17; Jn. 16:16-22

Lutheran Churches in America
Matins: II Sam. 12:15b-23; Jn. 14:1-14
Vespers: Prov. 4:7-18; Heb. 4:14-16
Holy Communion: Is. 40:25-31; I Pet. 2:11-40; Jn. 16:16-22

British Methodist
First Year, Morning: Deut. 6:4-9, 17-25; Lk. 8:40-56
First Year, Evening: Ex. 15:20-27; Jn. 15:12-27
Second Year, Morning: Ex. 32:1-6, 15-24, 30-35; I Cor. 15:12-28

Second Year, Evening: Is. 43:1-13; Jn. 11:17-28
Holy Communion: I Pet. 2:11-17; Jn. 16:16-22

Church of Scotland
First Year, Morning: Lev. 19:1-18; Rev. 22:1-5; Jn. 16:16-22
First Year, Evening: Deut. 8; Jn. 11:1-29
Second Year, Morning: Num. 21:1-9; I Cor. 15:20-28; Jn. 14:1-13
Second Year, Evening: Num. 22:1-21; I Cor. 15:42-58

American Presbyterians (Provisional)
First Year: Job 19:23-27; I Pet. 2:11-17; Jn. 10:11-16
Second Year: Is. 58:6-14; I Cor. 15:35-50; Jn. 15:1-17

United Church of Canada·
I Pet. 2:19-25; Jn. 10:11-16
Church of South India
Morning: Is. 60:15-19; II Cor. 4:1-6; Jn. 9:1-11
Evening: Zech. 14:1-7; Acts 26:1-20

Fourth Sunday after Easter Day

Roman Catholic Traditional
Jas. 1:17-21; Jn. 16:5-14
Roman Catholic Revised
First Year: Acts 6:1-7; I Pet. 2:4-9; Jn. 14:1-12
Second Year: Acts 9:26-31; I Jn. 3:18-24; Jn. 15:1-8
Third Year: Acts 14:20b-26; Rev. 21:1-5a; Jn. 13:31-33a, 34-35

Anglican (Protestant Episcopal, 1945 Revision)
Morning Prayer: *Job 19:21-27a or Ezek. 37:1-14; Jn. 12:44-50 or Acts 3:1-21
Evening Prayer: Dan. 12:1-4, 13 or Is. 60:13-22; I Thess. 4:13-18 or Jn. 8:12-30
Holy Communion: Jas. 1:17-21; Jn. 16:5-15
Lutheran Churches in America
Matins: Ezek. 37:1-14; Jn. 8:21-36
Vespers: Dan. 12:1-4, 13; II Cor. 5:14-21
Holy Communion: Is. 29:9-14; Jas. 1:17-21; Jn. 16:4b-15

British Methodist
First Year, Morning: Deut. 10:12-15, 17–11:1; Lk. 16:19-31

First Year, Evening: Ex. 16:2-15; Jn. 16:1-15
Second Year, Morning: Ex. 33:5-23; I Cor. 15:35-49
Second Year, Evening: Is. 62:1-12; Jn. 11:32-46
Holy Communion: Jas. 1:17-21; Jn. 16:5-15

Church of Scotland
First Year, Morning: Lev. 23:1-14; Jas. 1:17-27; Jn. 16:2-15
First Year, Evening: Deut. 26:1-11, 16-19; Jn. 11:30-54
Second Year, Morning: Num. 23:1-12; II Cor. 5:17-21; Jn. 16:2-15
Second Year, Evening: Num. 23:13-26; II Cor. 5:1-15

American Presbyterians (Provisional)
First Year: Mal. 3:16–4:3; Rom. 14:10-19; Jn. 16:1-15
Second Year: Is. 63:7-9; I Cor. 15:50-58; Jn. 16:16-33

United Church of Canada
I Pet. 2:11-17; Jn. 16:16-22

Church of South India
Morning: Prov. 4:10-18; I Jn. 1:1-4; Jn. 14:1-11
Evening: Is. 30:19-26; Jn. 16:1-15

Fifth Sunday after Easter Day

Roman Catholic Traditional
Jas. 1:22-27; Jn. 16:23-30

Roman Catholic Revised
First Year: Acts 8:5-8, 14-17; I Pet.
         3:15-18; Jn. 14:15-21
Second Year: Acts 10:25-26, 34-35, 44-
         48; I Jn. 4:7-10; Jn.
         15:9-17
Third Year: Acts 15:1-2, 22-29; Rev.
         21:10-14, 22-23; Jn. 14:
         23-29

Anglican (Protestant Episcopal, 1945 Revision)
Morning Prayer: *Ezek. 34:25-31 or II Es.
         14:27-35; Lk. 11:1-13
         or Acts 4:1-13, 33
Evening Prayer: Is. 48:12-21 or Ezek. 36:
         25-38; Rev. 5 or Mk.
         11:22-26
Holy Communion: Jas. 1:22-27; Jn. 16:23-33

Lutheran Churches in America
Matins: Ezek. 34:22-31; Jn. 17:1-
         19
Vespers: Is. 48:12-21; Rom. 8:24-
         28
Holy Communion: Is. 55:6-11; Jas. 1:22-27;
         Jn. 16:23b-30

British Methodist
First Year, Morning: Deut. 11:13-28; Jn. 16:
         16-33

First Year, Evening: Num. 14:11-24; Jn. 17:1-
         6, 9-11, 15-17, 20-26
Second Year, Morning: Dan. 9:1-10, 16-19; Rev.
         3:7-22
Second Year, Evening: Is. 65:17-24; Lk. 11:1-13
Holy Communion: Jas. 1:22-27; Jn. 16:23-33

Church of Scotland
First Year, Morning: Lev. 26:1-17; Jas. 3:2-13;
         Jn. 16:23-33
First Year, Evening: Deut. 28:1-14; Jn. 12:1-
         11
Second Year, Morning: Num. 24:10-25; I Jn. 2:
         7-17; Jn. 16:23-33
Second Year, Evening: Num. 27:12-23; Jas. 1:22-
         27

American Presbyterians (Provisional)
First Year: Is. 56:6-8; Jas. 1:22-27;
         Jn. 16:22-33
Second Year: Zech. 8:1-8; Eph. 1:15-
         23; Lk. 24:36-53

United Church of Canada
Jas. 1:17-21; Jn. 16:2-15

Church of South India
Morning: Dan. 7:9-14; Eph. 4:1-10;
         Jn. 16:25-33
Evening: Gen. 28:10-22; Mk. 14:
         55-62

Ascension Day

Roman Catholic Traditional
Acts 1:1-11; Mk. 16:14-20

Roman Catholic Revised
Each Year: Acts 1:1-11
Each Year: Eph. 1:17-23
First Year: Mt. 28:16-20
Second Year: Mk. 16:15-20
Third Year: Lk. 24:46-53

Anglican (Protestant Episcopal, 1945 Revision)
Morning Prayer: Dan. 7:9-10, 13-14; Eph.
         4:1-16
Morning Prayer: Is. 33:5-6, 17, 20-22; Heb.
         4:14–5:10
Holy Communion: Acts 1:1-11; Lk. 24:49-
         53

Lutheran Churches in America
Matins: Dan. 7:9-10, 13-14; Lk.
         24:45-53
Vespers: Is. 33:5-6, 17, 20-22; Eph.
         1:3-14
Holy Communion: II Kings 2:9-15 or Gen.
         5:21-24; Acts 1:1-11;
         Mk. 16:14-40

British Methodist
First Year, Morning: Ex. 24:1-18; Acts 1:1-14
First Year, Evening: Dan. 7:9-10, 13-14; Mt.
         28:16-20
Second Year, Morning: II Kings 2:1-15; Lk. 24:
         36-53
Second Year, Evening: Deut. 34:1-12; Rev. 19:6-
         16
Holy Communion: Acts 1:1-11; Mk. 16:14-20

Church of Scotland
First Year, Morning: II Kings 2:1-15; Acts 1:1-
         11; Lk. 24:44-53
First Year, Evening: Deut. 34; Heb. 4
Second Year, Morning: Dan. 7:9-14; Eph. 4:1-
         16; Lk. 24:44-53
Second Year, Evening: Ex. 24; Heb. 4

American Presbyterians (Provisional)
Gen. 5:21-24; Acts 1:1-11; Lk. 24:36-53

United Church of Canada
Acts 1:1-11 or Rev. 5; Mk. 16:14-20 or Lk. 24:44-53

Church of South India
Morning: II Kings 2:1-15; Acts 1:1-
         11; Lk. 24:44-53
Evening: Is. 65:17-25; Acts 1:12-26

Sixth Sunday after Easter Day
or Ascension Sunday

Roman Catholic Traditional
I Pet. 4:7-11; Jn. 15:26–16:4

Roman Catholic Revised

First Year: Acts 1:12-14; I Pet. 4:13-16; Jn. 17:1-11a

Second Year: Acts 1:15-17, 20-26; I Jn. 4:11-16; Jn. 17:11b-19

Third Year: Acts 7:55-60; Rev. 22:12-14, 16-17, 20; Jn. 17: 20-26

Anglican (Protestant Episcopal, 1945 Revision)

Morning Prayer: *Is. 33:5-6, 17, 20-22 or Is. 4:2-6 or Is. 65:17-25; Jn. 17 or Heb. 4: 14–5:10 or Rev. 41:1-14, 21-27

Evening Prayer: Wis. 9 or Is. 32:1-4, 15-20 or Dan. 7:9-10, 13-14; Eph. 1 or Jn. 3:16-21, 31-36a or Rev. 22

Holy Communion: I Pet. 4:7-11; Jn. 15:26–16:4

Lutheran Churches in America

Matins: Is. 4:2-6; Jn. 17:20-26

Vespers: Is. 32:13-20; Rom. 8:29-39

Holy Communion: Is. 32:14-20; I Pet. 4:7b-11; Jn. 15:26–16:4a

British Methodist

First Year, Morning: II Kings 2:1-15; Acts 1:1-14 or Heb. 1:1-12

First Year, Evening: Jer. 31:1-13; Eph. 4:1-16

Second Year, Morning: Dan. 7:9-10, 13-14; Lk. 24:36-53 or Mk. 16:9-20

Second Year, Evening: Ex. 24:1-18; Heb. 2:1-10

Holy Communion: I Pet. 4:7-11; Jn. 15:26–16:4

Church of Scotland

First Year, Morning: Dan. 7:9-14; Heb. 4; Mt. 28:16-20

First Year, Evening: Ex. 24; Acts 1:1-11

Second Year, Morning: II Kings 2:1-15; Acts 1:1-11; Mt. 28:16-20

Second Year, Evening: Deut. 34; Phil. 2:1-11

American Presbyterians (Provisional)

First Year: Joel 2:23-27; I Pet. 4:7-11; Lk. 11:5-13

Second Year: Dan. 7:9-14; I Jn. 2:28–3:3; Lk. 21:29-36

United Church of Canada
I Pet. 4:7-11 or Eph. 4:1-13; Jn. 15:26–16:4a or Jn. 14:12-21

Church of South India

Morning: Gen. 14:14-20; Heb. 4: 14-16; Jn. 12:20-33

Evening: Ex. 28:1-6, 15-30; Jn. 17: 1-19

Pentecost Sunday
or Whitsunday

Roman Catholic Traditional
Acts 2:1-11; Jn. 14:23-31

Roman Catholic Revised
Acts 2:1-11; I Cor. 12:4-7, 12-13; Jn. 20:19-23

Anglican (Protestant Episcopal, 1945 Revision)

Morning Prayer: Wis. 1:1-7 or *Joel 2:28-32; Jn. 4:19-26 or Rom. 8:1-11

Evening Prayer: Wis. 7:22–8:1 or Is. 11:1-9; I Cor. 2 or Jn. 6:53-69

Holy Communion: Acts 2:1-11 or I Cor. 12: 4-14; Jn. 14:15-31 or Lk. 11:9-13

Lutheran Churches in America

Matins: Ezek. 36:22-28; Jn. 14:15-21

Vespers: Is. 11:1-9; Acts 2:14-21

Holy Communion: Joel 2:28-32; Acts 2:1-11; Jn. 14:23-31a

British Methodist

First Year, Morning: Joel 2:28-32; Acts 2:1-13

First Year, Evening: Ezek. 36:22-28, 35-36; Rom. 8:1-17

Second Year, Morning: Ezek. 37:1-14; Acts 2:1-13

Second Year, Evening: Num. 11:16-17, 24-29; Jn. 14:15-31

Holy Communion: Acts 2:1-11; Jn. 14:15-31

Church of Scotland

First Year, Morning: Is. 11:1-10; Acts 2:1-11; Jn. 3:16-21

First Year, Evening: Joel 2:21-32; Rom. 8:1-18

Second Year, Morning: Is. 61; Acts 10:34-48a; Jn. 14:15-31

Second Year, Evening: Ezek. 37:1-14; Jn. 14:15-31

American Presbyterians (Provisional)

First Year: Ezek. 37:1-14; Acts 10:34-48; Jn. 20:19-23

Second Year: Ex. 19:1-11; Acts 2:1-21;
Jn. 14:23-31

United Church of Canada
Joel 2:23-32 or Ezek. 37:1-14; Acts 2:1-11 or 10:34-
48a; Jn. 3:16-21 or 10:1-10 or 14:15-31

Church of South India
Morning: Joel 2:28-32; Acts 2:1-12;
Jn. 14:15-26
Evening: Num. 11:16, 24-29; I Cor.
12:1-13

First Sunday after Pentecost
or Trinity Sunday

Roman Catholic Traditional
Rom. 11:33-36; Mt. 28:18-20

Roman Catholic Revised
First Year: Ex. 34:4b-6, 8-9; II Cor.
13:11-13; Jn. 3:16-18
Second Year: Deut. 4:32-34, 39-40;
Rom. 8:14-17; Mt. 28:
16-20
Third Year: Prov. 8:22-31; Rom. 5:1-
5; Jn. 16:12-15

Anglican (Protestant Episcopal, 1945 Revision)
Morning Prayer: *Is. 6:1-8 or Gen. 1:1–
2:3; I Pet. 1:1-12 or
Jn. 1:1-18
Evening Prayer: Ecclus. 43:1-12, 27-33 or
Job 38:1-11, 16-18, 42:
1-6; Eph. 4:1-16 or Jn.
1:29-34
Holy Communion: Rev. 4:1-11; Jn. 3:1-15

Lutheran Churches in America
Matins: Gen. 1:1–2:3; Mt. 28:19-
20
Vespers: Job 38:1-11, 16-18; II
Cor. 13:11-14
Holy Communion: Is. 6:1-8; Rom. 11:33-36;
Mt. 28:18-20 or Jn. 3:
1-15

British Methodist
First Year, Morning: Is. 6:1-8; Jn. 3:1-21
First Year, Evening: Ex. 34:1-10, 29-35; I Pet.
1:1-21
Second Year, Morning: Ex. 2:23–3:14; Rev. 4:1-
11
Second Year, Evening: Is. 63:7-16; Mt. 28:16-20
Holy Communion: Rev. 4:1-11; Jn. 3:1-15

Church of Scotland
First Year, Morning: Is. 6:1-8; Rev. 4:1-11; Jn.
3:1-15
First Year, Evening: Ex. 3:1-15; Mt. 28:16-20
Second Year, Morning: Is. 63:7-19; Rev. 4:1-11;
Jn. 4:1-26
Second Year, Evening: Job 23:3-10; I Pet. 1:1-12

American Presbyterians (Provisional)
First Year: Is. 61:1-7; Rom. 11:33-
36; Mt. 3:13-17
Second Year: Is. 6:1-8; I Pet. 1:10-21;
Jn. 4:7-24

United Church of Canada
Eph. 2:11-22 or 4:1-16; Mt. 16:13-18

Church of South India
Morning: Is. 6:1-8; Rev. 4; Mt.
28:16-20
Evening: Ezek. 1:15–2:2; Eph. 1:3-
14

Cross-reference comparisons between the lectionaries of several denominations is complicated after Pentecost or Trinity Sundays because not all churches number the Sundays the same. Most use the designation "Sundays after Trinity," though the more ancient usage is "Sundays after Pentecost." The latter terminology is being restored in some measure among churches which have been revising their liturgies in recent years.

The numbering system alone is not the main complication in arranging comparisons, however. The major complicating factor is the variations in adjusting the end of Post-Pentecost or Post-Trinity to the start of the fixed season of Advent. The number of Sundays after Pentecost or after Trinity is not the same every year, because both Pentecost Sunday and Trinity Sunday (always the next Sunday after Pentecost) are determined by the movable date of Easter Day. Advent, on the other hand, always begins four Sundays before Christmas Day. Accordingly, some years will include more Sundays after Pentecost or after Trinity than others. Different churches adjust between Post-Pentecost or Post-Trinity and Advent in slightly different ways, either by providing additional readings for longer Post-Pentecost or Post-Trinity seasons or by substituting readings from the Post-Epiphany season, which also may have more or fewer Sundays in any given year because of the movable date of Easter Day.

This situation is further complicated when the American Methodist or provisional American Presbyterian lectionaries are compared with those of more traditionally liturgical churches. The newer Methodist and Presbyterian lectionaries not only provide for adjustments just before Advent but also provide readings for more or fewer sets of lessons to match the number of Sundays which may occur in the division of Post-Pentecost or Post-Trinity into new seasons called by Methodists "Kingdomtide" and suggested by Presbyterians as "The Season of God the Father." Kingdomtide may include either thirteen or fourteen Sundays. The Season of God the Father is provided with readings for as many as eight Sundays.

Roman Catholic Traditional: Post-Pentecost

Sundays are numbered after Pentecost Sunday, although the first Sunday is named Trinity Sunday and the second Sunday is within the Octave of Corpus Christi. Epistles and Gospels are appointed for all Sundays through the Twenty-fourth after Pentecost. In years when more than twenty-four Sundays after Pentecost occur, Epistles and Gospels are supplied from the lectionary for the Fourth, Fifth and Sixth Sundays after Epiphany as may be required. In any year, however, the lessons for the Twenty-fourth Sunday after Pentecost are always to be read on the Sunday before Advent. The Post-Pentecost lectionary is as follows:

Second Sunday after Pentecost
I Jn. 3:13-18; Lk. 14:16-24

Third Sunday after Pentecost
I Pet. 5:6-11; Lk. 15:1-10

Fourth Sunday after Pentecost
Rom. 8:18-23; Lk. 5:1-11

Fifth Sunday after Pentecost
I Pet. 3:8-15; Mt. 5:20-24

Sixth Sunday after Pentecost
Rom. 6:3-11; Mk. 8:1-9

Seventh Sunday after Pentecost
Rom. 6:19-23; Mt. 7:15-21

Eighth Sunday after Pentecost
Rom. 8:12-17; Lk. 16:1-9

Ninth Sunday after Pentecost
I Cor. 10:6-13; Lk. 19:41-47

Tenth Sunday after Pentecost
I Cor. 12:2-11; Lk. 18:9-14

Eleventh Sunday after Pentecost
I Cor. 15:1-10; Mk. 7:31-37

Twelfth Sunday after Pentecost
II Cor. 3:4-9; Lk. 10:22-37

Thirteenth Sunday after Pentecost
Gal. 3:16-22; Lk. 17:11-19

Fourteenth Sunday after Pentecost
Gal. 5:16-24; Mt. 6:24-33

Fifteenth Sunday after Pentecost
Gal. 5:25—6:10; Lk. 7:11-16

Sixteenth Sunday after Pentecost
Eph. 3:13-21; Lk. 14:1-11

Seventeenth Sunday after Pentecost
Eph. 4:1-6; Mt. 22:35-46

Eighteenth Sunday after Pentecost
I Cor. 1:4-8; Mt. 9:1-8

Nineteenth Sunday after Pentecost
Eph. 4:23-28; Mt. 22:1-14

Twentieth Sunday after Pentecost
Eph. 5:15-21; Jn. 9:46-53

Twenty-first Sunday after Pentecost
Eph. 6:10-17; Mt. 27:23-35

Twenty-second Sunday after Pentecost
Phil. 1:6-11; Mt. 22:15-21

Twenty-third Sunday after Pentecost
Phil. 3:17—4:3; Mt. 9:18-26

Twenty-fourth Sunday after Pentecost
Col. 1:9-14; Mt. 24:15-35

Roman Catholic Revised: Post-Pentecost

The following table of lessons provides for two variable sequences of Sundays, the number of which any year depends on the date of Easter Day. Beginning the second Sunday after Epiphany Day (January 6) the lessons of this table are to be used in order until Lent for as many Sundays as necessary in any one year. Similarly, after Trinity Sunday (which follows Pentecost Sunday) the lessons from this table are resumed wherever they were discontinued at the end of the Sundays after Epiphany Day and are used in the post-Pentecost season for as many Sundays as may be needed. In some years there are thirty-four Sundays for which no specified lessons are prescribed; in other years, only thirty-three such Sundays. This table provides for all the Sundays for which no other particular lessons are otherwise listed in the Lectionary. To accommodate the difference between years with thirty-four such Sundays and the years with only thirty-three, one set of lessons in this table may be omitted when the post-Pentecost weeks begin. When this is done, the lessons omitted are the next set from the ones used for the Sundays after Epiphany Day. Always to be read, however, are the lessons for the last three Sundays in this table; they are provided for the three Sundays before Advent. Only to separate each set of lessons in the following table, the writer of this chapter has numbered each of the sets, and these numbers have no special meaning.

1.

First Year: Is. 49:3, 5-6; I Cor. 1:1-3; Jn. 1:29-34

Second Year: I Sam. 3:3b-10; I Cor. 6:13c-15a; Jn. 1:35-42

Third Year: Is. 62:1-5; I Cor. 12:4-11; Jn. 2:1-12

2.

First Year: Is. 9:1-4; I Cor. 1:10-13, 17; Mt. 4:12-23

Second Year: Jon. 3:1-5, 10; I Cor. 7:29-31; Mk. 1:14-20

Third Year: Neh. 8:1-4a, 5-6, 8-10; I Cor. 12:12-30; Lk. 1:1-4; 4:14-21

3.

First Year: Wis. 2:3–3:12-13; I Cor. 1:26-31; Mt. 5:1-12a

Second Year: Deut. 18:15-20; I Cor. 7:32-35; Mk. 1:21-28

Third Year: Jer. 1:4-5, 17-19; I Cor. 12:31–13: 13; Lk. 4:21-30

4.

First Year: Is. 58:7-10; I Cor. 2:1-5; Mt. 5:13-16

Second Year: Job 7:1-4, 6-7; I Cor. 9:16-19, 22-23; Mk. 1:29-39

Third Year: Is. 6:1-2a, 3-8; I Cor. 15:1-11; Lk. 5:1-11

5.

First Year: Ecclus. 15:16-21; I Cor. 2:6-10; Mt. 5:17-37

Second Year: Lev. 13:1-2, 44-46; I Cor. 10:31–11:1; Mk. 1:40-45

Third Year: Jer. 17:5-8; I Cor. 15:12, 16-20; Lk. 6:17, 20-26

6.

First Year: Lev. 19:1-2, 17-18; I Cor. 3:16-23; Mt. 5:38-48

Second Year: Is. 43:18-19, 21-22, 24b-25; II Cor. 1:18-22; Mk. 2:1-12

Third Year: I Sam. 26:2, 7-9, 12-13, 22-23; I Cor. 15:45-49; Lk. 6:27-38

7.

First Year: Is. 49:14-15; I Cor. 4:1-5; Mt. 6:24-34

Second Year: Hos. 2:14b, 15b, 19-20; II Cor. 3: 1b-6; Mk. 2:18-22

Third Year: Ecclus. 27:5-8; I Cor. 15:54-58; Lk. 6:39-45

8.

First Year: Deut. 11:18, 26-28; Rom. 3:21-25a, 28; Mt. 7:21-27

Second Year: Deut. 5:12-15; II Cor. 4:6-11; Mk. 2:23–3:6

Third Year: I Kings 8:41-43; Gal. 1:1-2, 6-10; Lk. 7:1-10

9.

First Year: Ex. 19:2-6a; Rom. 5:6-11; Mt. 9: 36–10:8

Second Year: Ezek. 17:22-24; II Cor. 5:6-10; Mk. 4:26-34

Third Year: II Sam. 12:7-10; Gal. 2:16, 19-21; Lk. 7:36–8:3

10.

First Year: Jer. 20:10-13; Rom. 5:12-15; Mt. 10:26-33

Second Year: Job 38:1, 8-11; II Cor. 5:14-17; Mk. 4:35-40

Third Year: Zech. 12:10-11; Gal. 3:26-29; Lk. 9:18-24

11.

First Year: II Kings 4:8-11; Rom. 6:3-4, 8-11; Mt. 10:37-42

Second Year: Wis. 1:13-15, 2:23-25; II Cor. 8:7, 9, 13-15; Mk. 5:21-43

Third Year: I Kings 19:16b, 19-21; Gal. 4:31b– 5:1, 13-18; Lk. 9:51-62

12.

First Year: Zech. 9:9-10; Rom. 8:9, 11-13; Mt. 11:25-30

13.

Second Year: Ezek. 2:2-5; II Cor. 12:7-10; Mk. 6:1-6

Third Year: Is. 66:10-14c; Gal. 6:14-18; Lk. 10: 1-12, 17-20

14.

First Year: Is. 55:10-11; Rom. 8:18-23; Mt. 13: 1-23

Second Year: Amos 7:12-15; Eph. 1:3-14; Mk. 6:7-13

Third Year: Deut. 30:10-14; Col. 1:15-20; Lk. 10:25-37

15.

First Year: Wis. 12:13, 16-19; Rom. 8:26-27; Mk. 13:24-43

Second Year: Jer. 23:1-6; Eph. 2:13-18; Mk. 6: 30-34

Third Year: Gen. 18:1-10a; Col. 1:24-28; Lk. 10:38-42

16.

First Year: I Kings 3:5, 7-12; Rom. 8:28-30; Mk. 13:44-52

Second Year: II Kings 4:42-44; Eph. 4:1-6; Jn. 6:1-15

Third Year: Gen. 18:20-32; Col. 2:12-14; Lk. 11:1-13

17.

First Year: Is. 55:1-3; Rom. 8:35, 37-39; Mk. 14:13-21

Second Year: Ex. 16:2-4, 12-15; Eph. 4:17, 20-24; Jn. 6:24-35

Third Year: Eccles. 1:2, 2:21-23; Col. 3:1-5, 9- 11; Lk. 12:13-21

18.

First Year: I Kings 19:9a, 11-13a; Rom. 9:1-5; Mt. 14:22-33

Second Year: I Kings 19:4-8; Eph. 4:30–5:2; Jn. 6:41-52

Third Year: Wis. 18:6-9; Heb. 11:1, 2, 8-19; Lk. 12:32-48

19.

First Year: Is. 56:1, 6-7; Rom. 11:13-15, 29-32; Mt. 15:21-28

Second Year: Prov. 9:1-6; Eph. 5:15-20; Jn. 6:51- 59

Third Year: Jer. 38:4-6, 8-10; Heb. 12:1-4; Lk. 12:49-53

20.

First Year: Is. 22:19-23; Rom. 11:33-36; Mt. 16:13-20

Second Year: Josh. 24:1-2a, 15-17, 18b; Eph. 5: 21-32; Jn. 6:61-70

Third Year: Is. 66:18-21; Heb. 12:5-7, 11-13; Lk. 13:22-30

21.

First Year: Jer. 20:7-9; Rom. 12:1-2; Mt. 16: 21-27

Second Year: Deut. 4:1-2, 6-8; Jas. 1:17-18, 21b 22, 27; Mk. 7:1-8a, 14-15, 21-23

Third Year: Ecclus. 3:19-21, 30-31; Heb. 12:18- 19, 22-24a; Lk. 14:1, 7-14

22.

First Year: Ezek. 33:7-9; Rom. 13:8-10; Mt. 18:15-20

Second Year: Is. 35:4-7a; Jas. 2:1-5; Mk. 7:31-37

Third Year: Wis. 9:13-19; Philem. 9b-10, 12-17; Lk. 14:25-33

23.

First Year: Ecclus. 27:33–28:9; Rom. 14:7-9; Mt. 18:21-35

Second Year: Is. 50:5-9a; Jas. 2:14-18; Mk. 8:27- 35

Third Year: Ex. 32:7-11, 13-14; I Tim. 1:12-17; Lk. 15:1-32

24.

First Year: Is. 55:6-9; Phil. 1:20c-24, 27a; Mt. 20:1-16a

Second Year: Wis. 2:17-20; Jas. 3:16–4:3; Mk. 9:29-36

Third Year: Amos 8:4-7; I Tim. 2:1-8; Lk. 16: 1-13

25.

First Year: Ezek. 18:25-28; Phil. 2:1-11; Mt. 21:28-32

Second Year: Num. 11:25-29; Jas. 5:1-6; Mk. 9:
37-42, 44, 46-47

Third Year: Amos 6:1a, 4-7; I Tim. 6:11-16; Lk.
16:19-31

26.

First Year: Is. 5:1-7; Phil. 4:6-9; Mt. 21:33-43

Second Year: Gen. 2:18-24; Heb. 2:9-11; Mk. 10:
2-16

Third Year: Hab. 1:2-3; 2:2-4; II Tim. 1:6-8,
13-14; Lk. 17:5-10

27.

First Year: Is. 25:6-10a; Phil. 4:12-14, 19-20; Mt.
22:1-14

Second Year: Wis. 7:7-11; Heb. 4:12-13; Mk. 10:
17-30

Third Year: II Kings 5:14-17; II Tim. 2:8-13;
Lk. 17:11-19

28.

First Year: Is. 45:1, 4-6; I Thess. 1:1-5b; Mt.
22:15-21

Second Year: Is. 53:10-11; Heb. 4:14-16; Mk. 10:
35-45

Third Year: Ex. 17:8-13; II Tim. 3:14–4:2; Lk.
18:1-8

29.

First Year: Ex. 22:21-27; I Thess. 1:5c-10;
Mt. 22:34-40

Second Year: Jer. 31:7-9; Heb. 5:1-6; Mk. 10:46-
52

Third Year: Ecclus. 35:15b-17, 20-22a; II Tim.
4:6-8, 16-18; Lk. 18:9-14

30.

First Year: Mal. 1:14b–2:2b, 8-10; I Thess. 2:
7b-9, 13; Mt. 23:1-12

Second Year: Deut. 6:2-6; Heb. 7:23-28; Mk. 12:
28b-34

Third Year: Wis. 11:23–12:2; II Thess. 1:11–2:
2; Lk. 19:1-10

31.

First Year: Wis. 6:13-17; I Thess. 4:12-17; Mt.
25:1-13

Second Year: I Kings 17:10-16; Heb. 9:24-28;
Mk. 12:38-44

Third Year: II Macc. 7:1-2, 9-14; II Thess. 2:15–
3:5; Lk. 20:27-38

32.

First Year: Prov. 31:10-13, 19-20, 30-31; I
Thess. 5:1-6; Mt. 25:14-30

Second Year: Dan. 12:1-3; Heb. 10:11-14, 18;
Mk. 13:24-32

Third Year: Mal. 4:1-2a; II Thess. 3:7-12; Lk.
21:5-19

33.

Feast of Christ the King

First Year: Ezek. 34:11-12, 15-17; I Cor. 15:20-
26a, 28; Mt. 25:31-46

Second Year: Dan. 7:13-14; Rev. 1:5-8; Jn. 18:
33b-37

Third Year: II Sam. 5:1-3; Col. 1:12-20; Lk. 23:
35-43

Anglican: Post-Trinity

Sundays are numbered "after Trinity" through the twenty-fourth. Provision is made for readings at Morning Prayer and Evening Prayer on three additional Sundays which may or may not occur in any given year. They are Third Sunday before Advent, Second Sunday before Advent, and Sunday Next before Advent, but the only one of these for which Epistle and Gospel lessons for Holy Communion are designated is the Sunday Next before Advent. If in any year there are twenty-six Sundays after Trinity, the Epistle and Gospel lessons for Holy Communion on the Sixth Sunday after Epiphany are to be read on the Twenty-fifth Sunday after Trinity. Similarly, if there are as many as twenty-seven Sundays after Trinity, the lessons appointed for Holy Communion on the Sixth Sunday after Epiphany are to be read on the Twenty-sixth Sunday after Trinity and those for the Fifth Sunday after Epiphany, on the Twenty-fifth Sunday after Trinity.

The Epistle and Gospel for Holy Communion on the Sunday Next before Advent are always to be read on the last Sunday after Trinity before the Fourth Sunday before Christmas Day, regardless of how many Sundays after Trinity there may be in any given year. The Post-Trinity lectionary is as follows:

First Sunday after Trinity
Morning Prayer: •Jer. 23:23-32 or Is. 5:8-12, 18-24 or Gen. 3; Mt. 7:13-14, 21-29 or Jas. 5 or Rom. 5
Evening Prayer: Deut. 30:11-20 or Job 21:17-33 or I Sam. 1:1-11, 19-20; Jn. 13:1-17, 34-35 or Lk. 16:19-31 or Acts 6
Holy Communion: I Jn. 4:7-21; Lk. 16:19-31

Second Sunday after Trinity
Morning Prayer: Job 31:13-28 or •Deut. 20:1-9 or Gen. 6:5-8, 13-22; I Cor. 13 or Lk. 9:57-62 or Mt. 24:32-42
Evening Prayer: I Sam. 20:1-7, 12-42 or II Kings 4:8-17 or I Sam. 3:1-18; I Pet. 1:17-25 or Lk. 14:12-24 or Acts 7:44—8:4
Holy Communion: I Jn. 3:13-24; Lk. 14:16-24

Third Sunday after Trinity
Morning Prayer: •Jer. 31:1-14 or Prov. 16:18-24, 32 or Gen. 9:1-17; Mt. 9:9-13 or Phil. 1:27—2:4 or I Pet. 3:17—4:6
Evening Prayer: Jer. 23:1-8 or Ezek. 34:20-24 or I Sam. 8; Lk. 19:2-10 or Lk. 15:1-10 or Acts 8:5-25
Holy Communion: I Pet. 5:5-11; Lk. 15:1-10

Fourth Sunday after Trinity
Morning Prayer: •Lam. 3:22-33 or Deut. 32:1-4, 34-39 or Gen. 12:1-9; Mt. 10:24-39 or Rom. 2:1-16 or Gal. 3:1-9
Evening Prayer: Is. 29:9-15 or Prov. 27:1-6, 10-12 or I Sam. 9:1-10, 18-19, 26—10:1; Mt. 15:1-20 or Lk. 6:36-42 or Acts 8:26-40
Holy Communion: Rom. 8:18-23; Lk. 6:36-42

Fifth Sunday after Trinity
Morning Prayer: •Eccles. 2:1-11, 18-23 or Prov. 15:1-10, 26 or Gen. 17:1-8; Mt. 19:16-30 or Jas. 3 or Heb. 11:1-16
Evening Prayer: Prov. 3:1-7, 11-12 or Judg. 6:11-23 or I Sam. 11; Lk. 14:25-35 or Lk. 5:1-11 or Acts 9:1-20
Holy Communion: I Pet. 3:8-15; Lk. 5:1-11

Sixth Sunday after Trinity
Morning Prayer: II Sam. 19:16-23 or •Is. 57:13b-19 or Gen. 18:1-16; Mt. 5:38-48 or II Tim. 2:7-13 or Rom. 4:13-25
Evening Prayer: Ex. 24:1-11, 16-18 or Gen. 4:1-16 or I Sam. 16:1-13; Heb. 9:18-28 or Mt. 5:20-26 or Acts 11:1-18

Holy Communion: Rom. 6:3-11; Mt. 5:20-26

Seventh Sunday after Trinity
Morning Prayer: •Hos. 14 or Ecclus. 6:5-17 or Gen. 22:1-18; Rom. 6:12-18 or Jn. 15:12-27 or Heb. 6
Evening Prayer: Dan. 5:1-9, 13-30 or Mic. 7:14-20; I Sam. 17:1-11, 32, 40-50; Rom. 1:17-21, 28-32 or Mk. 8:1-21 or Acts 11:19-30
Holy Communion: Rom. 6:19-23; Mk. 8:1-10a

Eighth Sunday after Trinity
Morning Prayer: •Ecclus. 1:18-27 or Zech. 4:1-10 or Gen. 24:1-27; Jn. 7:14-24 or Gal. 3:24—4:7 or Eph. 5:22-33
Evening Prayer: Ecclus. 6:22-37 or Prov. 11:24-31 or I Sam. 26:1-7, 12-17, 21-25; Lk. 10:38-42 or Mt. 7:15-21 or Acts 12:1-17
Holy Communion: Rom. 8:12-17; Mt. 7:15-21

Ninth Sunday after Trinity
Morning Prayer: Ezek. 14:1-11 or •Wis. 11:21—12:2 or Gen. 28:10-22; I Thess. 4:1-12 or Jn. 8:1-11 or II Cor. 9
Evening Prayer: Prov. 4:1-4, 20-27 or Lam. 3:40-58 or I Sam. 31; Heb. 12:1-13 or Lk. 15:11-32 or Acts 13:1-3, 14-31, 38, 44-49
Holy Communion: I Cor. 10:1-13; Lk. 15:11-32

Tenth Sunday after Trinity
Morning Prayer: •Ecclus. 1:1-10 or Jer. 26:1-7, 10-15 or Gen. 32:22-31; Jn. 8:25-36 or Mt. 23:34-39 or II Cor. 4:7-18
Evening Prayer: Is. 41:1-8, 21-23 or Lam. 1:1-12 or II Sam. 1:17-27; Rom. 12:1-9 or Lk. 19:41-47a or Acts 14:8-28
Holy Communion: I Cor. 12:1-11; Lk. 19:41-47a

Eleventh Sunday after Trinity
Morning Prayer: •Is. 26:12-16, 19 or Job 5:8-18 or Gen. 37:3-4, 12-35; Rom. 8:26-39 or Mt. 23:13-31 or Jas. 1:1-15
Evening Prayer: Ecclus. 35:10-19 or Eccles. 5:1-7 or II Sam. 7:18-29; Mk. 12:38-44 or Lk. 18:9-14 or Acts 15:1-21
Holy Communion: I Cor. 15:1-11; Lk. 18:9-14

Twelfth Sunday after Trinity
Morning Prayer: •Ecclus. 15:11-20 or Ecclus. 38:1-14 or Gen. 41:1a, 8, 14-40; Phil. 2:12-18 or Lk. 4:31-44 or Col. 3:22—4:6
Evening Prayer: Tob. 13:1b-5, 7-11 or Is. 29:18-24 or II Sam. 15:1-23; Rom. 15:14-21 or Mk. 7:

31-37 or Acts 15:36–16:5, 9-15

Holy Communion: II Cor. 3:4-9; Mk. 7:31-37

Thirteenth Sunday after Trinity

Morning Prayer: *Ecclus. 17:1-15 or Hab. 1: 2–2:4, 14 or Gen. 43:1-5, 11-16, 26-34; Mk. 3:20-21, 31-35 or Heb. 10:35-39 or Heb. 13:1-21

Evening Prayer: Deut. 15:7-15 or Deut. 24: 10-22 or II Sam. 18:1, 6-14, 19-33; Mt. 26:6-13 or Lk. 10:23-37 or Acts 16:16-34

Holy Communion: Gal. 3:16-22; Lk. 10:23-37

Fourteenth Sunday after Trinity

Morning Prayer: *Mic. 6:1-8 or I Chron. 29: 10-17 or Gen. 45:1-15, 25-28; Phil. 4:4-13 or Lk. 17: 5-10 or Rom. 12:9-21

Evening Prayer: Jer. 7:1-11 or Deut. 8:1-14, 17-20 or I Kings 3:4-15; Lk. 13:18-30 or Lk. 17:11-19 or Acts 17:16-34

Holy Communion: Gal. 5:16-24; Lk. 17:11-19

Fifteenth Sunday after Trinity

Morning Prayer: *Ecclus. 5:1-10 or Deut. 7:6-13 or Ex. 2:1-22; Lk. 12: 13-21 or Gal. 2:15-20 or Jas. 4

Evening Prayer: Eccles. 5:8-20 or Joel 2:21-27 or I Kings 8:22-30, 54-63; I Tim. 6:1-10 or Mt. 6:24-34 or Acts 18:1-17

Holy Communion: Gal. 6:11-18; Mt. 6:24-34

Sixteenth Sunday after Trinity

Morning Prayer: *Is. 12 or Jer. 32:36-42 or Ex. 3:1-15; Jn. 11:21-44 or Rom. 11:25-36 or I Pet. 5: 1-11

Evening Prayer: Ezek. 33:1-9 or I Kings 17:8-9, 17-24 or I Kings 12:1-20; Mt. 24:37-51 or Lk. 7:11-17 or Acts 19:21-41

Holy Communion: Eph. 3:13-21; Lk. 7:11-17

Seventeenth Sunday after Trinity

Morning Prayer: *Jer. 13:15-21 or Ecclus. 8: 1-9 or Ex. 5:1-9, 19–6:1; Mk. 10:35-45 or II Tim. 2: 19-26 or Heb. 3

Evening Prayer: Mal. 2:1-10 or Ecclus. 10:17-18 or I Kings 18:1-2, 17-39; Lk. 13:10-17 or Lk. 14:1-11 or Acts 20:17-38

Holy Communion: Eph. 4:1-6; Lk. 14:1-11

Eighteenth Sunday after Trinity

Morning Prayer: Prov. 2:1-9 or *Amos 8:4-12 or Ex. 14:5-14, 19-21, 24-28, 30; I Tim. 3:14–4:6 or

Jn. 7:37-52 or Heb. 11:23-29, 32-40

Evening Prayer: Deut. 11:18-21, 26-28, 32 or Deut. 5:1-21 or I Kings 19; Gal. 1:1-12 or Mt. 22:34-46 or Acts 21:7-19, 27-39

Holy Communion: I Cor. 1:4-8; Mt. 22:34-46

Nineteenth Sunday after Trinity

Morning Prayer: *Job 24:1-17 or Jer. 30:12-22 or Ex. 19:1-7, 16-19, 20:1-3; Titus 2 or Jn. 5:1-16 or Rom. 3:1-2, 19-31

Evening Prayer: Jer. 5:7-19 or Wis. 12:12-19 or I Kings 21:1-22; II Cor. 13 or Mt. 9:1-8 or Acts 22: 24–23:11

Holy Communion: Eph. 4:17-32; Mt. 9:1-8

Twentieth Sunday after Trinity

Morning Prayer: Mal. 2:14-17 or *Eccles. 9: 4-10 or Ex. 32:1-6, 15-20, 30-34; Mt. 19:3-9a, 13-15 or Eph. 6:1-9 or I Cor. 10:14-22

Evening Prayer: Jer. 31:31-37 or Jer. 2:1-9, 13 or II Kings 2:1-15; Jn. 13: 31-35 or Mt. 22:1-14 or Acts 24:10-27

Holy Communion: Eph. 5:15-21; Mt. 22:1-14

Twenty-first Sunday after Trinity

Morning Prayer: *Is. 59:15b-21 or Bar. 3:14-15, 29-37 or Ex. 33:1, 12-23; II Cor. 10:1-7, 17-18 or Jn. 9:1-38 or Heb. 4:1-13

Evening Prayer: Gen. 15:1-6 or II Kings 5: 1-15a or II Kings 6:8-23; Rom. 4:1-8 or Jn. 4:46b-54 or Acts 25:1-22

Holy Communion: Eph. 6:10-20; Jn. 4:46-54

Twenty-second Sunday after Trinity

Morning Prayer: *Ecclus. 27:30–28:7 or Bar. 5 or Num. 20:14-29; Mt. 18: 7-20 or I Jn. 2:24-29 or II Tim. 1:3-14

Evening Prayer: I Kings 8:46-53 or Zech. 7:8-14 or II Kings 9:1-6, 10b-13, 16-26; Lk. 7:36-50 or Mt. 18:21-35 or Acts 26

Holy Communion: Phil. 1:3-11; Mt. 18:21-35

Twenty-third Sunday after Trinity

Morning Prayer: Jer. 29:1, 4-14 or *Is. 64 or Deut. 34; Titus 3:1-8 or Mt. 23:1-12 or II Tim. 4: 1-8

Evening Prayer: Ezek. 33:30-33 or Wis. 6:1-11 or II Kings 25:1-4, 11-14, 21-23; I Cor. 4:8-16 or Mt. 22:15-22 or Acts 27:1-20, 27-32, 39-44

Holy Communion: Phil. 3:17-21; Mt. 22:15-22

Twenty-fourth Sunday after Trinity
Morning Prayer: *Mal. 3:13–4:3 or Ecclus. 36:
1-17 or Josh. 23:1-3, 11-16;
Lk. 10:17-24 or I Tim. 2:
1-8 or Lk. 13:1-9
Evening Prayer: Deut. 33:1-3, 26-29 or II
Kings 4:18-37 or II Chron.
36:11-23; Jude 1-4, 17-25
or Mt. 9:18-26 or Acts 28:
16-31
Holy Communion: Col. 1:3-12; Mt. 9:18-26

Third Sunday before Advent
Morning Prayer: Ruth 1:1-17 or *Hab. 1:12–
2:4, 9-14; Col. 3:5-11 or
Lk. 12:35-48
Evening Prayer: Joel 3:9-17 or Amos 5:14-24;
Mt. 13:36-52 or Gal. 6:1-10

Second Sunday before Advent
Morning Prayer: Is. 2:6-19 or *Is. 66:1-2, 10,
12-16, 18-23; Mt. 25:14-29
or II Thess. 1
Evening Prayer: Gen. 19:1-3, 12-17, 24-28 or
II Es. 8:63–9:13; Lk. 17:
20-37 or II Pet. 3:1-14, 17-
18

Sunday Next before Advent
Morning Prayer: Jer. 4:23-31 or *Jer. 3:14-18;
Mt. 25:31-46 or I Cor. 11:
17-32
Evening Prayer: Eccles. 11:9–12:8, 13-14 or Is.
25:1-9; Heb. 13:1-21 or Jn.
5:17-29
Holy Communion: Jer. 23:5-8; Jn. 6:5-14

Lutheran: Post-Trinity

Sundays are numbered "after Trinity" with subtitles "after Pentecost" for Holy Communion readings. Full sets of lessons are provided for twenty-seven such Sundays, the twenty-seventh being called "Last Sunday after Trinity." The Post-Trinity lectionary is as follows:

First Sunday after Trinity
Matins: Job 29:11-16; Lk. 12:13-21
Vespers: Is. 42:5-12; I Tim. 6:6-19
Holy Communion: Deut. 6:4-13; I Jn. 4:16b-21;
Lk. 16:19-31

Second Sunday after Trinity
Matins: Deut. 20:1-9; Lk. 14:25-33
Vespers: Jer. 7:25-28; Rev. 3:14-22
Holy Communion: Prov. 9:1-10; I Jn. 3:13-18;
Lk. 14:15-24

Third Sunday after Trinity
Matins: Jer. 31:1-14; Lk. 15:11-32
Vespers: Jer. 23:1-8; Acts 9:1-18
Holy Communion: Is. 12:1-6; I Pet. 5:6-11; Lk.
15:1-10

Fourth Sunday after Trinity
Matins: Deut. 32:1-4, 20-39; Mt. 5:43-48
Vespers: Gen. 18:20-33; Rom. 14:7-17
Holy Communion: Num. 6:22-27; Rom. 8:18-23;
Lk. 6:36-42

Fifth Sunday after Trinity
Matins: Eccles. 2:1-11, 18-23; Mt. 16:
13-25
Vespers: Prov. 3:1-7, 11-12; I Pet. 2:
1-10
Holy Communion: Lam. 3:22-33; I Pet. 3:8-15a;
Lk. 5:1-11

Sixth Sunday after Trinity
Matins: II Sam. 19:16-23; Mt. 19:16-30
Vespers: Gen. 4:1-16; Eph. 2:4-10
Holy Communion: Ruth 1:1-18; Rom. 6:3-11;
Mt. 5:20-26

Seventh Sunday after Trinity
Matins: Hos. 14:1-9; Mt. 10:24-31
Vespers: Dan. 5:1-9, 13-20; Acts 14:
8-23
Holy Communion: Is. 62:6-12; Rom. 6:19-23;
Mk. 8:1-9

Eighth Sunday after Trinity
Matins: Zech. 4:1-10; Mt. 7:21-29
Vespers: I Sam. 26:1-7, 12-17, 21-25;
Acts 20:17-38
Holy Communion: Jer. 23:16-29; Rom. 8:12-17;
Mt. 7:15-21

Ninth Sunday after Trinity
Matins: Ex. 32:1-6; Lk. 12:32-48
Vespers: Is. 38:1-8; II Tim. 1:3-14
Holy Communion: Prov. 16:1-9; I Cor. 10:1-13;
Lk. 16:1-9 or Lk. 15:11-32

Tenth Sunday after Trinity
Matins: Jer. 26:1-19; Mt. 11:16-24
Vespers: Lam. 1:1-12; Heb. 3:7-15
Holy Communion: Jer. 7:1-11; I Cor. 12:1-11;
Lk. 19:41-47a

Eleventh Sunday after Trinity
Matins: Is. 26:12-16, 19; Lk. 7:36-50
Vespers: Eccles. 5:1-7; Rom. 10:4-18
Holy Communion: Dan. 9:15-19; I Cor. 15:1-10;
Lk. 18:9-14

Twelfth Sunday after Trinity
Matins: Gen. 41:1a, 8, 14-40; Mt. 12:
31-42
Vespers: II Sam. 15:1-23; Jas. 3:1-12
Holy Communion: Is. 29:17-21; II Cor. 3:4-9;
Mk. 7:31-37

Thirteenth Sunday after Trinity
Matins: Hab. 1:12–2:4; Mt. 20:20-28
Vespers: Deut. 15:7-15; I Tim. 1:5-17
Holy Communion: Zech. 7:4-10; Gal. 3:16-22;
                       Lk. 10:23-37

Fourteenth Sunday after Trinity
Matins: Mic. 6:1-8; Jn. 5:1-15
Vespers: Deut. 8:1-14, 17-20; Acts 3:
                       1-10
Holy Communion: Prov. 4:10-23; Gal. 5:16-24;
                       Lk. 17:11-19

Fifteenth Sunday after Trinity
Matins: Deut. 7:6-12; Lk. 10:38-42
Vespers: Joel 2:21-27; Acts 8:26-39
Holy Communion: I Kings 17:8-16; Gal. 5:25–
                       6:10; Mt. 6:24-34

Sixteenth Sunday after Trinity
Matins: Jer. 32:36-42; Jn. 11:19-45
Vespers: I Kings 17:17-24; I Cor. 15:
                       21-28
Holy Communion: Job 5:17-26; Eph. 3:13-21;
                       Lk. 7:11-16

Seventeenth Sunday after Trinity
Matins: Jer. 13:15-25; Mk. 2:18-28
Vespers: Mal. 2:1-10; Jude 20-25
Holy Communion: Prov. 25:6-14; Eph. 4:1-6;
                       Lk. 14:1-11

Eighteenth Sunday after Trinity
Matins: Amos 8:4-12; Jn. 15:1-17
Vespers: Jer. 17:5-10; I Jn. 3:1-8
Holy Communion: II Chron. 1:7-12; I Cor. 1:
                       4-9; Mt. 22:34-46

Nineteenth Sunday after Trinity
Matins: Job 24:1-17; Jn. 1:35-51
Vespers: Jer. 5:7-19; I Cor. 12:12-27
Holy Communion: Gen. 28:10-17; Eph. 4:17-28;
                       Mt. 9:1-8

Twentieth Sunday after Trinity
Matins: Eccles. 9:4-10; Mt. 21:28-44
Vespers: Jer. 2:1-9, 13; Rom. 11:25-32
Holy Communion: Prov. 2:1-9; Eph. 5:15-21;
                       Mt. 22:1-14

Twenty-first Sunday after Trinity
Matins: Ex. 33:1, 12-33; Jn. 4:31-42
Vespers: Gen. 15:1-6; Rev. 3:7-13
Holy Communion: II Sam. 7:18-29; Eph. 6:10-
                       17; Jn. 4:46b-53

Twenty-second Sunday after Trinity
Matins: Num. 20:14-21; Mt. 18:1-20
Vespers: I Kings 8:46-53; Eph. 4:30-32
Holy Communion: Prov. 3:11-20; Phil. 1:3-11;
                       Mt. 18:21-35

Twenty-third Sunday after Trinity
Matins: Jer. 29:1, 4-14; Mk. 12:41-44
Vespers: II Kings 23:1-4, 11-14, 21-23;
                       Rom. 13:1-7
Holy Communion: Prov. 8:11-22; Phil. 3:17-21;
                       Mt. 22:15-22

Twenty-fourth Sunday after Trinity
Matins: Josh. 23:1-3, 11-16; Jn. 5:17-
                       29
Vespers: II Kings 4:18-37; II Cor. 5:
                       1-10
Holy Communion: I Kings 17:17-24; Col. 1:9-
                       14; Mt. 9:18-26

Twenty-fifth Sunday after Trinity
Matins: Dan. 12:1-4; Lk. 17:20-33
Vespers: Dan. 9:24-27; II Pet. 3:3-15
Holy Communion: Job 14:1-6; I Thess. 4:13-18;
                       Mt. 24:15-28

Twenty-sixth Sunday after Trinity
Matins: Jer. 3:14-18; Mt. 11:25-30
Vespers: Eccles. 11:9–12:7; Heb. 4:
                       9-13
Holy Communion: Dan. 7:9-14; I Thess. 5:1-11;
                       Mt. 25:31-46

Last Sunday after Trinity
Matins: Is. 2:6-19; Mt. 5:13-16
Vespers: Gen. 19:1-3, 10-17, 24-28;
                       Rev. 21:1-7
Holy Communion: Is. 35:3-10; II Pet. 3:8-14;
                       Mt. 25:1-13

British Methodist: Post-Trinity

Like the Anglican communion, the British Methodist calendar numbers Sundays "after Trinity" but provides morning and evening lessons for twenty-seven Post-Trinity Sundays. The Communion lectionary provides for the possible use of lessons for Sundays after Epiphany if they are needed after the Twenty-fifth Sunday after Trinity and before the Sunday next before Advent. The Post-Trinity lectionary is as follows:

First Sunday after Trinity
First Year, Morning: Num. 27:12-23; Jn. 4:1-
                       10, 13b-14, 19-26
First Year, Evening: Ex. 1:8-10, 22, 2:1-10;
                       Mk. 1:14-28

Second Year, Morning: Deut. 30:15-20; Mt. 11:
                       2-19
Second Year, Evening: Judg. 4:1-22; Acts 9:1-19
Holy Communion: I Jn. 4:7-21; Lk. 16:19-31

Second Sunday after Trinity
First Year, Morning: Deut. 34:1-12; Jn. 4:27-42
First Year, Evening: Ex. 2:11-22; Mk. 1:29-39
Second Year, Morning: Job 5:8-27; Lk. 7:36-50
Second Year, Evening: Judg. 5:1-12, 24-31; Acts 9:20-31
Holy Communion: I Jn. 3:13-24; Lk. 14:16-24

Third Sunday after Trinity
First Year, Morning: Josh. 2:1-9, 12-21; Acts 2:22-42
First Year, Evening: Ex. 6:2-12; Mk. 2:1-12
Second Year, Morning: Job 14:1-15; Mt. 12:22-37
Second Year, Evening: Judg. 6:1-6, 11-16, 33-40; Acts 14:8-27
Holy Communion: I Pet. 5:5-11; Lk. 15:1-10

Fourth Sunday after Trinity
First Year, Morning: Josh. 3:7-17, 4:4-7; Acts 3:1-19
First Year, Evening: Ex. 4:1-16; Mk. 2:13-28
Second Year, Morning: Job 40:6-24; Mt. 12:38-50
Second Year, Evening: Judg. 7:1-8, 16-21; Acts 15:1-20
Holy Communion: Rom. 8:18-23; Lk. 6:36-42

Fifth Sunday after Trinity
First Year, Morning: Josh. 5:13—6:5; Acts 4:1-12
First Year, Evening: Ex. 7:8-25; Mk. 3:1-12
Second Year, Morning: Job 42:7-17; Mk. 4:21-41
Second Year, Evening: Judg. 14:1-18; Lk. 8:26-39
Holy Communion: I Pet. 3:8-15; Lk. 5:1-11

Sixth Sunday after Trinity
First Year, Morning: Josh. 6:12-16, 20; Acts 4:13-32
First Year, Evening: I Sam. 1:1-11, 19-20; Jn. 5:1-15
Second Year, Morning: I Sam. 8:4-22; Acts 5:33-42
Second Year, Evening: Ruth 1:1-19a; Mt. 9:27—10:1
Holy Communion: Rom. 6:3-11; Mt. 5:20-26

Seventh Sunday after Trinity
First Year, Morning: Prov. 1:1-9; Acts 5:12, 17-32
First Year, Evening: I Sam. 4:1-11; Jn. 5:16-29
Second Year, Morning: I Sam. 9:15-19, 25—10:1; Acts 6:1-15
Second Year, Evening: Ruth 2:1-17; Mt. 10:2-15
Holy Communion: Rom. 6:19-23; Mk. 8:1-9

Eighth Sunday after Trinity
First Year, Morning: Prov. 4:5-27; Mk. 6:30-44
First Year, Evening: I Sam. 7:1-12; Jn. 5:30-47
Second Year, Morning: I Sam. 12:1-5, 13-15, 23-25; Acts 7:51—8:4

Second Year, Evening: Prov. 6:6-19; Mt. 10:16-33
Holy Communion: Rom. 8:12-17; Mt. 7:15-21

Ninth Sunday after Trinity
First Year, Morning: I Sam. 16:14-23; Mt. 14:22-36
First Year, Evening: Prov. 14:31—15:9, 13-17; Eph. 1:1-14
Second Year, Morning: I Sam. 15:10-23; Acts 8:26-40
Second Year, Evening: Prov. 10:1-12; Mt. 10:34—11:1
Holy Communion: I Cor. 10:1-13; Lk. 16:1-9

Tenth Sunday after Trinity
First Year, Morning: I Sam. 17:1-11; Jn. 6:22-40
First Year, Evening: Prov. 17:1-14; Eph. 1:15-23
Second Year, Morning: Prov. 20:1-12; I Pet. 4:7-19
Second Year, Evening: II Sam. 7:1-17; Mk. 6:14-29
Holy Communion: I Cor. 12:1-11; Lk. 19:41-47

Eleventh Sunday after Trinity
First Year, Morning: I Sam. 17:32-51; Jn. 6:41-51
First Year, Evening: I Sam. 18:1-16; Eph. 4:17-32
Second Year, Morning: Prov. 23:15-26; I Pet. 5:1-11
Second Year, Evening: II Sam. 12:1-10, 15-23; Jn. 13:1-20
Holy Communion: I Cor. 15:1-11; Lk. 18:9-14

Twelfth Sunday after Trinity
First Year, Morning: I Sam. 21:1-4a, 6-9; Jn. 6:52-71
First Year, Evening: I Sam. 26:5-25; Eph. 5:1-8, 14-21
Second Year, Morning: Prov. 25:11-28; Mk. 7:24-37
Second Year, Evening: II Sam. 18:5-15, 24-33; Acts 16:6-15
Holy Communion: II Cor. 3:4-9; Mk. 7:31-37

Thirteenth Sunday after Trinity
First Year, Morning: I Sam. 28:3-20; Mt. 18:15-35
First Year, Evening: II Sam. 1:1-10, 17-27; Eph. 6:5-20
Second Year, Morning: I Kings 3:4-15; Mt. 15:32—16:4
Second Year, Evening: I Kings 18:1-19; Acts 16:16-34
Holy Communion: Gal. 3:16-22; Lk. 10:23-37

169

Fourteenth Sunday after Trinity

First Year, Morning: I Kings 21:1-16; Lk. 9: 51-62

First Year, Evening: I Kings 22:1-17; II Cor. 5:20–6:10

Second Year, Morning: I Kings 10:1-13; Mk. 8: 13-26

Second Year, Evening: I Kings 18:20-46; I Cor. 12:4-14, 26-31

Holy Communion: Gal. 5:16-24; Lk. 17:11-19

Fifteenth Sunday after Trinity

First Year, Morning: II Kings 5:1-19; Acts 18: 24–19:6

First Year, Evening: II Kings 6:8-23; Lk. 5: 1-16

Second Year, Morning: I Kings 11:43–12:20; Jn. 7:53–8:11

Second Year, Evening: I Kings 19:1-18; I Cor. 13

Holy Communion: Gal. 6:11-18; Mt. 6:24-34

Sixteenth Sunday after Trinity

First Year, Morning: Hos. 2:14-23; Acts 19:21-41

First Year, Evening: II Kings 6:24-25, 7:1-6, 16; Mt. 21:33-46

Second Year, Morning: Is. 30:1-3, 7-17; Col. 1: 21–2:7

Second Year, Evening: Jer. 1:4-15, 18-19; Jn. 8: 12-30

Holy Communion: Eph. 3:13-21; Lk. 7:11-17

Seventeenth Sunday after Trinity

First Year, Morning: Hos. 6:1-6; Acts 20:17-38

First Year, Evening: II Kings 17:1-6, 24-28; Lk. 14:1-14

Second Year, Morning: Is. 32:1-5, 16-18; Col. 3: 1-17

Second Year, Evening: Jer. 2:1-13; Jn. 8:31-45

Holy Communion: Eph. 4:1-6; Lk. 14:1-11

Eighteenth Sunday after Trinity

First Year, Morning: Hos. 11:1-9c; Mt. 11:20-30

First Year, Evening: II Kings 22:3-11, 23:1-3; Acts 24:24–25:12

Second Year, Morning: II Kings 18:13-17, 28-37; I Tim. 6:6-19

Second Year, Evening: Jer. 5:1-3, 21-31; Jn. 8: 46-59

Holy Communion: I Cor. 1:4-8; Mt. 22:34-36

Nineteenth Sunday after Trinity

First Year, Morning: II Kings 23:4-14; Lk. 13: 1-17

First Year, Evening: II Kings 23:28–24:7; Acts 28:16-31

Second Year, Morning: II Kings 19:15-20, 32-36; II Tim. 1:1-14

Second Year, Evening: Jer. 6:9-16; Lk. 13:22-24, 31-35

Holy Communion: Eph. 4:17-32; Mt. 9:1-8

Twentieth Sunday after Trinity

First Year, Morning: Jer. 26:1-16; Lk. 16:1-15

First Year, Evening: Jer. 36:1-4, 21-28, 32; I Cor. 9:24–10:13

Second Year, Morning: II Kings 24:8-17; Mt. 20: 1-16

Second Year, Evening: Jer. 17:5-14; Lk. 14:15-35

Holy Communion: Eph. 5:15-21; Mt. 22:1-14

Twenty-first Sunday after Trinity

First Year, Morning: Jer. 22:1-5, 13-19; Lk. 17:5-21

First Year, Evening: II Chron. 36:11-21; Lk. 18:1-14

Second Year, Morning: Ezek. 2:1–3:3; Mt. 20:17-28

Second Year, Evening: Jer. 24:1-10; Lk. 15:1-10

Holy Communion: Eph. 6:10-20; Jn. 4:46-54

Twenty-second Sunday after Trinity

First Year, Morning: Ezek. 11:14-20; Lk. 18: 35–19:10

First Year, Evening: Jer. 38:1-13; Mt. 21:23-32

Second Year, Morning: Ezek. 3:4-21; Jas. 1:1-4, 12-27

Second Year, Evening: Jer. 28:1-14; Lk. 15:11-32

Holy Communion: Phil. 1:3-11; Mt. 18:21-35

Twenty-third Sunday after Trinity

First Year, Morning: Ezek. 18:1-4, 19-22, 27-32; Mk. 12:13-27

First Year, Evening: Ezek. 33:1-9; I Tim. 1: 12-17, 2:1-7

Second Year, Morning: Ezek. 33:21-33; Jas. 2:1-13

Second Year, Evening: Is. 45:1-13; Jn. 7:1-13

Holy Communion: Phil. 3:17-21; Mt. 22:15-22

Twenty-fourth Sunday after Trinity

First Year, Morning: Ezek. 33:21-33; Jn. 10:1-18

First Year, Evening: Ps. 119:9-24; II Tim. 2: 1-13

Second Year, Morning: Neh. 2:1-18; Jas. 3:5-18

Second Year, Evening: Ezra 1:1-8; Jn. 7:14-19, 24-36

Holy Communion: Col. 1:3-12; Mt. 9:18-26

Twenty-fifth Sunday after Trinity

First Year, Morning: Dan. 3:8-14, 16-27; Mt. 22:1-14

First Year, Evening: Ps. 119:33-48; I Jn. 5:1-12

Second Year, Morning: Neh. 4:1-9, 21-23; Gal. 5: 16–6:5

Second Year, Evening: Neh. 8:1-12; Jn. 7:37-52

Holy Communion, if Sunday next before Advent: Jer. 23:5-8; Jn. 6:5-14

170

Twenty-sixth Sunday after Trinity
First Year, Morning: Dan. 4:1-9, 19-27; I Cor. 1:18-31
First Year, Evening: Dan. 6:1-23; Mt. 17:1-13
Second Year, Morning: Neh. 6:1-16; Jn. 10:22-39
Second Year, Evening: Prov. 31:10-31; Philem. 1-19
Holy Communion, if Sunday next before Advent: Jer. 23:5-8; Jn. 6:5-14

Sunday Next before Advent
First Year, Morning: Hag. 2:1-9; II Cor. 4:5-18
First Year, Evening: Jer. 23:1-8; Jn. 12:37-50
Second Year, Morning: Mic. 6:1-8; Heb. 11:1-16
Second Year, Evening: Eccles. 11:9-12:8; Heb. 11:23-12:2
Holy Communion: Jer. 23:5-8; Jn. 6:5-14

Church of Scotland: Post-Trinity

Lessons for a complete season of twenty-seven Sundays are provided, each Sunday numbered "after Trinity" except the last, which is called "Next before Advent." The Post-Trinity lectionary is as follows:

First Sunday after Trinity
First Year, Morning: Josh. 1; Eph. 4:1-16; Mt. 16:13-19
First Year, Evening: Jer. 1; Lk. 7:19-35
Second Year, Morning: Joel 2:12-32; I Jn. 4:7-21; Lk. 16:19-31
Second Year, Evening: I Kings 3:1-15; Acts 3

Second Sunday after Trinity
First Year, Morning: Josh. 4:1-14; I Jn. 3:13-18; Lk. 14:16-24
First Year, Evening: Jer. 2:1-13; Lk. 7:36-50
Second Year, Morning: Joel 3:9-21; Gal. 5:16-25 or Rev. 19:4-9; Mt. 11:28-30
Second Year, Evening: I Kings 8:22-36; Acts 4:8-37

Third Sunday after Trinity
First Year, Morning: Josh. 6:1-20; Acts 3:1-10 or Acts 2:37-47; Lk. 15:1-10
First Year, Evening: Jer. 10:1-16; Mk. 4:1-20
Second Year, Morning: Amos 5:4-24; I Pet. 1:1-11; Lk. 15:1-10
Second Year, Evening: I Kings 8:54-66; Acts 5:11-42

Fourth Sunday after Trinity
First Year, Morning: Josh. 8:1-20; Acts 3:11-21 or Acts 4:5-13; Lk. 15:11-32
First Year, Evening: Jer. 17:1-14; Mk. 4:21-41
Second Year, Morning: Amos 6; Heb. 11:1-6, 8-10; Lk. 15:11-32
Second Year, Evening: I Kings 12:1-20; Acts 6, 7:54-60

Fifth Sunday after Trinity
First Year, Morning: Josh. 20; Acts 5:17-32; Lk. 5:1-11
First Year, Evening: Jer. 31:1-14, 31-34; Lk. 8:41-56
Second Year, Morning: Amos 7; I Cor. 6:9-11; Lk. 6:36-42 or Jn. 5:17-27

Second Year, Evening: I Kings 17:1-16; Acts 8:26-40
Sixth Sunday after Trinity
First Year, Morning: Josh. 24:1-15; Acts 7:51-60; Mk. 5:1-16
First Year, Evening: Jer. 35; Mk. 6:31-44
Second Year, Morning: Amos 8; I Cor. 10:14-24; Lk. 12:13-21
Second Year, Evening: I Kings 18:1-20; Acts 9:1-22

Seventh Sunday after Trinity
First Year, Morning: Josh. 24:16-28; Acts 8:1-13; Mt. 5:17-26
First Year, Evening: Lam. 3:22-41; Mk. 6:45-56
Second Year, Morning: Obad.; Rom. 6:19-23; Mk. 6:35-46
Second Year, Evening: I Kings 18:21-39; Acts 9:23-43

Eighth Sunday after Trinity
First Year, Morning: Judg. 5; Acts 8:14-24; Mt. 5:27-37
First Year, Evening: Ezek. 2:1-3:11; Mk. 7:24-37
Second Year, Morning: Jon. 1:1-16; II Cor. 4:1-10; Jn. 10:1-10
Second Year, Evening: I Kings 19; Acts 10:1-22

Ninth Sunday after Trinity
First Year, Morning: Judg. 7:1-21; Acts 8:26-40; Mt. 5:38-48
First Year, Evening: Ezek. 14:1-11; Mk. 8:1-13
Second Year, Morning: Jon. 3; Gal. 6:1-10; Lk. 16:1-13
Second Year, Evening: I Kings 20:1-21; Acts 10:24-48

Tenth Sunday after Trinity
First Year, Morning: Judg. 11:1-11, 29-40; Acts 9:1-9; Mt. 6:1-15
First Year, Evening: Ezek. 18:1-4, 19-32; Lk. 9:18-27

Second Year, Morning: Jon. 4; I Cor. 12:1-11; Lk. 19:41-48

Second Year, Evening: I Kings 20:28-43; Acts 11:1-18

Eleventh Sunday after Trinity

First Year, Morning: Ruth 1:1-17; Acts 9:10-22; Mt. 6:19-34

First Year, Evening: Ezek. 33:1-16; Lk. 9:28-45

Second Year, Morning: Mic. 4:1-8; I Cor. 15:1-11; Lk. 18:9-14

Second Year, Evening: I Kings 21:1-22; Acts 12:1-19

Twelfth Sunday after Trinity

First Year, Morning: Ruth 2:1-17; Acts 9:36-43; Mt. 7:1-6

First Year, Evening: Ezek. 34:1-24; Lk. 10:1-22

Second Year, Morning: Mic. 6; II Cor. 4:16–5:1; Mk. 7:31-37

Second Year, Evening: II Kings 4:1-17; Acts 13:1-33

Thirteenth Sunday after Trinity

First Year, Morning: I Sam. 3; Acts 10:9-16; Mt. 7:7-14

First Year, Evening: Ezek. 36:21-38; Lk. 10:25-42

Second Year, Morning: Mic. 7; Heb. 13:1-6; Lk. 10:23-37 or Mt. 18:1-9

Second Year, Evening: II Kings 4:18-37; Acts 14:1-18

Fourteenth Sunday after Trinity

First Year, Morning: I Sam. 4:1-18; Acts 13:14-52; Mt. 7:15-23

First Year, Evening: Dan. 1; Lk. 11:1-20

Second Year, Morning: Nahum 1; II Cor. 6:1-10; Lk. 17:11-19

Second Year, Evening: II Kings 5:1-14; Acts 16:1-18

Fifteenth Sunday after Trinity

First Year, Morning: I Sam. 9:1-20; Acts 14:8-18; Mt. 7:24-29

First Year, Evening: Dan. 2:1-3, 27-45; Lk. 12:16-40

Second Year, Morning: Hab. 2:1-4, 18-20; Gal. 6:11-18; Mt. 8:5-13

Second Year, Evening: II Kings 6:8-23; Acts 16:19-40

Sixteenth Sunday after Trinity

First Year, Morning: I Sam. 10:1-9, 17-27; Acts 16:11-18 or Acts 16:25-34; Lk. 7:11-17

First Year, Evening: Dan. 3:1-6, 16-30; Lk. 13:1-17

Second Year, Morning: Hab. 3; Eph. 3:13-21; Mt. 10:1-15

Second Year, Evening: II Kings 12:1-16; Acts 17:16-34

Seventeenth Sunday after Trinity

First Year, Morning: I Sam. 16:1-13; Acts 17:22-33; Lk. 14:1-11

First Year, Evening: Dan. 4:1-9, 19-27; Lk. 14:15-33

Second Year, Morning: Zeph. 3:8-20; II Cor. 9:6-15; Mt. 10:16-23

Second Year, Evening: II Kings 17:24-41; Acts 19:21-41

Eighteenth Sunday after Trinity

First Year, Morning: I Sam. 17:1-11, 32-49; Acts 18:1-11 or Acts 20:17-35; Mt. 22:34-46

First Year, Evening: Dan. 5:1-8, 17-30; Lk. 18:18-34

Second Year, Morning: Hag. 1; II Pet. 3:8-14; Mt. 10:24-33

Second Year, Evening: II Kings 18:1-18, 28-37; Acts 20:17-38

Nineteenth Sunday after Trinity

First Year, Morning: I Sam. 18:1-16; Acts 22:1-21 or Acts 26:1-20; Mt. 9:1-8

First Year, Evening: Dan. 6:1-23; Lk. 18:35–19:10

Second Year, Morning: Hag. 2; Eph. 4:17-32; Mt. 10:34-42

Second Year, Evening: II Kings 19:8-37; Acts 21:39–22:21

Twentieth Sunday after Trinity

First Year, Morning: I Sam. 24; Acts 28:16-31; Mt. 22:15-22

First Year, Evening: Dan. 7:1-14; Mk. 12:1-17

Second Year, Morning: Zech. 2; Eph. 5:1-14 or Eph. 5:6-21; Mt. 11:16-27

Second Year, Evening: II Kings 20:1-11; Acts 26

Twenty-first Sunday after Trinity

First Year, Morning: II Sam. 1:1-12, 17-27; Eph. 6:10-20; Lk. 21:1-9

First Year, Evening: Dan. 9:1-19; Mk. 12:28-44

Second Year, Morning: Zech. 7; Eph. 6:10-20; Lk. 20:19-26

Second Year, Evening: II Chron. 30:1-21; Rom. 1:1-17

Twenty-second Sunday after Trinity

First Year, Morning: II Sam. 7:1-17; Phil. 1:3-11; Mt. 18:21-35

First Year, Evening: Hos. 6; Mk. 14:1-17

Second Year, Morning: Zech. 8; I Pet. 5:1-11; Lk. 20:27-38

Second Year, Evening: II Kings 22:1–23:3; Rom. 5

Twenty-third Sunday after Trinity

First Year, Morning: II Sam. 12:1-10, 15-23;

Phil. 3:17-21; Lk. 12: 49-59

First Year, Evening: Hos. 10:12–11:12; Lk. 22: 14-30

Second Year, Morning: Zech. 11; I Cor. 1:18-31; Mt. 25:14-30

Second Year, Evening: II Chron. 36:1-21; Rom. 8:1-18

Twenty-fourth Sunday after Trinity
First Year, Morning: II Sam. 15:1-15; Col. 1: 3-18; Lk. 11:14-28

First Year, Evening: Hos. 14; Mk. 14:26-46

Second Year, Morning: Zech. 13; Col. 1:3-18; Mt. 9:18-26

Second Year, Evening: Ezra 3; Rom. 8:24-39

Twenty-fifth Sunday after Trinity
First Year, Morning: II Sam. 15:17-29; I Cor. 12:12-31; Lk. 19:11-26

First Year, Evening: Job 14; Mk. 14: 53-72

Second Year, Morning: Mal. 1; I Cor. 12:12-31; Mt. 9:27-38

Second Year, Evening: Neh. 2; Rom. 10

Twenty-sixth Sunday after Trinity
First Year, Morning: I Sam. 18:5-33; Eph. 2:1-10; Mt. 12:38-50

First Year, Evening: Job 28; Mk. 15:1-21

Second Year, Morning: Mal. 3; Eph. 2:1-10; Mt. 12:38-50

Second Year, Evening: Neh. 8:1-12; Rom. 12

Sunday Next before Advent
First Year, Morning: Eccles. 11:9–12:14; I Cor. 1:26-31; Lk. 4:16-24

First Year, Evening: Hag. 2:1-9; Lk. 23:27-47

Second Year, Morning: Mal. 4; I Cor. 2:1-10; Mt. 4:12-17 or Jn. 17

Second Year, Evening: Jer. 23:1-8; Rom. 13

Provisional American Presbyterian: Post-Pentecost

Lessons are provided for nineteen Sundays after Pentecost for a season called "God the Holy Spirit" and for eight Sundays of a season called "God the Father," which begins with Worldwide Communion Sunday (first in October) and includes the Sunday before Advent. These lectionaries are as follows:

Second Sunday after Pentecost
First Year: Is. 64:1-9; Eph. 1:3-14; Mk. 7:14-23
Second Year: Num. 14:11-24; Acts 4:1-12; Mt. 9: 9-17

Third Sunday after Pentecost
First Year: Amos 7:10-15; I Thess. 2:1-12; Mt. 5:27-37
Second Year: Deut. 6:1-9; Gal. 5:16-26; Lk. 16: 19-31

Fourth Sunday after Pentecost
First Year: Mic. 3:5-12; I Thess. 2:13-20; Mt. 5:38-48
Second Year: Deut. 30:11-20; Acts 6:1-7; Mt. 5: 17-26

Fifth Sunday after Pentecost
First Year: Jer. 15:15-21; I Thess. 5:12-24; Mt. 7:15-29
Second Year: Josh. 1:1-9; II Pet. 1:3-11; Lk. 6: 27-38

Sixth Sunday after Pentecost
First Year: Deut. 29:1-15; Eph. 2:11-22; Jn. 15: 18-27
Second Year: Judg. 7:1-8; Acts 9:1-18; Lk. 19:1-10

Seventh Sunday after Pentecost
First Year: Deut. 30:1-10; I Thess. 1:1-10; Jn. 17:6-11
Second Year: I Sam. 3:1-10; Rom. 12:9-21; Mt. 16:13-23

Eighth Sunday after Pentecost
First Year: Josh. 24:14-24; Col. 1:24-29; Jn. 17:20-26

Second Year: II Chron. 6:12-21; Acts 13:42-52; Jn. 17:1-11

Ninth Sunday after Pentecost
First Year: II Sam. 7:1-17; II Cor. 8:1-7; Mt. 12:46-50
Second Year: I Sam. 16:1-13; Rom. 15:1-13; Mt. 25:31-46

Tenth Sunday after Pentecost
First Year: I Sam. 12:6-15; Rom. 15:22-29; Mt. 9:35–10:4
Second Year: II Sam. 7:1-17; Acts 13:1-12; Mk. 6:30-44

Eleventh Sunday after Pentecost
First Year: I Sam. 17:41-47; Acts 26:12-23; Mt. 10:5-15
Second Year: II Kings 5:1-14; Acts 17:16-34; Mk. 12:1-12

Twelfth Sunday after Pentecost
First Year: I Kings 3:3-14; Acts 28:23-31; Mt. 10:16-25
Second Year: Is. 45:14-22; Rom. 10:8-17; Lk. 10: 25-37

Thirteenth Sunday after Pentecost
First Year: Hos. 14:1-9; Philem. 4-20; Lk. 18: 9-14
Second Year: Hos. 11:1-11; Rom. 3:21-31; Mt. 5:21-26

Fourteenth Sunday after Pentecost
First Year: Mic. 7:1-7; Heb. 13:1-8; Lk. 22:24-34
Second Year: Jon. 3:1–4:11; Eph. 4:25-32; Mt. 9: 1-13

173

Fifteenth Sunday after Pentecost
First Year: Zech. 10:1-7; Jas. 4:7-12; Lk. 22:54-62
Second Year: Is. 55:1-13; I Jn. 2:1-17; Lk. 7:36-50

Sixteenth Sunday after Pentecost
First Year: Ruth 1:6-18; II Pet. 3:3-14; Lk. 14:1-11
Second Year: Ezek. 37:1-14; II Cor. 5:1-15; Jn. 11:1-27

Seventeenth Sunday after Pentecost
First Year: Hag. 2:1-9; Jude 17-25; Lk. 14:12-24
Second Year: Dan. 12:1-4; Rom. 8:22-39; Mt. 22:23-33

Eighteenth Sunday after Pentecost
First Year: Ezek. 47:1-12; Rev. 7:9-17; Lk. 16:1-9
Second Year: Is. 65:17-25; Rev. 21:1-14; Jn. 14:1-19

Nineteenth Sunday after Pentecost
First Year: Jer. 23:5-6; Rev. 21:1-4; Mt. 24:45-51
Second Year: Zeph. 3:17-20; I Thess. 5:1-11; Mt. 25:1-13

First Sunday in God the Father
First Year: Is. 49:8-13; Heb. 10:11-25; Jn. 6:25-35
Second Year: Is. 53:1-11; I Cor. 11:17-26; Mk. 14:17-25

Second Sunday in God the Father
First Year: Job 38:1-18; Rom. 1:18-25; Mt. 14:13-21

Second Year: Gen. 1:1-5; I Jn. 1:1-4; Jn. 1:1-5

Third Sunday in God the Father
First Year: Gen. 3:1-15; I Tim. 2:1-7; Mt. 8:5-13
Second Year: Gen. 1:24-27; Rom. 8:18-23; Jn. 5:1-17

Fourth Sunday in God the Father
First Year: Gen. 3:22–4:7; Eph. 6:1-9; Mt. 8:14-22
Second Year: Gen. 2:15-25; Eph. 5:21-33; Mk. 10:1-9

Fifth Sunday in God the Father
First Year: Is. 41:8-13; I Pet. 4:12-19; Mt. 6:25-34
Second Year: Gen. 8:13-22; Jas. 1:12-18; Lk. 15:1-10

Sixth Sunday in God the Father
First Year: Gen. 17:1-8; II Cor. 3:4-11; Mt. 21:33-43
Second Year: Gen. 9:8-17; I Tim. 6:6-19; Lk. 12:13-21

Seventh Sunday in God the Father
First Year: Gen. 21:1-13; Phil. 1:12-18; Lk. 4:1-13
Second Year: Job 28:12-28; Jas. 3:1-13; Lk. 12:22-34

Sunday before Advent
First Year: Jer. 23:1-4; Jas. 1:12-18; Jn. 6:5-14
Second Year: Jer. 23:5-6; Jas. 4:1-10; Mt. 15:21-28

United Church of Canada: Post-Pentecost

Epistles and Gospels are appointed for twenty-six Sundays within the season of Pentecost, the first of which are for Trinity Sunday, though not so designated. The remaining lectionary is as follows:

Second Sunday in Pentecost
I Jn. 4:7-21; Lk. 16:19-31

Third Sunday in Pentecost
I Jn. 3:13-18; Lk. 14:16-24

Fourth Sunday in Pentecost
I Pet. 5:5-11; Lk. 15:1-10

Fifth Sunday in Pentecost
Rom. 8:18-23; Lk. 6:36-42

Sixth Sunday in Pentecost
I Pet. 3:8-15; Lk. 5:1-11

Seventh Sunday in Pentecost
Rom. 6:3-11; Mt. 5:20-26

Eighth Sunday in Pentecost
Rom. 6:19-23; Mk. 8:1-9

Ninth Sunday in Pentecost
Rom. 8:12-17; Mt. 7:15-21

Tenth Sunday in Pentecost
I Cor. 10:1-13; Lk. 16:1-13 or Lk. 15:11-32

Eleventh Sunday in Pentecost
I Cor. 12:1-11; Lk. 19:41-48

Twelfth Sunday in Pentecost
I Cor. 15:1-11; Lk. 18:9-14

Thirteenth Sunday in Pentecost
II Cor. 3:4-11; Mk. 7:31-37

Fourteenth Sunday in Pentecost
Gal. 3:16-22 or Heb. 13:1-6; Lk. 10:23-37

Fifteenth Sunday in Pentecost
Gal. 5:16-24; Lk. 17:11-19

Sixteenth Sunday in Pentecost
Gal. 6:11-18; Mt. 6:24-34

Seventeenth Sunday in Pentecost
Eph. 3:13-21; Lk. 7:11-17

Eighteenth Sunday in Pentecost
Eph. 4:1-6; Lk. 14:1-11

Nineteenth Sunday in Pentecost
I Cor. 1:4-9; Mt. 22:34-46

Twentieth Sunday in Pentecost
Eph. 4:17-32; Mt. 9:1-8

Twenty-first Sunday in Pentecost
Eph. 5:15-21; Mt. 22:1-14

Twenty-second Sunday in Pentecost
Eph. 6:1-20; Jn. 4:46b-54

Twenty-third Sunday in Pentecost
Phil. 1:3-11; Mt. 18:21-35

Twenty-fourth Sunday in Pentecost
Phil. 3:17-21; Mt. 22:15-22

Twenty-fifth Sunday in Pentecost
Col. 1:3-13; Mt. 9:18-26

Twenty-sixth Sunday in Pentecost
Jer. 23:5-8; Jn. 6:5-14

Church of South India: Post-Pentecost

The Sundays immediately following Eastertide are entitled "Pentecost," "Next after Pentecost: Trinity Sunday," and "Second after Pentecost." Beginning with the last of these, all further Sundays are numbered "After Pentecost" until the Sunday called "Next before Advent." Not counting the Sunday Next before Advent, the calendar lists twenty-seven Sundays after Pentecost, some of which may not occur in a given year, depending on the date of Easter Day. No recourse to lessons from Epiphany Season is required for the longest possible extension of the period between Pentecost and Advent. The Post-Pentecost lectionary is as follows:

Second Sunday after Pentecost
Morning: Ex. 3:1-15; I Cor. 1:26-31; Lk. 5:1-11
Evening: Judg. 6:1, 11-24; Lk. 14:15-24

Third Sunday after Pentecost
Morning: Josh. 24:14-24; Heb. 4:1-13; Jn. 6:53-69
Evening: Ex. 32:15-29; Acts 4:5-22

Fourth Sunday after Pentecost
Morning: Gen. 12:1-9; Heb. 11:1-16; Lk. 7:1-10
Evening: Is. 30:8-18; Lk. 18:9-14

Fifth Sunday after Pentecost
Morning: Ex. 12:51–13:10; Gal. 5:1-15; Jn. 8:31-38
Evening: Mic. 6:1-8; Rom. 8:12-27

Sixth Sunday after Pentecost
Morning: Deut. 6:1-9; Rom. 10:1-13; Mk. 12:18-27
Evening: Jer. 23:23-32; Lk. 4:16-30

Seventh Sunday after Pentecost
Morning: Ex. 19:1-8; I Pet. 2:1-10; Mt. 16:13-19
Evening: Is. 43:8-13; Mt. 18:1-20

Eighth Sunday after Pentecost
Morning: Ex. 16:11-15; Rom. 6:1-11; Jn. 6:47-58
Evening: Ezek. 36:22-28; Mk. 6:30-44

Ninth Sunday after Pentecost
Morning: II Chron. 30:1-9; Eph. 2:11-22; Jn. 17:20-26
Evening: Ezek. 37:15-28; I Cor. 3

Tenth Sunday after Pentecost
Morning: Is. 52:7-10; Rom. 10:11-17; Mt. 10:24-33
Evening: Is. 55:1-5; Acts 10:34-43

Eleventh Sunday after Pentecost
Morning: Ezek. 33:1-6; II Cor. 5:11-21; Jn. 21:15-19

Evening: Ezek. 2:3–3:3; I Cor. 4

Twelfth Sunday after Pentecost
Morning: Deut. 26:1-11; I Jn. 4:7-21; Mk. 12:28-34
Evening: Deut. 10:12-22; Lk. 17:11-19

Thirteenth Sunday after Pentecost
Morning: I Kings 18:36-39; Eph. 3:14-21; Mt. 6:5-15
Evening: Gen. 32:22-32; Rev. 8:1-5

Fourteenth Sunday after Pentecost
Morning: Is. 35; Gal. 5:16-25; Jn. 15:1-11
Evening: Neh. 8:1-3, 5-12, Jn. 16:16-24

Fifteenth Sunday after Pentecost
Morning: Ruth 1:8-18; Heb. 11:32–12:2; Mk. 13:3-13
Evening: Hos. 2:16-23; Rev. 2:1-11

Sixteenth Sunday after Pentecost
Morning: Jer. 45; Gal. 2:15-20; Mk. 8:27-38
Evening: Neh. 5:1-13; Phil. 3:3-11

Seventeenth Sunday after Pentecost
Morning: Gen. 1:31–2:3; Rev. 1:9-18; Jn. 20:19-23
Evening: Deut. 5:12-15; Mk. 2:23–3:6

Eighteenth Sunday after Pentecost
Morning: Lev. 19:9-18; I Cor. 13; Lk. 10:25-37
Evening: Ex. 23:1-12; Rom. 12:9-21

Nineteenth Sunday after Pentecost
Morning: Prov. 4:1-9; Eph. 5:21–6:4; Mk. 10:1-16
Evening: II Sam. 18:24-33; I Pet. 3:1-9

Twentieth Sunday after Pentecost
Morning: Zech. 8:16-23; Col. 4:2-6; Mt. 25:31-46
Evening: Job 31:13-22; Phil. 1:3-11

Twenty-first Sunday after Pentecost
Morning: Ex. 35:30–36:1; II Thess. 3:6-13; Mt. 25:14-30
Evening: Neh. 4; I Thess. 5:12-24

Twenty-second Sunday after Pentecost
Morning: Ex. 18:13-27; I Pet. 2:11-17; Mk. 12:13-17
Evening: Amos 5:1-15; Rom. 13:1-7

Twenty-third Sunday after Pentecost
Morning: I Chron. 29:1-9; II Cor. 8:1-9; Lk. 20:45–21:4
Evening: I Chron. 29:10-20; Acts 20:17-35

Twenty-fourth Sunday after Pentecost
Morning: Hab. 2:1-4; I Cor. 15:50-58; Lk. 12:22-34
Evening: Is. 55:6-13; Heb. 6:9-20

Twenty-fifth Sunday after Pentecost
Morning: Dan. 3:1-18; Phil. 3:17–4:1; Jn. 15:18-27
Evening: Dan. 3:19-30; Heb. 13:7-16

Twenty-sixth Sunday after Pentecost
Morning: Deut. 30:15-20; Jas. 1:19-27; Mt. 7:13-20
Evening: Jer. 6:16-21; Rom. 6:15-23

Twenty-seventh Sunday after Pentecost
Morning: Zeph. 1:14-18; I Thess. 4:13-18; Mk. 13:14-27
Evening: Amos 5:18-24; Mt. 25:1-13

Sunday Next before Advent
Morning: Mal. 3:13–4:2; I Thess. 5:1-11; Mk. 13:28-37
Evening: Amos 4:6-13; Lk. 21:25-36

Special Days

The widest variation between denominational lectionaries is to be found in the observance of special days. The older and more traditional communions have the more elaborate calendars, including most of the saints' days and such feast days as the Annunciation, the Transfiguration, Holy Innocents, Rogation and Ember days, etc. Some of these are being restored among the more recent lectionaries. The provisional lectionary for Presbyterian churches in America, for example, provides lessons for April 25, St. Mark's day; the fifth Sunday after Easter designated Rogation (or Rural Life) Sunday; June 29, Saints Peter and Paul; September 21 and September 26, Saints Matthew and John respectively; October 18, St. Luke; and November 30, St. Andrew.

Certain general subjects of Christian concern are provided for in the lectionaries of most churches. The Protestant Episcopal Church, for instance, Interest of Christian Education," and the like.

Similarly, several lectionaries include lessons for dedications, ordinations, and commemorations of one kind or another. The Church of South India offers collects and lessons for the remembrance of "Faithful Women" in addition to commemorations of the Apostles and Martyrs, and lists such other opportunities for special services as for Prophets and Reformers, Pioneers and Builders, Healers of the Sick, Doctors of the Church, and Preachers of the Gospel.

The same terminology is, of course, not uniformly used. Independence Day is Dominion Day in Canada. New Year's Sunday is Covenant Sunday in British Methodism. In the following, lessons of the several churches are listed when there is an actual identity with any of the special days listed in the American Methodist lectionary calendar, regardless of terminology.

New Year's Day or Watch Night

Anglican (Protestant Episcopal, 1945 Revision)
Eccles. 11:1-4, 6-10, 12:13-14; Rev. 21:1-7

Lutheran Churches in America
Circumcision and the Name of Jesus
Holy Communion: Josh. 24:14-24; Gal. 3:23-29;
Lk. 2:21

British Methodist
Covenant Sunday
First Year, Morning: Gen. 9:8-17; Rom. 6:1-14
First Year, Evening: Jer. 31:31-34; Mk. 14:17-31
Second Year, Morning: Gen. 17:1-9; Mt. 6:16-34
Second Year, Evening: Ezek. 37:21b-28; Heb. 8:1-13

Watch Night
First Year: Eccles. 3:1-15; Lk. 12:35-50
Second Year: Deut. 8:1-20; Lk. 12:13-21

Church of Scotland
Morning: Deut. 11:1-17; Phil. 3:7-14; Mt. 6:19-34
Evening: Is. 61; Lk. 9:57-62

American Presbyterians (Provisional)
Deut. 8:1-10; Rev. 21:1-7; Mt. 25:31-46

United Church of Canada
Rev. 21:1-7 or Phil. 3:1-14; Mt. 25:31-46 or Lk. 9:57-62

Church of South India
Gen. 17:1-8; Col. 2:8-15; Mk. 14:22-26

Race Relations Sunday

American Presbyterians (Provisional)
Gen. 11:1-9; Col. 3:1-11; Lk. 10:25-37

Festival of the Christian Home

American Presbyterians (Provisional)
Deut. 6:1-9; Col. 3:12-24; Mt. 8:5-17

Aldersgate Sunday

British Methodist
First Year, Morning: Is. 51:1-11; Mk. 12:28-37, 41-44
First Year, Evening: Is. 52:1-2, 7-12; Rom. 5:1-11

Second Year, Morning: Amos 4:4-13; II Pet. 1:1-11
Second Year, Evening: Is. 12:1-6; Lk. 10:1-12, 17-20

Independence Day

Anglican (Protestant Episcopal, 1945 Revision)
Morning Prayer: Is. 26:1-4, 7-8, 12; Jn. 8:31-36
Evening Prayer: Deut. 4:1-14; Gal. 4:26—5:1
Holy Communion: Deut. 10:17-21; Mt. 5:43-48

United Church of Canada
Dominion Day
Deut. 8 or Deut. 10:12-22, 11:8-12; Mt. 6:19-33

Church of South India
I Kings 3:5-14; Rom. 13:1-10; Mk. 12:13-17

Labor Day or Labor Sunday

American Presbyterians (Provisional)
Eccles. 2:18-26; Eph. 2:1-10; Jn. 5:1-17

Reformation Day or Reformation Sunday

Lutheran Churches in America
Matins: II Kings 23:1-25; Jn. 2:13-17
Vespers: I Kings 19:13-18; Gal. 2:16-21
Holy Communion: I Sam. 3:19-4:1a; Rom. 3:21-28; Jn. 8:31-36

American Presbyterians (Provisional)
Neh. 8:1-8; Rom. 3:21-26; Jn. 8:31-36

All Saints Day

Roman Catholic Traditional
Rev. 7:2-12; Mt. 5:1-12

Anglican (Protestant Episcopal, 1945 Revision)
Holy Communion: Rev. 7:2-17; Mt. 5:1-12

Lutheran Churches in America
Matins: II Kings 6:14-17; Heb. 11:32—12:2
Vespers: Dan. 12:1-3; Rev. 19:1-16

Holy Communion: Deut. 33:1-3; Rev. 7:2-17; Mt. 5:1-12

British Methodist

First Year, Morning: Wis. 5:1-16 or Dan. 12:1-4, 8-11; Rev. 19:6-16

First Year, Evening: II Es. 2:42-48 or Is. 25:1-9; Heb. 11:32–12:2

Second Year, Morning: II Es. 2:42-48 or Is. 51:1-11; Mt. 5:1-12

Second Year, Evening: Wis. 5:1-16 or Dan. 12:1-4, 8-11; Rev. 7:9-17

Church of Scotland

Morning: Is. 51:1-11; Rev. 7:9-17; Mt. 5:1-12

Evening: Dan. 12:1-4, 8-13; Heb. 11:32–12:2

American Presbyterians (Provisional)

Is. 61:1-11; Rev. 7:1-12; Mt. 5:1-12

United Church of Canada

Rev. 7:9-17 or Heb. 11:32–12:2; Mt. 5:1-12

Church of South India

Dan. 7:27 or Wis. 5:15, 16; Rev. 7:9-17; Mt. 5:1-12

World Order Sunday

American Presbyterians (Provisional)

Is. 2:1-4; Eph. 2:11-22; Jn. 4:7-26

Commitment Day or Temperance Sunday

British Methodist

First Year, Morning: Dan. 1:1-21; Rom. 14:1-12

First Year, Evening: Prov. 23:29-35; Rom. 14:13-23

Second Year, Morning: Jer. 35:1-10, 18-19; Rom. 13:1-14

Second Year, Evening: Is. 5:11-12, 18-24; Mt. 19:1-12

Thanksgiving Day

Anglican (Protestant Episcopal, 1945 Revision)

Morning Prayer: Deut. 8:1-11, 17-20 or Deut. 26:1-11; I Thess. 5:12-23 or Jn. 6:26-35

Evening Prayer: Is. 12 or Deut. 11:8-21; Phil. 4:4-7 or I Tim. 6:6-16

Holy Communion: Jas. 1:16-27; Mt. 6:25-34

Lutheran Churches in America

Matins: Deut. 26:1-11; Lk. 17:11-19

Vespers: Neh. 8:9-12; Gal. 6:7-10

Holy Communion: Deut. 8:1-20 or Is. 61:10, 11; I Tim. 2:1-8 or Acts 14:8-18; Mt. 6:25-33

Church of Scotland

Morning: Deut. 26:1-11 or Is. 55:9-13; Gal. 6:6-10; Lk. 12:13-34

Evening: Deut. 28:1-14 or Ruth 2:1-17; Jn. 4:31-38

American Presbyterians (Provisional)

Is. 61:10-11; I Tim. 2:1-8; Mt. 6:25-33

United Church of Canada

Deut. 26:1-11; I Cor. 3:6-15 or Gal. 6:6-10; Lk. 12:13-34 or Jn. 4:31-36 or Jn. 6:26-40

Church of South India

Deut. 26:1-11; II Cor. 9:6-15; Jn. 6:26-35

IX

Uses of "The Book of Worship" in the Home and with Small Groups

M. Lawrence Snow

Basic Aspects of Small Group Worship

Communities of Strangers and Estranged Communities

More than at any time since the primitive household church, large numbers of Christians have a feeling of being "resident aliens" in their society.[1] The feeling of foreignness is both a general mark of sin and a particular sign of grace. It is both man's problem and God's opportunity. They conspire for the minds and deeds of Christians in the work and worship of the twentieth-century church.

The first Christians used the Greek word for strangers (*paroikoi*) to describe the congregations or parishes of which they were members. They were like a nation within a nation, at once rooted and grounded in eternity and also resident *aliens* in the world community. Because of this dual character the church has often been tempted to become otherworldly, ascetic, mystical, escapist on the one hand, or secular, this-worldly, unspiritual, expediently humanistic on the other.[2]

---

[1] The Greek word for "alien" is *paroikos*. It is related to a cluster of biblical words rooted in the domestic, family image. *oikos, oikeios:* house, home, household. *paroikia:* congregation (cf. our modern "parochial" and "parish"). *oikumene:* one inhabited world (cf. our modern "ecumenical"). *oikonomia:* God's activity, church order (c. our modern "economy," e.g., of God's grace).

[2] E. G. Homrighausen's exposition of I Peter 2:11 in *The Interpreter's Bible*, XII, 112. Horton Davies, a historian of English and particularly Puritan worship, has remarked: "There is evidence that in the essential tension between fidelity to the historically given nature of

Today the Christian family or small group is being doubly rubbed: by the dated structures and services of the institutional church, and by the abrasive claims and eccentric activities of an urban, secular society. Christians can be most sensitive to this dilemma in their acts of worship. For more than a few this private and public discipline seems a desperate aid to piety (the "escapist" temptation) and a meaningless burden to be dropped (the "secular" temptation).

Familiar Worship, a Public Event

Familiar worship is intimate worship. Familiar worship is conducted by small groups, offered by families and individuals. Yet familiar worship should be accustomed to the public services of a historic church *and* to the public obligations of the secular world.[3]

Bishop Fulton J. Sheen's successor as national director of the Roman Catholic Society for the Propagation of the Faith recently observed: "It is no longer enough, nor is it time to be looking only up to Heaven. We must look out to the world to see its people and its needs." [4] The upward look and the outward look are the cross-views of Christianity.

Another way of talking about the vertical and horizontal dimensions of religion is by considering the "in's" and "out's" of worship.

In the past the theological understanding of worship has been developed mainly in one direction, i.e. *inwardly:* for example, it has been interpreted as that which builds up the Body of Christ. . . . I think the time has come when we must adopt another approach, which is complementary rather than an alternative; we must seek to understand worship *outwardly* in terms of mission.[5]

Christian revelation and the concern to communicate relevantly to the age, the liturgical church chooses fidelity and the non-liturgical churches select relevance." "The Expression of the Social Gospel in Worship," cited in *Worship and Mission*, J. G. Davies, p. 147, n. 12 (New York: Association Press, 1967). It needs to be noted that secularizing theologians like Harvey Cox (*The Secular City*) loosen this tension (i.e., between fidelity and relevance) when they urge: "We should now begin to emphasize the call of God to man to construct the Kingdom of God, to fashion the New Jerusalem, and to do so as an act, not a defiance, of praise and thanksgiving." (An unpublished paper presented to the International Congress on Religion, Architecture, and the Visual Arts, August, 1967.)

[3] Historically, the word "liturgy" (*laos*, people; *ergon*, work) embodies both meanings: public obligations to the state and public services of the church.

[4] Msgr. Edward T. O'Meara, *The New York Times*, August 23, 1967. Cf. this sentiment with the Gospel accounts narratively linking Jesus' transfiguration and his healing of the boy with the evil spirit. Matt. 17; Mark 9; Luke 9. Also the disciples looking up into heaven at the ascension and their mission. Acts 1.

[5] J. G. Davies, *Worship and Mission*, p. 8. This emphasis keeps worship rooted in history, i.e., human events, where God and men interact in their deeds and words. Cf. similar motifs in such books as John A. T. Robinson, *Liturgy Coming to Life* (Philadelphia: The Westminster Press, 1960); Alexander Schmemann, *For the Life of the World* (New York: National Student Christian Federation, 1963); J. C. Hoekendijk, *The Church Inside Out* (Philadelphia: The Westminster Press, 1966); James F. White, *The Worldliness of Worship* (New York: Oxford University Press, 1967).

This concern has so far modestly influenced the public practices of worship among the major denominations, and their revisions to hymnals and prayer books. It is beginning to influence the planning and building of new church edifices.[6] However, renewed attention to this two-sided responsibility (devotion—inward; mission—outward) could most readily revolutionize small group worship.

Problems of Methodist Worship

Methodists especially should not ignore the public implications of their private devotions. (As already indicated, "public" means both the services of the church and the affairs of the world.)

On the one hand, the end of the class meeting and the decline of the prayer meeting in Methodism have further loosed the ties of intimate discipline and personal devotion from the public services (work and worship) of the church. On the other hand, pivotal events, such as "the wet-dry controversy destroyed in the minds of many supporters of Prohibition any sense of the proportionate importance of social [i.e., public, worldly] issues" other than pietistic ones like abstinence.[7]

One of the consequences in recent times has been a dilution of Methodist notions of worship and particularly "devotions." Our devotional literature is deprived; our devotional practices are in a state of disrepair. They are individualistic, subjective, and faintly effeminate. They tend to be overly moralistic, "psychological"; sometimes an acrostic of mystical classics. They seem artificial because they are not public; they are unchurchly and unworldly. They are private to the point of unreality.[8]

Interestingly, the sermon, which Protestants have come to regard as the most important part of public worship, often mirrors the congregation's deprived spirituality. Widely popular preaching deals with how persons can "get along" and "be good." These themes narrow the responsibilities of worship and the humanity of the worshiper. They make God and his world too small.

For Church and Home

It is not accidental that *The Book of Worship* is intended for use in both church *and* home. Nor for our day should this dual purpose be incidental.

---

[6] Two useful primers, Catholic and Protestant, are: Louis Bouyer, *Liturgy and Architecture* (Notre Dame: University of Notre Dame Press, 1967) and James F. White, *Protestant Worship and Church Architecture* (New York: Oxford University Press, 1964).

[7] Paul A. Carter, *The Decline and Revival of the Social Gospel: Social and Political Liberalism in American Protestant Churches, 1920-1940* (Ithaca: Cornell University Press, 1954).

[8] It very much needs to be remembered that when John Wesley extracted and commended Puritan and medieval devotional literature in *A Christian Library* (50 vols.), he did it *because*, not in spite of, the fact he was first and foremost a *church* man, specifically a priest in the Church of England. Paul S. Sanders, a splendid student of the early history of Methodist worship, has commented on this matter in an essay, "Wesley's Eucharistic Faith and Practice" (available in reprint from The Order of St. Luke, Park Ave., Flanders, N. J.).

A glance at the acknowledgments following the title page shows that many of the resources come from familial prayer books and personal devotional manuals.

Further, we should recall that the original publication of *The Book of Worship* was not only to get Methodist rituals under one cover after the three-way merger in 1939, but also to provide resources for small group and family devotions. Older Methodists can remember some of its devotional forerunners: *A Book of Worship for Use at Table on Every Day of the Year,* compiled and edited by Wade Crawford Barclay; *The Table Altar: Meditations for a Month of Mornings,* edited by John H. Vincent; *Select Psalms Arranged for the Use of the Methodist Episcopal Church by John Wesley . . .* [divided into morning and evening lessons for every day in the month], edited by Charles S. Harrower.

The Small Group Movement and a Prayer Book

Like other denominations, modern Methodism has experienced the more or less spontaneous rise of a small group movement, and the planned publication (and now revision) of a church prayer book. These apparently unrelated events, considered together, quicken memories and expectations.

Methodism was born a small group movement within a prayer book church, the Church of England. From the earliest days of the Oxford Holy Club, Wesleyans created cells of practical piety within the body of the church catholic. These cells—society, class, band—were nourished by the *Book of Common Prayer* services of the church, particularly the Anglican liturgy of Holy Communion. In short, these disciplined groups generated an evangelistic elite serving a sorry society. It was a *church* piety with a mission of *social* holiness.[9]

The recent resurgence of small groups in the local congregation, gathered on the basis of common tasks, common study, and common questions, have the same twofold function as the whole church: serving God and the world.[10] As in former years, the youth of the Methodist movement, these smaller groups can perhaps again be the larger church's wellspring of devotion and its springboard for mission.

In many parts of the church, besides the existing smaller groups required or advised by the *Discipline,* countless new ones are springing up in the presence of specific opportunities and needs. Incidentally, some believe that local congregations ought to be authorized by the General Conference to reorganize

[9] *Church piety* is an intimate and personal spirituality fostered in and shaped by the services and orders of a historic church. A good example is *The Devotions of Bishop Andrewes,* originally published in the century before John Wesley and arranged anew the century after him by John Henry Newman.

[10] The late Carl Michalson recognized that some of these small groups are too "far out" to be called *ecclesiola in ecclesia* (a little church within the church). They "seem to be comprised of the faithless, those making a last desperate effort to remain in the church, but doing so under the auspices of the church." *Worldly Theology* (New York: Charles Scribner's Sons, 1967).

into flexible task forces, i.e., committed groups evolving mission, rather than fixed commissions "doing" programs.

Bible study groups (increasingly ecumenical), prayer cells, spiritual "laboratories," etc., usually have the prime purpose of creating informed piety. Neighborhood task forces, coffee-house committees, drama groups, etc., usually have the prime purpose of witnessing by doing, often outside the church's programs and buildings. (Political action groups are even "farther out," more controversial, and harder to relate to the visible church in terms of traditional criteria.) Both sorts of groups—and there are, of course, dozens of variations—have a way of doubling back upon each other. That is, Bible study leads to specific projects; neighborhood tasks lead to study and prayer.

The familiar uses of *The Book of Worship* in this time of experimentation should, therefore, provide greater opportunities than just one more "devotional" resource. Imaginative use can illuminate the intimate group's place within the total church and also encourage its sense of service for the world.

Liturgy, Devotion, Instruction

Whether with a large congregation or a small group, *The Book of Worship* is susceptible of three basic uses: *liturgical, devotional, instructional*. These distinctions are as much a matter of *how* the rites and resources are used as *what* ones are used or *who* uses them.

Historically, *the* Christian church's liturgy has been the sacrament of the Lord's Supper. Methodism acknowledges this tradition to the extent that only an elder (or one duly authorized by a bishop) may preside, and to the extent that a stipulated number of texts are required for a proper communion.[11]

Still, a general point worth making to Methodists is that prayers, orders, and other materials are understood as liturgical, devotional, or instructional easier by use than by text or leader.

The Lord's Prayer can be used liturgically, devotionaly, or instructionally, depending on the context for its use and the intent of the user (s) . All three uses could overlap, even coincide; for example, in an "instructed communion" (see below) .

When the editors write in the Preface to the *Book of Worship*, "Section II presents an anthology of Scripture, prayers, and other liturgical material . . . ," they are indicating that certain materials have been and can be used in *public services*, that is, for liturgical purposes. For Protestants, worship resources are not inherently liturgical. And in all instances the *size* of the worshiping group is utterly incidental.

Methodists are understandably careless about these nicer points because sacramental worship has for generations been secondary to "prayers and preaching" in their Sunday services. At this stage of liturgical revival and for our purposes in this chapter, we need only note that a Quaker meeting can be

---

[11] See, e.g., the second opening rubric to the Order for the Administration of the Sacrament of the Lord's Supper. *The Book of Worship*, p. 15.

as "liturgical" in its silence and spontaneity as a Catholic high Mass in its stipulated texts and sacramental action. They are both liturgical precisely insofar as they are offered as public service.

One final point. The pastor will be a key person in unlocking the *Book of Worship* in a parish. Nonetheless, maximum lay leadership and participation (the basic aim of liturgical renewal) is specifically required and implied in all suggestions for familiar use of the *Book of Worship*. Worship is not a clerical act, and only in the liturgy for Holy Communion need a pastor reserve the right of consecration, and this only because it is a matter of good order in The United Methodist Church. Of all the public services this sacrament needs maximum lay involvement, and it can best be obtained in the smaller groups, as we shall suggest below.

Practical Suggestions

Suggestions for Familiar Liturgical Uses of The Book of Worship

Now and in the immediate future some of the more creative and revitalizing acts in the church are going to be small, intimate group liturgies (i.e., public services, as defined above). The reason is simple: small groups of Christians, gathered with a common concern, committed to a specific task, deepen their intimacy with God and one another and sharpen their sense of servanthood in and for the world when they unite in a common public service.

As noted earlier, in the oldest and still widest sense, *the* liturgy is the celebration of Holy Communion. This sacrament is the normative public service within Roman Catholic, Eastern Orthodox, and Anglican communions.[12] Luther, Calvin, and Wesley all intended this sacrament to be the regular Sunday service. For various reasons it has not remained so within most Protestant churches. The trend, however, is toward renewal of this early church practice. The greatest impetus for frequent, even weekly, communions may have to come less from clerical mandate than from lay request. These requests will grow out of meaningful uses in small study and task groups.[13]

A. *An Order for Holy Communion* (pp. 15-22); *Also a Brief Form of the Order* (pp. 24-27)

    1. *Weekly chapel* celebrations, especially in larger churches and on college campuses. An early Sunday hour, e.g., 8 a.m. A regular midweek hour, e.g., Wednesday mornings or evenings (permitting men to commune). Families (or students) prepare and present the elements on the table, during opening hymn, if Brief Order is used. Laymen read lessons, offer prayers. After the post-communion

---

[12] Usually called the Mass, the Divine Liturgy, and the Eucharist. A few Protestant churches, e.g., the Disciples of Christ, commemorate the Lord's Supper weekly.

[13] Cf. the growing requests for the *agape* meal (a type of love feast) in countries like Holland. Edward B. Fiske, "The 'Love Feast' Is an Issue," in *The New York Times*, August 27 (Sunday), 1967.

Thanksgiving, let the concerns of the parish, campus, world be offered extemporaneously by members in the congregation (e.g., sentence prayers). Perhaps prayers for healing. A closing "collect" to gather them.

2. Regular administration to *sick* and *shut-ins* in hospitals, homes, and retirement homes. Whenever possible lay visitors ought to accompany the pastor (elder). They should assist, along with members of the family (if at home), making the whole service truly corporate. In some instances, the minister may lay hands on head of the sick person, even anoint with oil, after the communion. (See esp. prayers, pp. 233-38.) Services for laying on of hands will be discussed below.

3. *Household communions* around table, e.g., at outstanding family events such as a wedding anniversary. A minister who is an ordained elder would preside, of course. Let a hymn be sung. Use a piano when possible. Emphasize the "eucharist"—the joy and thanksgiving. Personal words of testimony. A meal as part of the occasion could be (in several senses) a Love Feast. (See p. 389.) Love Feast discussed in greater detail below. Intimate house communions are fitting with particular task-force groups: drama, coffee-house planners, ghetto-workers, workers with migrants, etc.

4. Small group use of Communion with a *Covenant Service* is discussed below.

5. Small *Communion breakfasts* or other meals. Possible variations with parts or all of Love Feast (p. 389) are possible with preparation, even at a businessmen's luncheon if pastor has spent time with his laymen. Confirmation classes, Methodist Men in small face-to-face gatherings. With members of other communions, e.g., C.M.E., A.M.E., and A.M.E. Zion Churches.

B. *The Love Feast* (p. 389) [14]

1. Excellent as a regular part of an *ecumenical Bible study group,* or at the end of a period of study and fellowship. Use water and buns. (When bread and wine or grape juice are used it blurs the distinction between the "meal" and Communion. The Shalom group in Holland is doing this "blurring" intentionally; but it can create as many difficulties as it overcomes, especially when Roman Catholics are participating.) Let the "offering for the poor" be sacrificial and go to some definite cause in the neighborhood. Depending on the nature and will of the group, the offering could go for anything from migrant work to legal aid for conscientious objectors. If

---

[14] See Richard N. Ryley, "The Love Feast: Yesterday and Today" (available in reprint from The Order of St. Luke, Park Ave., Flanders, N. J.). Several variations on how to use the "love feast" in contemporary situations are discussed in this essay. See also Frank Baker's *Methodism and the Love Feast* (London: Epworth Press, 1957).

Roman Catholics are involved, try to secure the (or a) parish priest's participation. Let there be testimonies about what the fellowship and study mean and imply. Especially popular with college-age youth. *It is not a substitute for, or a shortcut to, the Sacrament of Holy Communion.*

2. Love Feast can be effectively used as a "high point" in small group retreats, e.g., a senior high camp. (Better alternative than the overdone, semi-pagan campfires.) On retreats, fasting or sacrificial meals could provide for the "offering." "Voluntary Prayers": Let there be silence and sentence petitions.

C. *The Covenant Service* (pp. 382-88) with/without *A Brief Form for Holy Communion* (pp. 24-27)

Beginning a *new church year* with such commissions as Membership and Evangelism, Missions, Christian Social Concerns, Education; officers of the Official Board, W.S.C.S., Methodist Men, etc. Around table in church hall, church school room, or at home. Try to celebrate where the work is going to be done. Let laymen lead all parts. In Communion the offering can include (in addition to the elements) symbols of the services to be rendered, e.g., church school curricula, statements promising particular amounts of time and types of work. Emphasize the *particular implications* of the Covenant to which the group is binding itself, e.g., teachers to teaching.

D. *The Order for Morning Prayer, from John Wesley's Sunday Service, 1784* (pp. 377-81)

Early weekday services in college and university chapels; also chapels of larger churches. An excellent 8 a.m. Sunday service which can be alternated with early weekly Sunday communions (see above). For evening prayer the *Book of Common Prayer* (from which Wesley's service of course comes) can be used. The whole service can be done entirely with or without service music. It is a prayer service (with or without sermon or meditation) and probably ought not to be used as an ante-communion, i.e., an introduction to the sacrament. Can be used in small discussion groups, e.g., local Consultation on Church Union or COCU) disclosing the common heritage of the Anglo-Saxon churches, i.e., Presbyterians, Episcopalians, Methodists, Congregationalists, etc.

E. *NOTE:* On *The Order for the Burial of the Dead* (pp. 32-43)

The fourth rubric (p. 32) indicates that "in the event of cremation the service may be adapted at the discretion of the minister." Small family memorial services are becoming increasingly common. The Order in such instances can be adapted for greater group participation. The psalms should be read responsively. Psalm 23 is Psalter 7 (p. 256); Psalm 27 is Psalter 10 (p. 257), etc. Hymns should be sung. (See suggestions in Chapter V of the Handbook.) Members of the family could read scriptures. A brief scriptural meditation is desirable.

F.   *NOTE: An Office for Blessing a Dwelling* (pp. 373-74)
     Can be used (with or without a minister) by a family after moving into a new or newly built house.

Suggestions for Familiar Devotional Uses of The Book of Worship ["Prayers"]
     Small group and private devotions should support, not substitute for, the church's regular public services. While (in the words of Charles Williams) they need not "twiddle and twist . . . to the supposed momentary needs of the crowd," regular and occasional devotional acts do serve as bridges between the public services of the church and the private claims of conscience in a secular society.[15]

     They personalize church piety [see n. 9]. They offer the practice in the daily discipline of "centering down" loyalty to a living God. They provide insights into specific claims of God's rulership, that is, his Kingdom. Through devotional habits, especially personal and family, the conscience is sensitized, the intellect informed, the will disposed to obey; the whole person kept resilient. They create a tempered will, or at least a temperament, for the services of the church and the serving of Christ in our neighbor.

A.   *Regular Devotions:* Form for Family Prayer or Worship in a Small Group (p. 249)
     1.   *Daily morning/evening chapel services* in larger congregations and on campuses, etc. Depending on hour and location, services can have participation by church staff, folk going to/returning from work, classes, etc. Led by laymen as much as possible. (Calendar of leadership?)

          Rubrics (p. 249) suggest the possible resources in *The Book of Worship*. See also Confessions, pp. 171-74. These are good occasions for specific *intercessory prayers*. Rubrics list pages for many special types. Pray by *name* for sick, special needs, birthdays, anniversaries, etc. Publicize in calendar form for parish, so people will know when and why they are being lifted up in prayers. Thanksgiving for recoveries of all sorts. Prayers for special neighborhood needs and opportunities; and of course the larger issues of the day. See pp. 184-95.

          Encourage laymen to use other prayer books such as Michel Quoist, *Prayers;* Malcolm Boyd, *Are You Running with Me, Jesus?* and those cited in the *Book of Worship* acknowledgments following the title page.

          When possible allow for at least a couple of sentences or minute

---

[15] "The Liturgy" in *The Image of the City and Other Essays* by Charles Williams, selected by Anne Ridler (London: Oxford University Press, 1958).

comment, a reading, a quotation. Anything from the newspaper to *The Upper Room* to a medieval mystic.

Though the *Book of Worship* provides only a Sunday lectionary (pp. 62-64), there are five readings for each Sunday so they can be spread through a week, especially if there is no Saturday service, and the Sunday one used twice. It is helpful in regular prayers to follow a lectionary, particularly if the assigned ones are used the week preceding their reading in the Sunday service. Groups having daily devotions, morning *and* evening, may wish to supplement the present limited Methodist lectionary with assignments from other sources (*Book of Common Prayer, Lutheran Service Book,* etc.) or make their own.

2. *Family or Private Devotions at Home.* See above. Also Order for Morning Worship for Family, and Order for Evening Worship for Family, in the first edition of the *Book of Worship,* pp. 119-21. Again it is helpful, even with young children, to have a regular daily order (i.e., routine) and of course a fixed time. Some "said" prayers, for example: "Home and Kindred," pp. 222-29. "Morning, Day, Evening," pp. 218-22. Vary the versions of scriptures used. Sometimes read same passage, if brief, from two or more versions at same devotion. That is a message in itself. Especially good in families are: *Young Readers Bible* (RSV), *Today's English Version of the New Testament* (in paperback: *Good News for Modern Man*); *New English Bible* (New Testament); *The Children's Bible;* various versions and adaptations by Ronald Knox, J. B. Phillips, James Moffatt, W. R. Bowie (The Story of the Bible); *The Jerusalem Bible* (Catholic), and *The Torah, The Five Books of Moses* (Jewish Publication Society, 1962), *et al.,* make good comparative reading in this ecumenical age.

In family devotions all members should have assignments.

3. *Table Graces,* pp. 229-32. Many can be sung, e.g., the Wesley Graces 1 & 2.

Note: Many of the table graces can be said together (children memorize) *after* a meal in addition, or as an alternate, to grace *before* eating. The Doxology is a fitting grace to be said or sung before or after meals.

B. *Occasional Devotions and Prayers*

1. *Prayers before public services.* See Prayers for Use on Entering the Church, p. 166; Prayers with Choir, pp. 167-68. For Ministers of the Gospel, p. 241. In British Methodism lay stewards regularly lead their pastors or visiting preachers in prayer before he enters the church and pulpit. It would be a deeply affecting habit if various laymen, such as the lay leader and other church officers, regularly led their pastor (s) and choir (s) in prayer before services.

2. *Prayers before and after* commissions, committees, and other small group meetings. Lay led as much as possible. See especially pp. 205-7; pp. 242-49.

3. *Church School devotions: class, department, etc.* Methodist church school curricula make helpful suggestions for uses of *The Book of Worship* with all ages. The book should be a standard resource in all classes, and teachers encouraged to use it regularly, as advised in the lessons, and perhaps with some general instruction from the pastor. By the time of confirmation young people should be thoroughly acquainted with it through liturgical use in public services and through devotional and instructional uses in church school. *The Book of Worship* is a meaningful gift, after such background, for confirmation classes. The "Handbook" will be a helpful classroom tool. Young people should be encouraged to use the book themselves in preparing devotions.

Laying on of Hands and Intercessory Prayers for Healing

This type of service, growing in significance and use in our churches, deserves special mention. While there is no office in *The Book of Worship* for this (usually) small group service, prayers "For the Sick and Sorrowing" (pp. 233-38) may be useful. Such a service may be regular (perhaps midweek, early morning, or evening) or occasional, depending upon the sensitivities of a parish and the gifts of a pastor.

The service may move from silence; in any case a minimum of music is required. The direction should be for creative prayer, starting with brief readings from, e.g., Scriptures, Quaker writers (George Fox, Douglas Steere, Rufus Jones, Elton Trueblood, *et al.*) and other appropriate devotional readings. Reading of Scriptures giving antecedent and authorization: Epistle of James, passages on Jesus' ministry, Paul's epistles, etc. Brief exposition. Confession. Silent prayer and intercessions with reading of names of those for whom prayer has been specially requested. Invitation to altar rail for laying on of hands. A sample invitation: "Those who wish to use the New Testament rite of the laying on of hands as a time of special intercession for another, or to meet some special need in their own lives, may now come to the altar . . . ,"

A sample prayer by pastor while laying on of hands: "In the name of God Most High may you find set at work in the depths of your being the power and purpose of God to release you from anxiety, illness, and distress. May you sense anew the indwelling of the Holy Spirit as God alive and at work in you now to restore you to wholeness of being in body, mind, and spirit, through Jesus Christ our Lord. Amen."

There would be a dismissal and benediction.[16]

---

[16] I am indebted to my friend and colleague Dr. Edgar N. Jackson for permission to cite material and ideas he has put to work, especially in a regular midweek service of intercessory prayer for healing during his lengthy pastorate in Mamaroneck, New York. Another resource is

Suggestions for Familiar Instructional Uses of The Book of Worship

Reinhold Niebuhr is reputed to have told the late Archbishop of Canterbury, William Temple, that it was not the bishops but the *Book of Common Prayer* which kept the Church of England in the apostolic tradition. This quip suggests an important fact. A prayer book, among other things, abets the preservation of faith. *The Book of Worship* has had too short a history and too limited a use for such prestige. Still, much of its material, especially in "The General Services," "The Christian Year," "The Psalter," and "Services in the Methodist Tradition," gathers orders which have in part shaped the liturgies and pieties of Methodism for 200 years and of the Church for 2,000 years.

Liturgy and devotions are always inwardly forming faith as trust and outwardly forming faith as right belief (i.e., doctrine or teaching). This informative and instructional function is most evident in the texts and words of sermons, scriptures, prayers, hymns, etc. It is less evident but equally important in the overall duties and disciplines of worship which influence the total person, from his moral posture in public to his physical posture in the pew!

We agree with many like James White who have said: "Worship and education go together. Both are parts of the same process of formation." [17] In particular there are some small group *teaching* opportunities with *The Book of Worship* which merit special mention, in addition to those implied in the familiar liturgical and devotional uses of the book.

A. *Teaching about the Services*

The texts and rubrics of "The General Services" (pp. 3-58) and "Services in the Methodist Tradition" (pp. 377-92) are particularly excellent teaching resources for confirmation classes, acolyte corps, Commissions on Worship, W.S.C.S. study groups, ecumenical study groups (laity and/or clergy), church school classes, liturgical retreats, lay academies, etc.

Background study and preparation must be done by the teacher and often assigned to the class or study group. Approaches to studying the services are almost unlimited. Here are some examples: Comparison with liturgies of other churches; history of a particular liturgy's development; the theology embodied in the shape of the liturgy, the texts and rubrics of the services; modern variations and experiments with the liturgies; biblical origins of the services; the uses and abuses of scriptures in the liturgies . . . , etc.

Seminary polity courses and conference Boards of the Ministry ought

---

the International Order of St. Luke the Physician (not to be confused with a liturgical fellowship of Methodists known as The Order of St. Luke). The former group has an Episcopal origin but is interdenominational in influence and membership. Material can be obtained by writing: The Rev. John J. Park, executive secretary, 2243 Front Street, San Diego, California 92101.

[17] *The Worldliness of Worship*, p. 28.

to give time to the ordinands (classes of deacons and elders) for more than just the mechanics of the ordinals. In this ecumenical era it is important that Methodist ordinations assume greater significance than just adjunct ceremonies to entering conferences on trial and in full membership. (Since such classes would be composed of seminarians, they can be advanced theological seminars, considering the related yet discreet ministries of clergy and laymen within the church.)

Resources for background teaching about the liturgies and service are boundless. A few are listed below:

Book of Common Prayer (Episcopal); *The First and Second Prayer Books of Edward VI; Roman Missal; The Taizé Office* (London: The Faith Press, 1966); *The Book of Common Worship* (The Church of South India) (London: Oxford University Press, 1963); *English Ritual* (Roman Catholic) (Collegeville: The Liturgical Press, 1964); *The Book of Catholic Worship* (Washington: The Liturgical Conference, 1966); For other prayer books, see the "Acknowledgment of Sources" in *The Book of Worship,* pp. 393-95. Also general reading: Gregory Dix: *The Shape of the Liturgy* (Westminster: Dacre Press, 1945); John C. Bowmer, *The Sacrament of the Lord's Supper in Early Methodism* (Westminster: Dacre Press, 1951); Frank Baker, *Methodism and the Love Feast* (London: Epworth Press, 1957); John Bishop, *Methodist Worship in Relation to Free Church Worship* (London: Epworth Press, 1950); H. G. Hardin, J. D. Quillian, Jr., J. F. White, *The Celebration of the Gospel* (Nashville: Abingdon Press, 1964); Nathaniel Micklem, ed., *Christian Worship* (Oxford: Oxford University Press, 1936); Ecumenical Studies in Worship, 17 titles now in print (General eds., J. G. Davies and A. Raymond George; Richmond: John Knox Press); Albert C. Outler, ed., *John Wesley* (New York: Oxford University Press, 1964), esp. "Church and Sacraments," pp. 306-44; Rupert Davies, Gordon Rupp, eds., *A History of the Methodist Church in Great Britain* (London: Epworth Press, 1965-   ; Vol. I published to date); *The History of American Methodism,* 3 vols. (Nashville: Abingdon Press, 1964); M. L. Snow, "Confirmation and The Methodist Church" (Park Ave., Flanders, N. J.: The Order of St. Luke, 1964). Many of these books have extensive bibliographies, and more specialized theological texts would be readily accessible in colleges and seminaries.

B.   *Instructed Liturgies*

In addition to "teaching about the liturgy," some churches have been reviving the custom of instructed communions. The celebrant comments on the meaning, theology, history, etc., of the different parts of service (rubrics, prayers, actions) *in the process of using the order for worship.* Thus the sermon or lesson becomes the overall instruction. It is a quite feasible technique for a large public service. However, a good way to begin is with small groups, e.g., a confirmation class, a study group, a church school class, a commission on worship, etc.

In some special instances it is conceivable that "instructed" baptisms and confirmations may be edifying not only in the regular morning service (when it is most desirable) but now and again in smaller (e.g., afternoon) public acts of worship.

C. *Teaching the Christian Year*

As mentioned above, the lectionary when regularly followed in the Sunday service can be used for small group study, encouraging (1) lay participation in sermon preparation, and (2) informed discussions in post-service "talk-backs." These conversations can be part of weekly prayer group or Bible class. Mature biblical exegesis and historical criticism should be expected.

Examination of the liturgical-devotional resources for the Christian Year (pp. 61-317) ought to be a regular part of confirmation courses. Visual aids, including paraments, church symbols, etc., are helpful. *The Methodist Hymnal* (1966) provides hymn texts arranged for the Christian Year.

X

Other Occasional Services

Roy A. Reed

The Occasional Offices of the *Book of Worship* may be described as services of consecration or dedication. To be sure, these terms are not always used in the titles of the services; some of the sixteen services are designated as acts of "recognition," "commissioning," or "blessing." In effect, however, all the occasional offices are ceremonies in which persons or things are set apart, usually named, and dedicated to a specific task in the work of Christ's church.

Appropriately, the terms "dedication" and "consecration" dominate the titles of these services. The terms are synonymous. Despite their different roots, the Latin words *consecro* and *dedico* have the same meaning. Likewise, the Greek terms which these Latin words translate have essentially equivalent meanings.

In popular understanding, however, there exists at least a nuance of difference between the two words. "Consecrate" implies especially an action of setting apart by "making sacred." "Dedicate" implies more an action of setting apart by "giving special purpose."

"Dedication" and "consecration" refer to the naming of a special purpose proposed for a person or a thing; thus the meaning and intention of the ceremony in which this purpose is stated are clear and uncontroversial. Insofar as "dedication" and "consecration" mean or imply the making sacred of a person or thing, certain classical theological problems are raised. What it may mean to "make sacred" is a question that has bothered generations of Christians. Moreover, in the twentieth century when many problems concerning the doctrine of God are under discussion, the notion of divinization or consecration is particularly difficult. We may be tempted to ignore the idea of the

193

consacre (old English spelling which makes the meaning of the term clear), the "making sacred," and the whole idea of holy existence, in favor of the idea of purpose, stressing dedication as specific action.

This temptation doubtless will not be indulged primarily because of the close connection made in the New Testament between who a person *is* and what he *does*. Perhaps the best citation to illustrate this point, in connection with our discussion, is Christ's prayer for the disciples in the seventeenth chapter of John's Gospel:

Sanctify them in the truth; thy word is truth. As thou didst send me into the world, so I have sent them into the world. And for their sake I consecrate myself, that they also may be consecrated in truth. (Vs. 17-19 RSV)

As the prayer indicates, whoever and whatever is made sacred in this world, is made to enter into the consecration of the Christ. This point is made many times in the New Testament. Paul calls Christians into a transforming commitment which he calls the renewal of the mind (Rom. 12:2). The transformation which he intends is a self-conscious commitment to discover and emulate the "mind" of Christ. It is a call to new being, to existence as a holy and reasonable living sacrifice (Rom. 12:1). The reality of consecration is, thus, a function of the work of Christ in the world (I John 3:11-24). What the disciple *does* cannot be abstracted from what he *is*.

The Christ who is the "Holy One of God" (Mark 1:24) calls his disciples into his own sanctity through his life and death (John 17:17; Heb. 13:12; I Peter 1:15; I Cor. 6:11). The holiness—the *consacre* of Christ—is not an otherworldly transcendent essence which can be conveyed through particular "religious experiences" or authorized rites and ceremonies. It is the very power of being which was holy in Christ—not life itself but the agape life, which is his gift to us. It is the grace of discipleship which is bestowed upon those who are being made into "holy temples in the Lord" (Eph. 2:21) and given the task of a missionary priesthood as a consecrated people (I Peter 2:9).

This consecration and dedication are not enjoined upon some Christians such as ministers, deaconesses, or directors of Christian Education and withheld from others. All are consecrated and dedicated. The content of the ceremonies of Baptism and Confirmation proclaims this clearly. This is exactly their purpose. Why then, we might ask, do we need Occasional Offices to do what has already been done? True, the Spirit is one; insofar as we are consecrated we are all in the one Spirit. But there are many varieties of service; we have different gifts and talents (I Cor. 11:4-12; Rom. 12:4-8).

The purpose of the Occasional Offices is to recognize some of the varieties in which the one consecration in Christ is realized in the life of the church. The group of services provided in *The Book of Worship* is not an exhaustive collection of the possibilities for liturgical acts of dedication and consecration. Other services, composed by groups or individuals for special purposes, are possible and desirable. The specific ministries into which the one consecration may be channeled are multiplying continually; it is appropriate for these "vocations" of the ordained clergy and laity to be recognized and entered into prayerfully through special liturgical celebrations.

Such services, or "moments" within services, help the Christian community to recognize its identity and mission. They might be unnecessary were human nature different than it is. Consecration and dedication are "spiritual" qualities whose essence and meaning cannot be objectified in a liturgical event. This is surely a fact. Many Protestants have pointed to this fact in objection to some of the rites and ceremonies of the church, including sometimes the sacraments, where the subjectivity of the divine presence is perhaps threatened by the objectifying possibilities inherent in ritual forms of worship. The history of the church demonstrates that such objections are valid. No ceremony properly executed becomes the guarantor, through ritual words and actions, of the actuality of consecration and dedication. The gifts of Christ, the presence of the Holy Spirit, are not coaxed down by our incantations. Our words do not have this power; our services do not have this goal.

In liturgies of consecration and dedication we recognize the divine presence, affirm it, and celebrate it; we do not create it. In such ceremonies we may experience together the power of which we speak. The words and actions themselves do not guarantee this experience.

Individual celebrations of the different directions of the one consecration are helpful because our experience of the one consecration is not homogenous and undifferentiated. It is of the essence of faith, as well as of existence itself, that our lives in time and space are not static but dynamic. One moment is different from another moment; one place is different from another place. Some *times* are filled with great meaning; some *places* assume special significance. This psychological phenomenon creates the Christian, and every other, cultus. Certain events in the cultus, such as the Holy Communion, are repetitions of times (the last supper) and places (the upper room) of special meaning which the church recalls because they actualize her very life. They proclaim the Christ, the discipleship, and enable us to affirm our own acceptance of Christ and discipleship. The Communion is obviously not repeated as a law—a mandatory recollection of Maundy Thursday. If we repeat the events of that meal, it is not simply to remember an objective fact, but to be a part of a dynamic and continuing reality—the Christ, his sacrifice, the community of discipleship gathered around him, and the participation by this community in the self-giving of her Lord. Liturgical event as time-of-meaning and place-of-meaning is thus not static, objectifying experience, but the celebration of the one consecration in a particular manifestation.

Such events have their own life; they take place at a given time and in a given place, but only in order that the consecration celebrated can be extended beyond the time-and-place boundaries of a particular service of worship.

An individual dedication of a church building, for instance, is not a ceremony in which a secular building is made holy. It is a ceremony where the *one* consecration is recalled as it relates to the life and work of the Christian community which will make its headquarters in this building. The building is dedicated, not that the walls may be magically sacred, or even that a people be sanctified exclusively within the walls, but "for the extension of the kingdom of God."

Such ceremonies are *sacramental* in effect. At the heart of the Holy Communion is the *consecration,* where ordinary elements of bread and wine are placed before us and the words of Jesus are said over them: "This is my body; this is my blood." What takes place is not magic; what takes place is the celebration of the one consecration, which concerns the life of the Christ and his life in us. The bread and wine, the prayers, the action, all are symbols of this one consecration. The dedication of a church building, of a church organ, the blessing of a dwelling, or consecration of deaconesses, are ceremonies of consecration analogous to the prayers of consecration in the Lord's Supper. Such services are not called sacraments, but they are sacramental.

Prior to the late medieval settlement of sacramental theology and the establishment of seven liturgical acts as sacraments, many ceremonies were referred to as sacraments. The term had no absolutely fixed reference. After the dogmatizing of sacramental theology (1439), it became necessary to refer to "occasional" services which were not part of the system of the seven sacraments as "sacramentals." Protestants have generally not used this term and have reserved the use of the word "sacrament" for the two biblical sacraments of Baptism and the Lord's Supper. Methodists have customarily referred to occasional services as "ordinances." The term is not defined in the *Discipline*. By implication it refers to services of worship other than the sacraments. District superintendents are instructed to "promote the administration of the ordinances and Sacraments" (¶ 362.15 [1964 *Discipline*]). But the term also refers to laws of the church (¶ 352.12) and, in the General Rules, to such disciplines as "family and public prayer," "searching the Scriptures," and "fasting or abstinence" (¶ 97).

"Ordinance" is not used in *The Book of Worship*. "Office" has the same general root meaning (*officium* means duty or rule and became a common Latin term for any solemn assembly). The word was employed by the early monastic communities to refer to the daily hours of worship. In contemporary liturgical usage, the phrase "divine office" refers in the Roman Catholic Church to the whole collection of daily services known as the *Breviary,* and in the Anglican or Episcopal Church to the services of morning and evening prayer. It is difficult to judge what term is appropriate for our usage. "Ordinance," the historical Methodist designation, and "office," a more ecumenical as well as historical term, are both suitable, though archaic, and probably confusing to some people. "Sacramental" may be the most appropriate designation, though its use is hardly to be recommended; there is no historical-

Methodist nor Protestant-ecumenical tradition for its usage. In the 1944 *Book of Worship,* and in issues of the *Discipline,* prior to 1964, the services were designated simply as "orders."

The title may be unimportant. What is important is that we relate these acts of consecration and dedication to the one *consacre* in Christ which is the primordial sacrament. Every prayer which consecrates, whether said over bread and wine, missionaries, church buildings—over any person or thing—is a proclamation of God in Christ, of us in him, and of his rule over the whole created order. Every prayer which consecrates is a petition that creation should partake of the Lordship of Christ, grow into his likeness, and dwell in him.

An Office for the Consecration of Deaconesses

The office of deaconess was authorized in the former Methodist Episcopal Church during the General Conference of 1888.

Precedent for this office exists both in church history and the New Testament. Paul commends Phoebe to the church at Rome as a deaconess of the church at Cenchreae, the eastern port of Corinth (Rom. 16:1). This is the single explicit reference to deaconesses in the New Testament. The women referred to in I Tim. 3:11 may be either wives of deacons, or themselves deaconesses. The disciple named Dorcas, the subject of the miracle story of Acts 9:36-43, is not referred to as a deaconess. However, her ministry—"she was full of good works and acts of charity"—defines the ideal of the office of deaconess as it has existed in the church. Both Dorcas and Phoebe are New Testament symbols of the *diakonia* of a specially consecrated group of women in the church.

The early existence of this order is further attested in a letter of Pliny, Governor of Bithinia (*ca.* A.D. 112) to the Emperor Trajan. Pliny reports the torture of two servant girls "who were called deaconesses." After the fourth century, references to the work of the deaconesses increase in Christian literature, especially in the Eastern church, where deaconesses were ordained in a special ceremony similar to that for the deacon and were appointed to work in local congregations.

Their exact function in the West is more obscure. With the development in the West of an authoritarian hierarchy and the withdrawal of devout laity into monastic communities during the Middle Ages, the diaconate for women declined and finally disappeared.

Reforming movements in the church have periodically revived the office of deaconess. Such revivals occurred among the Waldenses and the Hussites before the Reformation. The Reformation churches did not immediately reestablish the diaconate for women; this development in Protestantism occurred first among Mennonites in Holland during the eighteenth century. In 1833, Theodor Fliedner, an Evangelical-Reformed pastor, founded a community of deaconesses at Kaiserswerth in Germany. In 1871 the Church of England revived the office of deaconess and instituted an ordination ceremony. In 1888 the Church of Scotland and the Methodists in Great Britain and the United States did the same.

An ecumenical organization, consisting primarily of Lutherans, unites deaconesses of the world; the International Federation of Deaconess Associations, called *Diakonia,* was founded at Copenhagen, Denmark, in 1947.

While Deaconess work was instituted in American Methodism in 1888, it was not until 1908 that a "Form for Consecration of Deaconesses" first appeared in the *Discipline.*

This early liturgy included the first two verses of "Savior, Thy Dying Love," as the opening of the service, and the hymn "Take My Life and Let It Be." This latter hymn was prescribed in the service until the order assumed its present shape in 1944.

Since its establishment in 1908 the order of service for the consecration of deaconesses has included the following elements: (1) Presentation of the candidates. (2) A scripture reading; since 1916, Matt. 25:31-40 (omitted, 1924-28). (3) A brief address to the prospective deaconesses, which defines their serving ministry. (4) Vows assumed by the candidates. (5) A consecrating prayer. (6) Provisions for a hymn or hymns.

The shape of the service and of these specific elements has changed over the years, but these elements have remained constant, and their content fundamentally the same. In the 1908 service the question was asked of the candidates, "Will you strive to walk so close to your Saviour's side that you will ever carry his blessed presence to the hearts and homes of those to whom you minister?" The answer: "I will endeavor so to do." In 1916 this was altered to read, "Will you strive to live that you may convey the blessed sense of God's presence to the hearts and homes of those to whom you minister?" This question disappears from the list of vows in 1944.

The other vows have been consistently represented in the service since 1908, with the single exception of the present final vow promising obedience, which was omitted in the service from 1924 to 1932.

The central action of this service consists of the vows of the candidates and the consecrating prayer. The essential meaning of the service is located here.

In the vows the prospective deaconesses affirm that they have been *called* to ministry, and covenant that they will *serve* in *obedience* in the church; they promise that they will *nurture* their ministries of service through *prayer* and the *study* of the Bible. The consecrating prayer which follows the taking of vows is a petition that the promises of the vows may be fulfilled.

Suggested Hymns:

74 All Praise to Thee, for Thou, O King Divine
107 Jesus Calls Us o'er the Tumult

130 What Shall I Do My God to Love
152 Forth in Thy Name
186 Servant of All, to Toil for Man

Psalms, Canticles, or Acts of Praise: nos. 13, 36, 38, 51, 59, 67, 83, 85, 96, 99, 100.

Prayers: p. 186, no. 8; p. 235, nos. 13-16; p. 246, no. 13.

Litany: p. 207, no. 1.

An Office for the Commissioning of Missionaries and Deaconesses

This service of commissioning is essentially an abbreviation of a longer service which first appeared in the 1944 *Book of Worship*. It is the concluding portion of the earlier service, containing the act of commissioning. An opening rubric which reads, "This office may be included in an order of worship, following the sermon," substitutes for the full order provided in the 1944 service.

When this office is performed *within* an order of worship, the person responsible for planning the service may wish to consult the 1944 order for appropriate scripture sentences, prayers, and lessons.

The simple service contained in the present *Book of Worship* is generated out of the statement entitled, "The Aim of Missions," found in the *Discipline* at ¶ 1176 (1964 *Discipline*). This concise formulation in its entirety opens the service, prepared only by three brief scripture sentences. It is followed by an address to the deaconesses and missionaries which attempts to relate the principles of "The Aim of Missions" to the *lives* of men and women who undertake to make the missionary task their professional vocation. This "charge" is followed by public commitment through the taking of vows, a consecration prayer, and an individual commissioning of each missionary or deaconess.

This central act of the service is followed by a unique series of addresses and prayers which joins the whole congregation to the missionary task of the persons being commissioned. The Christian mission is, thus, in this conclusion of the service defined as the work of the whole people of God as well as a professional and particular responsibility of the persons being commissioned.

Suggested Hymns:

10 Let All the World in Every Corner Sing
14 From All That Dwell Below the Skies
39 Let All on Earth Their Voices Raise
46 Captain of Israel's Host
47 God of Our Life
74 All Praise to Thee, for Thou, O King Divine
131 Come, Holy Ghost, Our Hearts Inspire
137 Spirit of Faith, Come Down
149 I Love to Tell the Story
150 A Charge to Keep I Have
151 Faith of Our Fathers
160 Take Up Thy Cross
170 O Master, Let Me Walk with Thee
171 O Master Workman of the Race
186 Servant of All, to Toil for Man
187 Take My Life, and Let It Be Consecrated
192 In Christ There Is No East or West

199 O Brother Man, Fold to Thy Heart
200 The Voice of God Is Calling
201 O Thou Who Art the Shepherd
202 We Bear the Strain of Earthly Care
203 We Thank Thee, Lord
204 Where Cross the Crowded Ways of Life
292 Christ for the World We Sing
299 O Zion, Haste
339 Lord of the Harvest, Hear
340 With Thine Own Pity, Savior
342 Go, Make of All Disciples
406 Heralds of Christ
407 O Master of the Waking World
408 Christ Is the World's True Light
409 Ye Servants of God
469 Father Eternal, Ruler of Creation
472 Jesus Shall Reign
479 Lord, Whose Love Through Humble Service
481 O Holy City, Seen of John

Psalms, Canticles, or Acts of Praise: nos. 13, 23, 30, 31, 45, 49, 55, 58, 83, 85, 86, 89, 94, 95.

Prayers: p. 185, no. 6; p. 168, nos. 7-9; p. 241, nos. 12-16; p. 242, p. 17.

An Office for the Consecration of Directors of Christian Education and Directors of Music

Since 1948, annual conference boards of education have been authorized to certify directors or ministers of education, and since 1956, directors or ministers of music.

The decision concerning certification has involved considerable discussion concerning the terms "director" and "minister." The language of the 1948 and 1952 *Disciplines* designates "directors" of Christian education (¶ 1454). In 1956, when certification of musicians is added, the *Discipline* refers to "directors of Christian education and ministers of music" (¶ 1451). In 1960 this is altered to read "ministers and directors of Christian education and ministers and directors of music" (¶ 1451). In 1964 the designation is reversed to read, in both cases, "directors and ministers." If this ambiguity reveals a controversy, it is apparently a still unsettled one, since the present *Book of Worship* service of consecration refers only to "directors" of education and music.

The designation may be insignificant; the decision of 1964, creating this service whereby bishops may consecrate Christian educators and musicians, is a step which recognizes the actual "ministry" of many devoted men and women who have chosen vocations in the church.

Suggested Hymns:

150 A Charge to Keep I Have
170 O Master Let Me Walk with Thee
186 Servant of All to Toil for Man

187 Take My Life, and Let It Be Consecrated
467 Come, Holy Ghost, Our Souls Inspire

Psalms, Canticles, or Acts of Praise: nos. 2, 5, 15, 19, 22, 30, 40, 41, 50, 53, 54, 76.

An Office for the Recognition of Officials in the Church
An Office for the Recognition of Church School Officers and Teachers
An Office for the Recognition of Choristers

Lay leadership in our churches is consecrated ministry. Regular use of these simple offices can reinforce recognition of this fact.

The history of the use of these three brief acts of worship extends no further than the 1944 *Book of Worship*.

Suggested Hymns:

187 Take My Life, and Let It Be Consecrated
301 All Praise to Our Redeeming Lord
307 Father, We Thank Thee Who Hast Planted
1 O For a Thousand Tongues to Sing
2 Angel Voices, Ever Singing
3 Come, Thou Almighty King

4 Sing Praise to God Who Reigns Above
5 Come, Ye That Love the Lord
23 Come, Let Us Tune Our Loftiest Song
77 Come, Christians, Join to Sing
343 All Nature's Works His Praise Declare

Psalms, Canticles, or Acts of Praise: 1, 2, 3, 4, 12, 22, 26, 30, 43, 54, 55, 76.

An Office for the Organizing of a Church

The organization of a new congregation of Christian people surely requires a significant liturgical celebration. This service which first appeared in the *Discipline* of 1956 fills a real void previously existing in the "occasional offices."

Suggested Hymns:

161 Hope of the World
292 Christ for the World We Sing
297 The Church's One Foundation

301 All Praise to Our Redeeming Lord
307 Father, We Thank Thee Who Hast Planted

An Office for the Breaking of Ground for a Church Building
An Office for the Laying of the Cornerstone of a Building
An Office for the Opening or Consecrating of a Church Building
An Office for the Dedication of a Church Building

It was natural for a growing church in a growing nation that the first orders of worship to appear in the *Discipline* alongside orders for the sacraments, marriage, burial, and ordination were services for the laying of a cornerstone and for the dedication of a church building. These services were adopted by the Methodist Episcopal Church in 1864 and by the southern church in 1870.

Ritual acts of prayer at the beginning of important ventures and thanksgiving upon the first use of significant things are traditional cultural celebrations. Today, ceremonies at the breaking of ground for a new building are often more important events than the traditional act of "laying a cornerstone." Many modern buildings require no cornerstone; the ceremonial stone which once functionally united two walls at their intersection is now often a nominal starting place in construction, upon which a date or other inscription is carved and in which memorabilia are sometimes placed. In many buildings such a stone is replaced by a metal plaque which may be attached to the building in the last stage of construction or after the building is completed.

In 1956 an order for the breaking of ground was introduced to the *Discipline*. The service opens, after two brief scripture sentences, with a shortened form of the "exhortation" from the Anglican rite commonly used since 1712 for the consecration of church buildings. The exhortation is simply an introduction, paying respect to "devout and holy men" who erect houses of worship, which serves as a preparation for the prayer which follows imploring the inspiration of the Holy Spirit. One phrase of the exhortation needs special consideration in our day. It refers to houses of worship being separated "from all unhallowed, worldly, and common uses." Such a phrase should drive us to consider seriously what it means to "hallow" the things of this world or to "profane" those things which belong to the gospel. It would be tragic indeed if this phrase would lead us to limit the use of a church building either to the exercise of the Christian cultus or "church activities."

The ritual action of sacralizing space has its roots in Old Testament practice and human experience. The vision of Jacob recorded in Genesis 28 demonstrates how personal experience may hallow a particular place. Jacob's response to his vision was a sense of awe: "Surely the Lord is in this place. . . . This is none other than the house of God, and this is the gate of heaven," and a ritual act setting the place apart from "profane" places: "He took the stone which he had put under his head and set it up for a pillar and poured oil on the top of it. He called the name of that place Bethel."

Blessings and curses were once a rule of life and nothing significant was undertaken without proper consecration: "What man is there that has built a new house and not dedicated it (Deut. 20:5)?" The more important the event, the more elaborate was the ceremony.

And at the dedication of the wall of Jerusalem they sought Levites in all their places, to bring them to Jerusalem to celebrate the dedication with gladness, with thanksgivings and with singing, with cymbals, harps, and lyres. (Neh. 12:27.)

The paradigm of all consecrations of Christian houses of worship is the dedication of Solomon's temple recorded in the eighth chapter of I Kings. A portion of the prayer attributed to Solomon on this occasion remains an appropriate petition for our times:

"But will God indeed dwell on the earth? Behold, heaven and the highest heaven cannot contain thee; how much less this house which I have built! Yet have regard to the prayer . . . which thy servant prays before thee this day; that thy eyes may be open night and day toward this house, the place of which thou hast said, 'My name shall be there,' that thou mayest hearken to the prayer which thy servant offers toward this place."

The earliest record concerning the dedication of a church building is Eusebius' description of the dedication of the cathedral at Tyre in 314 (*Church History*, X, 3-4). Church buildings certainly existed prior to this time; Eusebius refers, for instance, to the fact that "the houses of prayer were thrown down to the very foundations" (*Church History*, VIII, 2) during the persecution under Diocletian. Indeed, the splendid basilica at Tyre described in Eusebius' oration was itself apparently the reconstruction of an older house of worship destroyed in the persecution.

We do not know when Christians first used church buildings or how they consecrated them. From the records of the ceremonies held in the fourth century it is clear that the consecration of buildings was effected by their use. Dedications were impressive inaugural ceremonies which consisted of lengthy orations, many prayers, and the celebration of the Lord's Supper. That these ceremonies were important and obligatory is attested by Athanasius' defense, in 357, of his use of an uncompleted and undedicated church for public prayers (*Apology to Emperor Constantius*, 17-18).

In this same century a distinction appeared between the "dedication" and "consecration" of a church building. An excerpt from a letter of Ambrose to his sister Marcellina (386) explains the difference. "For after I had dedicated the basilica, many, as it were, with one mouth began to address me, and said: 'Consecrate this as you did the Roman basilica.' And I answered: 'Certainly I will if I find any relics of martyrs.' "

The custom of consecrating church buildings by enshrining in altars the bodies of martyrs, or things which had been in contact with them, apparently originated in Rome where many churches were constructed over the tombs of martyrs. The practice soon became normative, and the distinction between simple dedication and consecration with the relics of martyrs disappeared.

Disposition of relics in or below the altar became the central act in the rite of consecration; these tokens were regarded as essential to the "sacredness" of the building.

The Latin ritual of consecration, hence, developed in imitation of funerary rites, with the procession of relics, preparation of their "tomb," and their deposition forming the core of the ceremony.

Development of rites of consecration after the edict of toleration did not, however, universally stress the sacralizing power of relics. In the Gallican church, practices of consecrating buildings evolved which were imitative of Christian baptismal rites. The central emphasis was upon exorcism of demonic powers, the use of water to sprinkle the altar, consecratory prayers, and the anointing of the altar and portions of the church building.

After the ninth century, these two traditions in the Western church fused, and a Roman ritual emerged, consisting of: preparatory rites, including prayers and the consecration of water before the doors of the church, the sprinkling of exterior walls, and the entry procession with litany; a blessing performed in the middle of the church; preparation of the altar and church interior with holy water; consecration of the altar; procession with relics and blessing of altar vessels and other articles; and the celebration of the Mass. This is still the pattern of the Roman consecration.

The consecration service as it developed through the Middle Ages attempts essentially a transubstantiation of space; a building is made holy through association with sacred relics and by being baptized and confirmed.

Rites of consecration developed by churches of the Reformation vary greatly. In conception they attempt a return to the pre-medieval functional understanding of consecration where a church building is inaugurated by first use. The ceremonies include, as did those of the fourth century described by Eusebius, ordinary worship, special dedicatory prayers, and appropriate "orations."

Since 1944, the Methodist *Book of Worship* has made a distinction between the dedication of a church building and the opening of a church for worship. In the *Book of Worship* of 1964, the service intended for first use of a building is titled, "An Office for the Opening or Consecrating of a Church Building."

The difference between these services does not, of course, concern the use of relics of saints which we observed in the distinction between "dedication" and "consecration" in the fourth century, although a paragraph might be inserted here concerning plaques on doors, windows, and various church furnishings. The difference concerns the possible distinction between the *de facto* commencement of use of a building and the naming or specific dedication of the building.

Not infrequently a "sanctuary, a church school building, or a parish house (see rubrics for both services, pp. 351 and 355)," is completed and in use before a name or dedication is decided upon. Sometimes the event of dedication must wait upon the time schedules of persons who should appropriately be involved in the ceremony.

In the 1964 *Book of Worship* these services refer to the dedication or con-secration of a "church building" rather than a "church." This is a change from the previous *Book of Worship* and all previous *Disciplines*. This distinction is not superficial. The New Testament never applies the word "church" to a building, but to a people. The church which meets to proclaim the *consacre* of Christ in the place of its "gathered" worship needs the awareness that its identity and its meeting with Christ are not confined to architectural space.

Both the service for the opening of a church and the rite of dedication are brief orders of worship which may appropriately be followed by the Sacrament of the Lord's Supper; the brief form found on pp. 24-27 is to be preferred, since prayers, reading of scripture, and preaching will naturally have preceded the Eucharist.

Suggested Hymns:

For the Breaking of Ground for a Church Building
59 We Gather Together

For the Laying of the Cornerstone of a Church Building:
293 Glorious Things of Thee Are Spoken
297 The Church's One Foundation
298 Christ Is Made the Sure Foundation
348 On This Stone Now Laid with Prayer
349 O Living Christ, Chief Cornerstone

For Opening or Consecration of a Church Building or the Dedication of a Church Building:
257 Blessed Jesus, at Thy Word

293 Glorious Things of Thee Are Spoken
294 I Love Thy Kingdom, Lord
295 How Lovely Is Thy Dwelling Place
296 One Holy Church of God Appears
297 The Church's One Foundation
298 Christ Is Made the Sure Foundation
345 Thou, Whose Unmeasured Temple Stands
347 All Things Are Thine
350 How Blessed Is This Place
351 Eternal God and Sovereign Lord
352 Come, O Thou God of Grace
461 Spirit Divine, Attend Our Prayers
467 Come, Holy Ghost, Our Souls Inspire

An Office for the Dedication of a School, College, or University Building

This service was introduced into the Methodist cultus in 1932, when it was titled, "The Order for the Dedication of an Educational Building." In 1939 an additional title before the service read, "The Dedication of a College or University Building." The service was intended to be appropriate for the dedi-cation of both educational buildings of local churches and college buildings. In 1944 a distinction between these educational enterprises was recognized in the designation of separate services for "the Dedication of a Church-School Building or Parish House," and "An Order for the Dedication of a School, College, or University Building." In the present *Book of Worship,* no distinc-tion is made between consecration of church school buildings, parish houses, and church buildings generally (see rubrics on pp. 355 and 361), but this sep-arate service is included for school buildings not directly a part of a local church.

The contents of the service are essentially the same as the original dedication for an educational building included in the 1932 *Discipline.*

Suggested Hymns:

344 Come, Father, Son, and Holy Ghost
346 The Lord Our God Alone Is Strong
206 God of the Ages, by Whose Hand
 84 O Guide to Every Child

An Office for the Dedication of a Hospital

This service also originated in 1932 and has remained essentially the same to the present day.

Suggested Hymns:

485 From Thee All Skill and Science Flow
479 Lord, Whose Love Through Humble
     Service

An Office for the Dedication of a Church Organ or Other Instruments for Sacred Music

This simple dedication is a much shortened and changed version of the first service for the dedication of an organ which was first published in the *Discipline* of 1932.

Suggested Hymns:

 9 I'll Praise My Maker While I've
    Breath
15 Praise the Lord Who Reigns Above

An Office for the Dedication of a Memorial

Since 1936, Methodists have had an official act of worship appropriate for the dedication of a memorial. The present service is a simplification of earlier versions. The central act of the rite, accepting the gift, dedicating it, and naming the donor has remained virtually unchanged.

Suggested Hymns:

  8 Holy God, We Praise Thy Name
 66 Praise, My Soul, The King of Heaven
352 Come, O Thou God of Grace

Psalms, Canticles, or Acts of Praise: 36, 39, 44, 60.

An Office for the Blessing of a Dwelling

The provision for the Lord's Prayer is the only element the present and the original service for the blessing of a house (1932) have in common. The early service was a sentimental exaltation of the virtues of the Christian family. Our service is an appropriate, simple rhythm of scripture and prayer which consecrates the home in the name of the Trinity and commends its occupants to God's love and care.

Suggested Hymns:

516 Happy the Home When God Is There
517 Lord of Life and King of Glory

518 Be Present at Our Table, Lord
520 O Lord, May Church and Home Combine

Psalms, Canticles, or Acts of Praise: 42, 47.